From Abolition to Rights for All

From Abolition to Rights for All

The Making of a Reform Community in the Nineteenth Century

JOHN T. CUMBLER

PENN

University of Pennsylvania Press

Philadelphia

Published by
University of Pennsylvania Press
Philadelphia, Pennsylvania 19104-4112

Printed in the United States of America on acid-free paper

10 9 8 7 6 5 4 3 2 1

A Cataloging-in-Publication record is available from the Library of Congress

ISBN-13: 978-0-8122-4026-9
ISBN-10: 0-8122-4026-X

To all those who have dedicated their lives to the struggle for social justice "till every yoke is broken"

Contents

Preface

I began this project as an investigation into the life of Henry Ingersoll Bowditch, father of American public health and long-time radical reformer. Bowditch's radicalism began with abolition, so I soon expanded my scope of research to the broader reform community beginning with the abolitionists. In their personal papers many of these reformers, whether in public health, tenement house reform, immigrant rights, or women's rights, talked about having been educated in reform through their struggle against slavery. For me their stories struck a chord of familiarity. Like many of them, I was bred "in an old . . . reform"—in my case, civil rights. And, like these reformers, I took from that involvement lessons and a worldview that informed me not just about civil rights but of a larger social justice vision. In the middle of the voter registration campaign, I went south to Mississippi as a young undergraduate to become a civil rights worker as part of the COFO voter registration project. When I returned to the University of Wisconsin I continued working for civil rights, marching for open housing in Milwaukee, but I also joined SDS, worked for Indian and worker rights, and became involved in the antiwar movement. When women began to organize and push for women's rights, my friends and wife made sure I understood that the struggle for women's equality was an equal part in the campaign for social justice. It was never clear to me what impulses brought me to civil rights and social activism, but it is clear to me now that my initial involvement in that community had a fundamental formative influence on my life and world outlook. When the environmental and gay rights movement spread across the world, I understood where I had to stand on those issues. And if I had questions about where I should stand, I had plenty of friends to help me find my way.

My involvement in the social justice community has been as central to my understanding of myself as my role as a parent or a historian. My history as an activist informs my worldview, and the people I know and have known through that activity make up and have made up my community, my friends, my loves, and my opponents. Opponents because, even though we have shared a larger common vision and membership in a larger community of social justice activists, there have been and still are multiple divisions and conflicts within that community. Some of my fellow activists I cannot abide. Some I find insufferable, as I am sure many find me. Disagreements over strategies, tactics, and even philosophies have divided us, sometimes forever. But I know, as do most involved in any social movement, that divisions within the movement usually do not mean that we don't understand that those with whom we disagree are still within the movement.

Although I am a social activist, I am also a historian, and after publishing five traditional history books I found in the story of these nineteenth-century reformers, especially the less-known ones, a story I needed to tell. As I immersed myself in the historical literature about abolitionism and read more of the abolitionists' letters and papers, I was struck by a disjuncture between what was said about them and the world that was reflected in those letters and papers. It was not that what the historians were saying was untrue so much as that it missed the essential social exchanges of a political movement.

Certainly one does not have to experience something to know it, any more than one has to have played football to know and appreciate the game, yet much of the history of abolitionism, with some significant exceptions, seemed to be written by people who had never experienced being in a social justice movement. As historians we are trained to avoid imposing the present on the past. But as historians we should be careful that in maintaining the integrity of the past experience as past we do not divorce that experience from reality. In our efforts to keep the present out of the past we are in danger of keeping life out of the past as well.

As much as we should keep our historical distance and objectivity, we should also keep our historical empathy. The past was different from the present. Childhood was a far different experience for young people expected to add their labor to the family farm at an early age or enter a workshop or factory rather than go to school and summer camp. The reality of childhood death was much closer to nineteenth-century families than for those of the late twentieth century. Yet real people grew up, lived, and struggled in the nineteenth century, and they did so not fundamentally that differently from the way we do today. They did not have Social Security, cars, airplanes, atomic bombs, cell phones, televisions, VCRs, central heating and air conditioning, Medicare, or antibiotics—those things that make up our world and give us a sense of our place in that world—but they did have parents, fell in love, married, and had children, even if they experienced those things in a different context from ours today. They tried to give their lives meaning by leading a good life, as they understood the idea. They tried to maintain and provide for their families. They suffered loss and also understood happiness.

Too often in an attempt to keep historical distance, historians present the people in the past as if they were cut from cardboard. We lose so much of history when we do so. Parents in the past agonized about their children and their children's future as much as parents do today. We can better understand their struggles if we also use our experiences as parents or children to understand their experiences. Historical characters loved and experienced failed love. We must use our love or failures at love to understand their experiences, while at the same time remembering that the context of that love was different, and the understanding of it by those in the past may have been different. An agricultural historian, for example, might well gain insights into how farmers worked the land in the nineteenth century if she or he had worked at farming.[1] Although I do not believe one has to experience something to write knowledgeably about it, certainly we do appreciate that female historians have brought insights into our understanding of women's history that might have been missed by male historians. Historical empathy is not the fallacy of presentism, but a tool of historians to better understand the past.

Introduction: "Till Every Yoke Is Broken"

In 1886 James Olcott, an old Connecticut farmer, gave a speech before the Agricultural Board of Connecticut urging the farmers of Connecticut to join the battle against the "social evil" of pollution. Olcott introduced himself with the pronouncement that he had "been bred in the old anti-slavery reform," and went on to claim a link between abolitionism and anti-pollution agitation. The connection between the struggle against slavery and the campaign to end pollution was clear to Olcott even if it might be seem strained to us today. It was a connection that would not have surprised Wendell Phillips, one of the stalwarts of the campaign against slavery, who in 1884 wrote, "Let it be seen that our experience made us not merely abolitionists, but philanthropists." Phillips wrote not only to his friends but to historians as well, that abolitionists "sought to establish a principle, the right of human nature."[1]

What would have surprised Phillips is how historians have come to see the postwar period.[2] For the most part historians have presented antebellum reformers (with the exception of women suffrage activists) as having retired from the historical stage, unwilling or unable to engage the complex world of government and commerce in the postwar era.[3] And most historians argue that reform would have to wait until a new generation of progressives took up the banner of social change. Although there is an element of truth to this telling of our national story, it misses as much as it captures. What it misses tells us much about the nature of reform movements, their continuity and their disruption. Abolitionist reformers did not voluntarily leave the historical stage, nor did their views relegate them to the sidelines. In the postwar years abolitionists, who rooted their critique of slavery in natural rights, led the way in expanding on Lockean (after the philosopher John Locke) ideas of rights and the role of the state to encompass the ideal of an activist state animated by social justice and working to secure and advance freedom and basic rights to decent housing, health care, safe and well paying jobs, prison reform, and equal rights at home and abroad.[4]

To achieve their expanded vision of human rights for all, these old abolitionists vigorously engaged in the struggle for power as much as they had in their earlier campaign against slavery. The postwar story is not one of gradual retirement and retreat but one of aggressive engagement and defeat. But even in defeat these activists and their struggles significantly influenced the next generation, the progressive reformers. Indeed, the defeat of these activists' broader reform agenda set the stage, tone, and limits of the later progressive program. Yet despite the failure of the abolitionists to achieve their broad program, the heart of American reform came out of the gathering of those individuals committed to opposing an institution so deeply rooted in the American experience.

Focusing on the abolitionist community as a broader social movement, this work looks to uncover the world of nineteenth-century radical New England reformers, its expansion and its ultimate defeat. Abolitionism politicized those involved by mounting a moral and philosophical critique of slavery. In that process abolitionists fashioned institutions and traditions that bound them together and developed and expanded the nation's natural rights tradition and carried it into the postwar era raising the banner of rights for all Americans.

The process of building a social movement to end slavery created bonds between various activists and politicized them in ways that moved them in the postwar period into a broad range of activism. It was from old networks and contacts that reformers brought people together to fight for what Thomas Wentworth Higginson called the "sisters of reform"—for the extension of civil rights, tenement house reform, public health, women's rights, workers' rights, immigrant rights, fair wages, care of the poor, a healthy environment, and social justice abroad and against the expanding racism at home.[5] As they expanded their activity into new areas, reformers built on movement connections that were forged during the struggle against slavery and reinforced each other's activism in these new areas. Community sustained the abolitionist movement, but that community and movement also affected how and where these reformers defined themselves and their politics and acted as the vehicle for moving old abolitionists into the wider reform agenda after the war.

The ultimate collapse of this reform impulse under the combined weight of Social Darwinism and the defeat of Reconstruction also informs this story. Its failure in the last quarter of the century not only ended a long campaign for social justice begun with the abolitionists almost forty years earlier, it also influenced the scope and tactics of the progressives who followed. The progressives did not try to rally the country to reform under the banner of natural rights. Accepting Darwinism and believing that the radical call for social justice and equal rights based on a sweeping and egalitarian understanding of natural rights was what led to the "failure of Reconstruction," the progressives tailored their reforms to a more limited, pragmatic, and self interested program. "Philanthropy and Five Percent" was Jacob Riis's slogan for reform. Riis, Theodore Roosevelt, Gifford Pinchot, and many of the other reformers of the progressive age argued for paternalistic reform to protect the middle class. It was not an accident that in speeches and historical references the progressives harkened back not to the abolitionist struggle but to Abraham Lincoln.[6]

A movement is larger than an organization; it is also a gathering of individuals. To succeed, it has to hold people together and maintain commitment over time. As Lawrence Goodwyn has shown in his work on the Populists, a movement has to construct a common culture and belief system with which people can identify.[7] It has to be able to sustain itself in the face of opposition and provide a reason for people to join and stay active. A social movement is made up of multiple and overlapping organizations. Individuals belonging to one or more of these organizations are also tied together by bonds that transcend a particular group or affiliation. Abolitionism was a community and a movement, and to understand it and why the individuals involved continued their reform activities on a wide range of fronts after the ending of slavery, it is important to understand the individuals involved and how they were linked together in a variety of ways and how their activism took many and varied forms.[8] We need to study them as they understood themselves.[9]

Henry Ingersoll Bowditch and Julia Ward Howe will anchor this narrative, but the work will be more than biographies of Bowditch and Howe since it hopes to tell the story of the larger reform movement that included people like Wendell Phillips, James Olcott, Maria Weston Chapman, Lewis Hayden, Thomas Wentworth Higginson, Lucy Stone, William Lloyd Garrison, Abby Kelley Foster, and Charles Sumner. Biographies allow the author to put the reader into the eyes of real historical actors. They also provide the historian with the opportunity to see the impact of history on real people's lives. But biographies' strengths are also their weakness. To look at a few leaders tells us little about the movement or about the lives of the rank and file. In the detail of an individual's life the larger social reality can be lost. No individual's experience can be truly typical of a time. And this is particularly true of those individuals who have left behind a rich enough record for historians to recreate past lives. By intertwining the lives of Henry Ingersoll Bowditch and Julia Ward Howe with those who shared with them the work of justice "till every yoke is broken," this work hopes to tell a personal yet more inclusive history of a community of reformers.[10]

Bowditch is an appropriate figure for this task because his world linked together so many of the strains of this vibrant yet diverse and contested community. He was an early activist drawn to abolitionism by his already formed radical idealism. Bowditch became vice president of the Massachusetts Anti-Slavery Society and a friend to many of the Garrisonians, yet he was also active in party politics: a Liberty Party candidate for office, a supporter of the Free Soil Party, and a friend to political abolitionists like Charles Sumner, Samuel Gridley Howe, and John Andrew. He was centrally involved in the Vigilance Committee, organized the campaign to free the fugitive slave Latimer, and was an active participant in the riots to free the runaway slaves Sims and Burns. He was an agent of the Underground Railroad. With the failure to free Burns, Bowditch spearheaded the creation of an underground paramilitary abolitionist organization. In the midst of the Civil War, while volunteering as a doctor in Virginia, Bowditch defined himself to another doctor by saying, "you know Wendell Phillips, he is a pro-slavery man compared to me."[11] Bowditch led the campaign for public health in America, what he called "state medicine." He was president of the nation's first state board of health and a reform president of the American Medical Association. He was a leader in the tenement house reform campaign. He was an active supporter of women's rights, suffrage, and women's equality in medicine. He was a founding figure in creating a women's hospital in Boston and campaigned for women's admission to Harvard Medical School and the Massachusetts Medical Society. He helped maintain Carney Hospital, the first Catholic hospital in New England, in its early years. He supported immigrant rights and championed the cause of the downtrodden and poor until the end of his life in 1892. He was a doctor, an intellectual, and part of the Boston intelligentsia, yet he was also an activist. The tension between one's role as a professional and as an activist is an inevitable fate for an activist professional, and Bowditch did not escape it.

Like Bowditch's, Julia Ward Howe's life touched on a variety of reformers and reforms. But unlike Bowditch she came late and reluctantly to the movement by way of her intellectual involvement and friendships with Theodore Parker, James Freeman Clarke, and Thomas Wentworth Higginson. She was at the social center of Boston's intellectual community and a coeditor of the abolitionist journal, *The Commonwealth*. She became a central figure in the Woman's Club movement and the struggle for women's rights, suffrage, racial justice, and international peace. Her personal life also reflected the tensions and conflicts strong and gifted women faced in the nineteenth century.

Although this work uses Bowditch and Howe to center its narrative, it is not a biography of either. Julia Ward Howe's life has already been covered in earlier biographies.[12] Bowditch's life will get more thorough coverage because little has been written about this important reform figure.[13]

Bowditch was a person deeply committed to his profession and deeply committed to the advancement of knowledge in medicine.[14] He was a published scholar and intellectual who did not step back from what he believed was his social responsibility to the world. He publicly attacked Emerson for sitting on the sidelines in the abolitionist campaign. "I judged Mr. Emerson by his acts as I judge other people. Whenever there was an antislavery case in Boston, Emerson was not among the abolitionists as . . . other abolitionists were."[15] Bowditch felt that "by my antislavery acts I had been made in reality a man."[16] Not only was his conception of masculinity linked to his activism, he also believed that activism gave him strength and purpose: "thank God that I early became an abolitionist. The thought of the fact seems to strengthen me for the other failures."[17]

Julia Ward Howe was a scholar and intellectual who was drawn first into the campaign for abolitionism and then to woman's rights. Her intelligence, her integrity, and her forceful character in an age that had little patience for women with such characteristics did not make for an easy life. Yet despite the caviling of society, her husband, and her family, she pushed forward and eventually found a community and acceptance with others struggling for ideal of human rights.

Bowditch and Howe are important foci for study because unlike their better known fellow activists neither was a "professional abolitionist" or reformer. As such their experience more typified that of those drawn to the movement than those whose profession was abolitionism.[18]

Although neither Julia Ward Howe nor Henry Ingersoll Bowditch represented the typical New England abolitionist, it is hard to imagine what such a typical abolitionist would be. Howe was intensely religious, but belonged to James Freeman Clarke's rather free nontraditional church, having previously attended Theodore Parker's radical church.[19] Bowditch also held a strong belief in God, but "had no dogma but love and affection toward him and reverence for man."[20] He was a militant anti-cleric who "hailed from no church" and denounced organized religions while at the same time claiming that none of the dominant religions of the region, Protestant, Catholic, or Jewish, had a monopoly on truth and all were equally valid.[21] Bowditch's God was very personal. Bowditch believed he experienced God when he acted from "a lofty sense of right."[22] His brother William, also an active reformer and member of the Board of the Anti-Slavery Society, was a "nonbeliever." The Bowditches, like Howe, Wendell Phillips, Edmund Quincy, and the Chapmans, came from the upper reaches of society, while William Lloyd Garrison, a "plain, unlettered man" as he called himself, did not attend college and apprenticed as a printer; Elizabeth Buffum Chace, Parker Pillsbury, and Abby and Stephan Foster were also common folk.[23]

Abolitionists lived in a contested time. For much of the early period of struggle their views were held in contempt by their neighbors and peers. Even many of those who had no sympathy with slavery held aloof from the struggle or at best were "lukewarm" in their support of abolition. For activists social isolation was common, as was the real possibility of being violently set upon. New England was a small place in 1831 when William Lloyd Garrison published his first edition of the *Liberator*, where he challenged the mainstream American Colonization Society and called for immediate emancipation. When Garrison wrote in that issue that he would "be heard," he knew it was Boston that would hear him first. Boston had barely 93,000 inhabitants in 1840. Most of its residents could easily walk to one another's homes, and although they did not tend to socialize together, wealthy merchants, artisans, and even the poor lived within a few blocks of each other. Just on the north side of the State House from Boston's fashionable Beacon Hill was Boston's black community, both within a five-minute walk from the office of the *Liberator*. People knew each other, they went to school together, and they visited back and forth. As the conflict over slavery heated up people divided. Those who became vocal in their opposition to slavery found they were no longer welcome in the homes of their peers.[24]

Yet if the abolitionists suffered exclusion, they also developed networks among themselves to provide support and to recruit others to the cause.[25] Henry Ingersoll Bowditch recruited his younger brother William. William married Julia Ward Howe's friend Thomas Wentworth Higginson's sister, Sarah Rhea Higginson. Higginson's courtship of abolitionist Mary Channing involved him with Theodore Parker and ultimately abolitionism.[26] Charles Sumner, a school friend of Wendell Phillips, introduced Phillips to Ann Terry Greene, who pushed Phillips into the movement.[27] Parker, Pillsbury, and William Chase also married activist abolitionists who pulled them into the movement.[28] And Charles Sumner, Henry Longfellow, and Theodore Parker worked on the Howes to bring them into abolitionism.[29]

Abolitionists not only gathered at each other's homes but also organized conferences, festivals, and bazaars.[30] In 1857, while Lucy Stone was on tour lecturing against slavery, she longed for the community of New England, specifically the community of abolitionists. She wrote James Buffum, "I suppose you are at Framingham today [for an abolitionist gathering on the Fourth of July] with the other good souls who live more and better in Massachusetts than anywhere else. God bless them and you and let us who are out of the healing of their atmosphere still

hold on our way."[31] The abolitionists of Boston held a large and successful annual Bazaar where they sold goods, works of art and crafts fashioned by members from across the globe. By the 1850s the fair became
a major community event and fundraiser drawing hundreds of people
anxious to support the movement and purchase Christmas gifts. Soon
the success of the fairs led to a concluding celebration where blacks and
whites met, interacted, and ate together as equals.[32] People came into
radical reform from a variety of places and for a variety of reasons, but
their time in the anti-slavery campaign sharpened their politics and gave
form to their outlook. They came to believe the world was organized
around power. Garrison and the moral suasionists may have avoided political party activities, but they understood power and politics. And that
mastery even more completely characterized activists like Phillips,
Bowditch, Higginson, Howe, Richard Dana, and John Whittier and professional politicians like Charles Sumner, John Palfrey, or John Albion
Andrew. In their battle against slavery these radicals constructed a vision
of themselves and their opponents. In that world of political struggle,
they labeled their enemies as a type: the wealthy privileged "Hunkers."
By contrast they viewed themselves as of the people, despite the fact that
as many of those who opposed abolitionists came from the common folk
as those who supported them.[33] Bowditch claimed of the abolitionists
that "all classes were represented, all three professions, various trades,
and not a few laborers."[34] There is some irony in the fact that the abolitionists construed themselves as "of the people" while they depicted
their opponents as "lords of the loom" and "hunkers" since many abolitionists came from elite families with traditions of paternalism.[35]

Like many other activists in American politics, the abolitionists
viewed the world as a conflict over the defense of liberty. The contest
pitted privileged wealth against the common people.[36] The abolitionists
constructed the conflict as the wealthy privileged classes defending slavery for their self-interest and profit against the poor slave and those in
support of liberty.[37] Theodore Parker asked Bostonians in 1854, "have
you forgotten the 1500 gentlemen of property and standing who volunteered to conduct Mr. Sims to slavery?" and reminded them that "the
men of property and standing all over New England" supported the
Fugitive Slave Law. Parker believed that the enemies of freedom and
justice were the "wealthy capitalists."[38] In a letter to his brother, Thomas
Wentworth Higginson argued "that the capitalists" have "muzzled" the
politicians.[39]

The abolitionists fashioned an ideal of themselves that enabled
them to contest power not only on moral grounds but on social, political and egalitarian grounds as well.[40] Julia Ward Howe noted that slavery was "upheld by the immense money power of the North."[41] For

many abolitionists state power was not the problem, but how it was exercised, and for whom. The abolitionists felt that since the wealthy privileged were using state power to undermine popular will and rights, the people had a responsibility to seize that power. For abolitionists this was without question a conflict between right and wrong—a struggle for human rights, but it was also a contest for power.

In such a highly politicized world, justice became an overarching issue. New England radicals came to argue that slavery was wrong not only because it was morally reprehensible but also because it violated fundamental natural rights. Out of the struggle against slavery came an expanded vision of rights and freedoms. Parker preached that "the instinct of commerce is adverse to the natural rights of labor, so the chief leaders in commerce wish to have the workingman but poorly paid; the larger gain falls into their hands; their labor is a mill, they must run him as cheap as they can."[42]

The story of the struggle against slavery and later activism is the story of a community and a social justice movement. In all social movements there are conflicts, disputes, personality clashes, and ideological divisions. Some of these conflicts, disputes, and divisions lead to bitter antagonisms and break people away from the larger social goal, while others smolder below the surface, while still others blow over, or are kept within bounds. In a letter to William Lloyd Garrison's son, Bowditch noted that, although many in the Garrison camp opposed Henry Wright's radicalism and anti-clericalism, he found them, "at times extravagant [in speech and writing], but true . . . to their ideas of anti-slavery." Bowditch went on to critique Wendell Phillips and Edmund Quincy as "often quite as distasteful to me and as unjust to others as either Bradburn or Wright. All four of them at times, were, I thought, offensively sharp on anti-slavery men who did not agree with them. I could bear with equanimity anything from your father . . . , although I not infrequently differed from him in thought and actions. . . . I allowed his denunciation of the course pursued by the Liberty Party and the Free Soil party to pass quickly from my mind."[43]

Social movements are personal. The more intensely one is involved or committed to an issue or ideal the more one's involvement in the social movement defines one's personal social life. Social movements are also seldom one-dimensional. People come into movements for multiple reasons, some philosophical, some religious, some personal, some psychological, and some ideological. Most join for a combination of motivations. Historians looking for a tale to tell often shortchange this complexity and focus on one or another reason. In the case of the New England radical reformers, religion plays a big role in the story told. But people come to radical reform for a variety of reasons, and when historians have sought to find a common religious motivation among abolitionists it has led to strained arguments that forced differently shaped pegs into a single shaped hole.

Religion provides a comforting explanation for the motivations that led individuals to become militant reformers. Many historians have explained the abolitionists as products of the perfectionist religious enthusiasms that swept through early nineteenth-century America.[44] But this explanation has weaknesses. Thousands if not hundreds of thousands of Americans got caught up in the religious revivals of the period 1820 to 1850, yet only a small portion of those people moved into radical abolitionism.[45] And as mentioned above there were many abolitionists who were not connected to perfectionism or the religious revivals.[46]

Yet few nineteenth-century Americans could escape the intense religiosity that was sweeping America at the time, including most abolitionists. Most of these activists were deeply religious, some were committed to traditional religious denominations, others were caught up with the perfectionist evangelicals, some held deeply religious beliefs but were intensely anti-clerical, others considered themselves free thinkers. Religious metaphors, symbols, and images, even for free thinkers, provided a common vocabulary shared by most Americans. It should not surprise us that they were part of the language and experience of abolitionists as it was for much of the rest of American society. But that religious language, and, for many, belief system and frame of reference, should not blind us to the equally prevalent language of natural rights that permeated abolitionists' writings.[47]

Like most nineteenth-century Americans, abolitionists adopted the natural rights position from philosophers such as John Locke. Locke proposed that basic rights were grounded in nature, not in government. They were inborn, timeless, and universal, transcending particular governments or human laws. He argued that man had these basic natural rights in "a state of nature," but in practice exercising of those rights might be threatened by others. Locke argued that governments were created and humans through social contract subordinated themselves to those governments in exchange for the protection of fundamental rights and governments did not have rights individuals did. In America those fundamental rights were delineated as life, liberty, and pursuit of happiness. For conservatives, natural rights implied a limitation of government to protecting property and not interfering with individual exercise of rights. The radical abolitionists took two fundamental notions from this tradition. One was that rights were inherent to all individuals and not created by governments. The other was that the purpose of governments was to protect and by extension advance those rights. Slavery, no matter how deeply rooted in tradition and the constitution, violated the right of the slave to liberty, let alone happiness.[48] Rather than enter the search for original motivations, this work looks at the reformers as they looked at themselves.[49] True, many saw their abolitionism as an expression of their religious commitment, and that fact should not be minimized. Yet in explaining themselves these radicals also continually wrote of their desire for social justice.[50] Rather than dismiss their understanding of themselves, this book takes seriously their claim that they "went forth for justice of the oppressed."[51] Taking seriously their own explanation for their involvement in the struggle against slavery helps us better understand what happened to the movement after slavery was formally ended. Because these activists saw themselves as struggling for social justice, they continued that struggle after the war. Slavery commanded so much of their attention in the prewar period because it was such a glaring abuse; once it ended, for the most part the community of activists who organized themselves to fight slavery continued in their quest to break "every yoke."[52]

Historians have made much of the different strains of abolitionism: the moral suasionists, who shunned electoral politics and who hoped to convert the nation to the immediate end of slavery by their moral arguments, versus the political activists; the pacifists versus those advocating violence; the socially conservative versus those advocating the broad platform.[53] These divisions certainly existed, but I think we often overlook the commonality among those who struggled against slavery, as noted in Bowditch's earlier quote. Many held differing views but continued to socialize together and considered each other companions in the struggle. It is also true, however, that sometimes personalities or personal dispute disrupted their ability to work together. A social movement is by definition a mixed bag. Thomas Wentworth Higginson noted at the end of a long lifetime involvement in reform activity that "internal feuds among philanthropists are, alas no new story and few bodies of reformers have escaped this peril."[54] John Greenleaf Whittier could not abide Maria Weston Chapman, and she saw him as a cowardly waffler and said so publicly. Chapman rejected political party activity as compromising with a slavery-corrupted system, while Whittier was involved in the Liberty Party and then the Free Soil Party. Yet both Whittier and Chapman understood they were in the same movement.[55] Higginson saw Whittier as his mentor and friend, but Higginson committed himself to women's equality while Whittier was appalled at the actions of his "good friend Abby" Kelley in demanding a seat on the executive committee of the American Anti-Slavery Society.[56]

The focus of this book is on the radical New England reformers. New

England seems a most appropriate place to locate this story, not only because it was a hotbed of abolitionism and produced many of the movement's leading figures, but it was also, contrary to general assumptions, one of the most diverse communities of abolitionism. It had within its ranks, in both leadership and rank and file, Quakers, Unitarians, Radical Free Church Come-outers, Congregationalists, religious anti-clerics, and nonbelievers. Its ranks included merchants, lawyers, doctors, teachers, farmers, shoe-workers, sailors, and sea captains. Along with Philadelphia community it had significant African American participation.

Although New England abolitionism was a struggle of both blacks and whites, this work focuses most of its attention on the white community.[57] It begins with the abolitionists and follows them to their last days. Many historians make a distinction between radical abolitionists, by which they mean abolitionists involved in the Liberty Party or radical wing of the Free Soil Party or the Republican Party, and Garrisonian abolitionists. This is a distinction I am *not* making in this work. I am including within the term "radical abolitionists" all those abolitionists, Garrisonians or political party activists, who demanded an immediate end to slavery and supported some form of racial equality.[58] Included in that group were those who opposed political action, like Garrison, the Chapmans, and the Westons, and those who were involved in political party activity, such as Higginson, Whittier, Samuel Gridley Howe, Charles Sumner, Richard Dana, John Andrew, the Buffums, and Henry Ingersoll Bowditch. It also included some, like William Bowditch, who supported the Liberty Party and Free Soil Party but would not vote because such an act would be supporting a system that supported slavery. The group included nonresisters, or pacifists, again like Garrison, but also resisters, those who accepted violence as a means of opposing slavery, like Howe, Higginson, Bowditch, Franklin Sanborn, and Lewis Hayden, and those who moved from one view to the other, like Phillips and Theodore Parker. Although I believe that those who bolted from the Garrisonians over women's rights, such as Amos Phelps, were still abolitionists, they played a smaller role in New England once their position was defeated in 1840 and do not figure significantly in this work.

Using Bowditch and Howe as the central figures in this narrative also redirects attention away from those few abolitionists such as Garrison or Phillips for whom abolitionism was effectively a career to those who had constantly to balance their social activism with their other commitments. Like any social movement, the nineteenth-century reform community involved intertwining but shifting circles of groups of people. Many were linked by friendship, family, and love; others were at odds over one or another issue or tactic; still others were bitter opponents on one or another issue. And as is always the case in the course of human affairs, personalities played a part in these conflicts. To visualize the New England reform community one needs to think about intersecting circles.[59]

For many radicals, the defeat of formal slavery was only the beginning. Success in the war against slavery represented one step along the road to ending racism and creating a truly inclusive society. The struggle for women's rights, workers' rights, and the rights of the poor and disadvantaged also continued. When slavery ended, a significant number of former abolitionists moved in this expansive direction, although along different paths. Wendell Phillips ran for governor as a candidate for the Massachusetts Labor Party; with Parker Pillsbury and Stephan and Abby Foster, he championed worker rights and the eight-hour work day.[60] William Bowditch worked for prison reform and joined Phillips, the Fosters, Thomas Wentworth Higginson, James Buffum, James Freeman Clarke, Julia Ward Howe, and Lucy Stone and Henry Blackwell in the campaign for women's rights, while Parker Pillsbury joined Elizabeth Cady Stanton and Susan B. Anthony. Franklin Sanborn and Samuel Gridley Howe worked to empower the state Board of Charities. Henry Ingersoll Bowditch and Clarke worked for tenement house reform, while Bowditch and Robert Davis led the movement for "state medicine." Henry Ingersoll Bowditch accurately predicted his own future in 1848, when he stated, "I seemed called to do battle for justice and the oppressed."[61]

Others joined these new campaigns, but in their beginning days abolitionists were in the forefront. In general abolitionists had always been concerned about the poor and downtrodden. Slavery was but one, although the most grievous, example of tyranny of the powerful over the poor. Though he occasionally supported curious notions (such as his wildly misconceived idea about annexing Santo Domingo), Samuel Gridley Howe fundamentally believed that the world contained injustice and that people of conscience had a duty to respond with action. Once slavery was ended Howe, despite old age and poor health, continued to work for human rights around the world and in Massachusetts (though his wife would note his blindness to justice within his own home).

If the obvious injustice of slavery called for equivalent commitments of time and energy, slavery's end opened the space for these social justice agents to focus their attention in areas more closely linked to their professional orientation. Howe's adult life had been centered on his role as the director of the Perkins School for the Blind and his work on establishing a school for the mentally disabled. By mid-century he was identified with that role. With the Civil War's end Howe turned his "reform" energies to the newly created state Board of Charities, where he expected to bring his broad vision of reform and philanthropy to bear.[62] In this his acolyte, and fellow member of John Brown's "secret six," Franklin Sanborn, joined him. Sanborn, an intellectual as well as a social justice activist, hoped to bring science and information about the true causes of disorder and crime, which he believed to be rooted in poverty, to the public conscience. The rising of public consciousness would lead in turn to social reform, including tenement house reform, limited hours of labor, and easier working conditions.

It was an exciting time in Boston.[63] For these old abolitionists, talk was all about the future. The Bowditches, Higginson, Phillips, Clarke, Stone, Blackman, and Julia Ward Howe were all activists in the newly formed American Equal Rights Association, soon to be named the New England Woman Suffrage Association. Henry Ingersoll Bowditch's 1862 call for preventive health care, or what he called "state medicine," was about to bear fruit in the creation of the nation's first state board of health. Phillips and others were talking about the rights of workers. As leaders of the State Board of Charities, Howe and Sanborn were convinced that a union of the new social science with the natural rights tradition would lead the state into newly expanded action on behalf of the poor and feeble.[64]

The optimism of that moment would not last. Within twenty years Reconstruction would be in shambles. The national mood and political direction turned once again to the privileged. Lynching, segregation, and limits to black political influence increased in the South. When in January 1875 Wendell Phillips attempted to defend the use of federal troops to stop lynching and mob rule in Louisiana, he was booed off the stage of Faneuil Hall. That same stage had been the scene of his earlier triumphant trouncing of those who failed to condemn the mob killing of the abolitionist Elijah Lovejoy. The Massachusetts Board of Health would retreat from its sweeping early vision of state medicine and focus its attention on personal hygiene. The state Board of Charities would find more reasons to condemn paupers and would call for more Christian charity than state action on behalf of the rights of the poor. The expansion to universal suffrage failed to materialize and by 1890 the two suffrage organizations would merge, with African Americans left at the back of the parade. Increasingly suffrage supporters were arguing that as educated and refined white women they had earned the privilege of the vote.[65]

Frederick Douglass noted with sadness the death of Henry Ingersoll Bowditch in 1892. Douglass sat down and dashed off a letter to the *Boston Globe* in praise of his fellow activist.[66] He wrote to the people of Boston, who were remembering Bowditch as a great doctor and civic leader, that Bowditch was also a "loved and venerated friend" who invited Douglass into his home and showed him respect and equality.[67] Douglass's comments, however, might not have registered in the minds of the people of Boston in 1892. The struggle against slavery was long over, and Massachusetts had long ago outlawed segregation. Six years earlier Boston had placed Olin Levi-Warner's statue of William Lloyd Garrison on Commonwealth Avenue, and within five years the city would put the Augustus Saint-Gaudens monument commemorating Robert Shaw and the Fighting 54th (the Massachusetts black regiment that fought so valiantly in the attack against Fort Wagner) at the edge of the Commons across from the State House. Boston of 1892 felt smug about its history of fighting slavery. Yet, as the old abolitionist Harriet Winslow Sewall stated in 1889, "it does not require much moral courage to decry the injustice of fifty years ago."[68]

Chapter 1
The People and the Times

Freedom isn't like the bird on the wing
Freedom isn't like the summer rain
You have to work for it, fight for it
Live and die for it
And every generation has to win it again

—old folk song

A Life Long Earnest Worker in Every Good Cause
—Henry Ingersoll Bowditch about Samuel Sewall

On a wet November morning in 1868 Julia Ward Howe, author of numerous books of poetry, two plays, travel books, and the Battle Hymn of the Republic, set off for Boston's Horticultural Hall wearing her "rainy-day suit." She had not really wanted to go to the Horticultural Hall that morning. Earlier her old friend, Thomas Wentworth Higginson, had prodded her to lend her name to a call for a women's rights meeting. But women's rights was not where Julia Ward Howe wanted to put her energy in 1868. On her mind at the time were the condition of the freedman and the question of black suffrage and rights. She was also interested in the New England Women's Club that she had helped found only six months earlier.[1] However, Higginson was a very old friend, a member with her husband of the secret six, the Northern supporters of John Brown's Harpers Ferry raid, and a fellow member with her in the intellectual circle behind the *Atlantic Monthly*. Julia just could not say no to Higginson, so she lent her name to the call for a woman's rights meeting. Having done so, she felt she had to at least put in an appearance. "Nothing was further from my mind than the thought that I should take part in the day's proceedings. . . . [She] hoped not to be noticed."[2]

Unfortunately for Julia, she was noticed. Higginson spotted her in the back of the hall and insisted that she come up on the platform. She did so "very reluctantly." Walking up to the platform she had an epiphany. "I was now face to face with a new order of things. Here, indeed were Phillips, Colonel Higginson, my dear pastor, James Freeman Clarke. But here was also Lucy Stone [along with her husband, Henry Blackwell]. . . . These champions, who had fought so long and so valiantly for the slave, now turned the searchlight of their intelligence upon the conditions of woman and demanded for the mothers of the community the civil rights which had recently been accorded to the Negro."[3] Seeing these old champions, Julia realized not only that they made up her community, but that their battle was also hers. She told her daughter that at that moment she felt that she "belonged with them, that she must help draw the car of progress not drag like a brake on its wheel."[4] When Lucy Stone finished talking she turned to Julia and asked her to speak. Julia "could only say, 'I am with you.'" And she was "with them ever since."[5]

Out of that meeting came the New England Woman Suffrage Association with Julia as its first president. She became the organization's most effective and popular speaker and went on to help form the American Woman Suffrage Association. By the end of the century Julia Ward Howe was as famous for her struggle for women's rights as for the Battle Hymn of the Republic.

Howe was perhaps more ready to join the women's rights campaign on that wet November morning than she may have realized or remembered. Before 1868 she may not have seen herself as a women's rights advocate, but her writings and behavior clearly indicate a woman ready to move in that direction. In a book manuscript begun in 1860 and finished in 1865, she noted "the primal truth, the intrinsic necessity from which the extrinsic necessities follow. The beauty and justice of all that depends upon this first necessity, out of which I hope to demonstrate the equality, the dignity, and the eternal dissimilarity of the two sexes."[6] In her diary in 1866, she noted that her "family" opposed her public lectures but that she would not give in. That same year she argued, "Slaves had no rights. Women have few."[7] Even so, her remembered experience of "a new light com[ing] to [her of a] new domain . . . of true womanhood, woman no longer in her ancillary relation to man, but . . . as a free agent fully sharing with man every human right and every human responsibility," captures much about the world of New England reformers in the nineteenth century.[8] In it we can see community, the role of friendship, loyalty, and love, and the power of a social justice ideal.

Born in 1819, Julia Ward Howe was strong-willed, well-educated, cultured, and very bright. She grew up in a prosperous New York family. Her father, Samuel Cutler Ward, banker and founder of New York University, was a harsh, domineering, though loving father. The death of

Julia's mother when Julia was five hardened him and increased his religious piety. Samuel Ward came to believe the outside world was corrupt and evil, and he attempted to guard his daughter from it. After his wife's death he moved the family to Bond Street, where Julia's grandfather and uncles also bought homes. There Samuel attempted to hold his children within the tight net of family and away from the influence of the outer world.

Although her father was conservative, he recognized Julia's intense intellectual curiosity and ability and gave her, if not social freedom, space to develop her intellectual talents. Julia immersed herself in studies. She mastered French, Latin, and Italian, studied music, and wrote poetry. Mathematics eluded her, but she found philosophy exciting and stimulating. She also wrote drama, although her father frowned on performances as frivolous. Julia's love of art, drama, and music were constantly rubbing up against her father's rigidity. She did manage to persuade him to let her attend private school for seven years, but at sixteen she decided she had mastered all she could from school and turned to private study to advance her mind. Julia's self-discipline and love of study never left her, and her children commented on how important study time ("precious time" she called it) was to her.

Although for Julia, Samuel Ward could be her "jailer" who "shut me up within an enchanted castle," he was a failed jailer to his sons, who were committed to the "social tie."[9] With her brothers' active social life dangling before her, Julia enlisted them in her campaign to enter the larger world. When she was nineteen her brother Sam's marriage to Emily Astor opened a door to New York City Society. Her father's death on November 27, 1839, allowed Julia and her sisters to walk in.

The excitement of New York Society was tempered by the death of her brother Henry a year later, which briefly plunged Julia into the conservative religion of her father. But her intellectual curiosity and romantic bent soon turned her away from strict orthodoxy and she again engaged in the wider world, both the social world of dances and theater and intellectual intercourse.[10]

Julia's brothers opened doors of New York Society for Julia and her sisters, and they became known as the Three Graces of Bond Street. By her early twenties, Julia was intellectually accomplished, well read in several languages (especially poetry of the romantics and dissertations of philosophers), and eagerly involved in the social scene of the time.

The upper-class world of the northeast stretched from Philadelphia to Boston, and Julia was soon visiting friends in Boston, Newport, and Philadelphia. One summer in Boston she became part of a social set that included Charles Sumner, later a radical abolitionist senator, and Henry Wadsworth Longfellow. Samuel Gridley Howe was a close friend of Sumner and Longfellow. Howe was a dashing figure, a Byronesque hero of the failed Greek liberation struggle. Many considered him Boston's most handsome bachelor. In Boston, Howe established an international reputation for his work with the blind, in particular a blind and deaf student named Laura Bridgman. Visiting Boston with her sisters, Julia accepted an offer from Sumner to visit Howe's institute. During the visit, the dashing Howe galloped up on horseback and Julia was smitten, at least until the two were married in 1843.[11]

Married life did not prove to be what Julia had hoped. Although Howe was sexually attracted to women and Julia was an attractive woman, he preferred the company of men. On their honeymoon in Europe, the couple took with them Julia's sister Annie and Howe's closest friend Horace Mann and his new wife Mary. Julia was fortunate to have Annie along, for Howe regularly abandoned her for social engagements of his own with European reformers. On returning to Boston Julia and "Chev," as she called him, now accompanied by their first child, Romana—named for the city of her birth—initially set up house at the Institute for the Blind, a bleak house set off from the city by two miles of rugged countryside.

Although during courtship Howe delighted in Julia's accomplishments as a poet and intellectual, as a wife he wanted a subservient homemaker.[12] As a companion, Julia noted that Howe would have happier married to Charles Sumner. She was not particularly interested in being a successful household manager, and the difficulties of managing a home that was also an institution for the blind and those who tended to them were compounded by Howe's constant undermining of her authority with the staff. Even after they moved to their own place in South Boston, it was Howe's dream home, not Julia's. She continued to feel isolated from the social whirl of Boston itself.

Howe expected his wife to be devoted to him and avoid public life, to focus on raising the family and keeping house.[13] He ceaselessly criticized her for her shortcomings in these affairs, at times punishing her by refusing to speak. In 1854 Julia published her first book of poetry, *Passion Flowers*. Correctly believing her husband would not approve of publishing her work for the general public, she did not tell him and published the book anonymously. The book was a success, but not with Howe. When he found out that Julia was the author and that some of the poems addressed conflicts in marriage, he exploded with rage.

There were other problems between them as well. Julia was terrified of childbirth and had three difficult deliveries between 1844 and 1848. By 1849 she was pregnant again. To avoid pregnancy she tried to avoid sex. Her husband responded with hostility, threatening to divorce her.[14] Divorce meant the loss of the children, so Julia relented.

Although a critical thinker and intellectual, Julia shared many of the assumptions of her social class. She remembers arriving in Boston "supposing the abolitionists to be men and women of rather course fiber, abounding in cheap easy denunciations and seeking to lay rash hands on the complex machinery of government."[15] But she was also drawn to abolitionist Theodore Parker's intellectual rigor, honesty, and friendship. (Parker's library, Boston's largest, was also an appeal.) Soon Parker and his wife were Julia's closest friends and confidants. At social gatherings at the Parkers', Julia met Wendell Phillips and his radical wife Ann, William Lloyd Garrison, abolitionist poet John Greenleaf Whittier, and other radical Boston abolitionists. Her husband's closest friends, Henry Longfellow and Charles Sumner, were also committed to abolitionism. Sumner was a regular visitor to the Howe home, and the Howes and Longfellows, Henry and Fanny, spent significant time at each other's homes and shared a summer cottage in Newport.

Despite these early associations, the Howes were not initially involved with the abolitionists. Julia thought them reckless and Samuel thought them ineffectual.[16] But they were increasingly pulled into abolitionism. The formation of the Vigilance Committee to fight against slave renditions was too exciting for Howe to resist, and Julia's social world immersed her in what she called "a community that was still forming" of abolitionists.[17] Her friendships with the Parkers and Clarkes dispelled notions that abolitionists were irresponsible. Soon Julia "cast my lot with those who protested against new assumptions of the slave power."[18] And in doing so she found herself alienated from her "society friends."[19]

Although alienated from Boston society by both the physical isolation of her home and her growing sympathy for abolitionism, Julia was developing links to a new community. Despite the hostility of her husband, she slowly developed a world independent of his domineering. She increasingly found companionship among Howe's intellectual companions—Horace Mann, Sumner, Longfellow, and particularly Boston's leading intellectual, Theodore Parker. Longfellow encouraged Julia's poetry writing and Parker supported her study of philosophy. Among Boston intelligentsia Julia became the center of a vibrant literary scene that included not only Longfellow and Parker but also Thomas Wentworth Higginson and Harriet Beecher Stowe. When Samuel decided to take on publishing the abolitionist paper, *The Commonwealth*, Julia took the job of coeditor. Although it galled him to depend on her, he realized he needed her skills to broaden the paper's reach.

Yet her behavior fed an ever-flowing spring of conflict with her husband. Samuel admired and supported public women such as Florence

Nightingale and Dorothea Dix,[20] but he wanted a wife like the one Parker had critically called a "domestic drudge" and "domestic doll."[21] Despite his public reputation as a liberal, Howe found Parker's radical theology too extreme. He objected to Julia taking the children to Parker's egalitarian church and pushed her to attend a more traditional service. Eventually the Howes compromised, with Julia and the children attending James Freeman Clarke's less notorious but equally radical church, and the families became lifelong friends. Young Sarah Clarke would often visit, and Abby May, daughter of radical abolitionist Samuel May, would spend the summers with the Howe family as a helpmate for Julia.

Struggling with a husband who expected subservience in a wife, Julia also pondered the role of women in society. Yet in the 1850s she was not yet ready to go as far as Parker, who was calling for radical equality between the sexes. In an essay on the "Women's Rights Question," written in the 1850s, Julia noted that the statutes of New England, like the customs of "savages," vest women's rights in the husband. "To him belong the functions of the outer world . . . to her belong the restrictions of the inner world-the bearing and rearing of children, domestic economy and elementary instruction." Although under these laws and customs women enjoyed some general benefit, they also were "unduly subject to some evils and excluded from some benefits which we might enjoy." Despite these reservations, in the 1850s Julia did not see the system of gender relations as fundamentally flawed and did not accept Parker's rejection of separate spheres for women. Admitting that under existing practices women were denied many of the opportunities men enjoyed, Julia still held that women were morally independent and must be given moral equality. She felt that some women could move into the male sphere—after all, she studied and wrote on philosophy and theology—but these women must "study like a man." The ability to concentrate, study, and think, she argued, "belonged to men and women who greatly love and who holding to one object can achieve ends they want."[22] In a lecture prepared in the early 1860s she posited "the equality, the dignity and the eternal dissimilarity of the two sexes."[23]

For the first twenty years of her married life, Julia stood in the shadow of her more famous husband, whose work with Laura Bridgman brought visitors from around the world to his Perkins School. But ultimately she eclipsed him in fame and honor.[24] In 1870, Thomas Wentworth Higginson took two visiting English radicals to see "Mrs. Howe, but found only the Dr. [Samuel Gridley Howe] and Laura." By this time Julia Ward Howe had become the primary draw, while her husband, still an active reformer, was "only the Dr."[25]

For some abolitionists, like Julia Ward Howe, friendship served to heighten interest in anti-slavery issues from a vague concern to active involvement in a vibrant social community. Others, like Henry Ingersoll Bowditch, came to abolitionism from an already heightened political sensitivity. As he walked home from work down Washington Street on the evening of October 21, 1835, Bowditch found his way blocked by a crowd, later referred to by Theodore Parker as a mob of persons of "property and standing," at Court Street.[26] Not accustomed to such gatherings, Bowditch asked what the occasion was. "They are trying to smoke out Garrison and Thompson," the man replied, "for holding a meeting in opposition to slavery." Bowditch was outraged at this attack on free speech. "Then it has come to this," he cried, "that a man cannot speak on slavery within sight of Faneuil Hall and almost at the foot of Bunker Hill. If this is so, it is time for me to be an abolitionist."[27] Bowditch would later recall this event as the pivotal moment that launched him into social action.[28] Yet like Julia Ward Howe, Bowditch was far more predisposed to social action than he acknowledged in his remembrance.

Bowditch was born August 9, 1809, in Salem and, like Julia Ward Howe, grew up in a solidly respectable household. His father, Nathaniel Bowditch, had recently retired from the sea and his mother, Mary Ingersoll, was the daughter of a sea captain.[29] Nathaniel left school at ten and two years later apprenticed as a clerk, while pursuing independent study of mathematics. He taught himself algebra and then, in order to study Newton's *Principia*, he mastered calculus and Latin. By the 1790s Bowditch's local reputation in math and astronomy earned him a navigator's berth on a series of merchant ships.[30]

By 1802 Bowditch was captaining his own ship and had published the *New American Practical Navigator*, a work that used logarithmic tables and trigonometric functions to enable a sailor with simple mathematical skills to navigate.[31] By then Bowditch was already publishing works on mathematics and astronomy; in 1799 he was elected to the American Academy of Arts and Sciences and offered the professorship of mathematics and physics at Harvard. Between 1802 and 1804, during various sea trips he perfected his French and read Pierre-Simon Laplace's *Traité de mécanique celeste*. In 1804 he retired from the sea and became president of the Essex Fire and Maine Insurance Company. He also continued his study of mathematics and astronomy and published on these subjects in Europe and America. This work earned him membership in several prestigious European scientific societies. Between 1829 and 1839 he translated and published with comments and corrections Laplace's four-volume work on astronomy.

By the time of Henry's Bowditch's birth, his father was a successful scientist and business manager. The Bowditch children played with the children of Salem's other notable families, the Peabodys, Peirces, Pick-erings, and Putnams. Nathaniel Bowditch was an intellectual but stern father who believed that study should prepare one for life's "hard strug-gle." Mary Ingersoll was a religious woman. The children (Henry was the third of five surviving offspring, three boys and two girls) were ex-pected to be at church on Sunday. Except for Mary Ingersoll's prohibi-tion against playing outside on the Sabbath, Nathaniel believed that children should enjoy the open air and nature's wonders.[32]

Nathaniel Bowditch was known to be scrupulously honest and hard working with a head for details. Now a new career beckoned. In 1818 the state chartered the Massachusetts Hospital Life Insurance Company (MHLIC). Its original mission was life insurance and charity—it was to pay one-third of its profits to Massachusetts General Hospital. But MHLIC soon became much more than a charitable life insurance com-pany. At a time when state legislatures were reluctant to grant broad charters to banking institutions, the investors behind the growing tex-tile industry in New England needed an institution that could accumu-late large amounts of trust capital for investment in their mills and other interests. MHLIC's charitable purpose encouraged the legislature to provide it with a liberal charter that enabled it to accumulate signif-icant amounts of capital for investment.[33]

The MHLIC began operations in 1823, and the board of directors ap-pointed Nathaniel Bowditch as actuary, the company's chief officer.[34] Boston's leading families felt secure in depositing their wealth with the well-managed company. The names of those who were building the re-gion's textile empire, Appleton, Cabot, Perkins, Lawrence, and Eliot, were dominant among those with large trusts managed by the MHLIC, but Boston's older merchant princes also put their faith and funds in the institution run by the mathematician from Salem.

This new job required that the family leave Salem and move to Boston, where Henry enrolled in Boston Latin School.[35] After complet-ing his studies there, he entered Harvard as a sophomore in 1825, join-ing Henry Pickering, his childhood friend from Salem, and his soon-to-be-friend Richard Dana.[36] Henry's studies could not suppress his zest for life. Although he reluctantly deferred to his father and turned down invitations to dances in Boston because they violated Har-vard College rules, he spent much of his leisure time fishing and visit-ing the Athenaeum, where "some very pretty girls" were to be found.[37]

Even as a young man, Bowditch felt his privilege and understood it contributed to his good life. He reminded himself that he had no reason "for discontent," for his "lot has fallen in pleasant places."[38] But he was also his father's son. His father's life of hard work, brilliance, and self-discipline were constantly held up to the younger generation. It was a standard Henry worried he would not live up to as he went about enjoy-ing life. He reminded himself in his notebooks, "if I intend to get along at all it must be perseverance . . . [and] the performance of duty."[39]

In 1828 Bowditch graduated from Harvard with little idea what he would do with his life. He did not want to go into law, business, or the ministry. By default he entered Harvard Medical School, studying under Dr. James Jackson and Dr. Jacob Bigelow. He continued his edu-cation as a house physician at Massachusetts General Hospital in 1830–1831.[40] After he finished his Boston studies he decided to com-plete his medical education in Europe, a common practice among nineteenth-century New England intellectuals.[41] In the summer of 1832 he sailed for France carrying his father's letter to some of Europe's most important intellectuals. Nathaniel Bowditch's scientific reputation "introduced me certainly to some of the greatest men of Europe. It car-ried me [into] . . . the elite of the French Academy of sciences."[42]

In the 1830s France was an auspicious place to begin medical study. Subsequent to the French Revolution, the Paris École de Médicine was established to unite surgery and medicine as the same branch of sci-ence. More important, the medical school used Paris hospitals for train-ing. Lectures, laboratories, and careful, systematic observation of hospital patients provided the basis for Paris's new medical education.

By the time Bowditch arrived in Paris, a new school of empirical cli-nicians was challenging the older version of medicine that looked to purges and heroic interventions.[43] The clinicians believed in the power of nature to heal and that a physician should study disease in order to understand its cause.[44] Bowditch fell in with the new clinicians as they challenged the old school. Linking up with fellow Bostonian James Jackson, son of Bowditch's Boston teacher, Bowditch entered Pierre Charles Alexander Louis's seminar and quickly became a partisan in the battles over the direction of medical education.[45] Louis had founded the Société Médicale d'Observation, stressing the importance of science, statistics, and observation of large numbers of patients with similar symptoms.

Jackson, already in Paris studying under Louis when Bowditch ar-rived, introduced Bowditch to Louis and got him special privileges in the hospital.[46] Bowditch remembered the time fondly: "Louis and I be-came very intimate. He allowed me to visit and record the cases in his wards at any hour of the day. I attended also his autopsies, saw his care-ful method of examination . . . I felt at one with his analysis of a new case as if new scenes in Medical diagnosis were clearly offered before me."[47] Under Louis's tutorage Bowditch came to appreciate medicine as a profession of caring and intellectual challenge. In Louis, Bowditch saw a doctor "with a noble heart, [and] a delightful kind disposition."[48]

Louis's "numerical way," as Bowditch called it, enabled Bowditch to combine his interest in science as a field to help patients and medicine. Since his days at Harvard, where he was influenced by John Ware, Bowditch was fascinated with the problem solving of science. In remembering Louis's contribution to medicine, Bowditch compared Louis's method to that of the astronomer who derives his laws from a comparison of many careful observations.[49] Science opened up nature for Bowditch. He felt that through scientific investigation he would capture the wonder of God's creation.[50] Louis lectured to his students about the human "need for truth; that state of soul which does not allow us to stop in any scientific labors at which is only probable, but compels us to continue our researches until we have arrived at evidence."[51] Bowditch also wanted to help and serve humankind. Louis stressed to his students that doctors should pursue both rigorous science and human nurturing and appreciation of the dignity of the patient.[52] He offered Bowditch the opportunity to serve both science and humanity.

While Bowditch was taking up the banner of the new clinicians, he also immersed himself into the culture and community of French intellectuals. His father's name opened doors for him, but it was the ideas and community he found within that helped transform him.[53] Scientists and doctors were very much a part of the French campaign for greater liberty and equality. Only two years before Bowditch arrived in Paris, Parisians had risen up and overthrown Charles X, and installed what Bowditch sarcastically called "the citizen king," Louis Philippe. But Paris was still awash in revolutionary rhetoric and fervor. The "citizen king," in an attempt to control growing popular radical republicanism, increasingly clamped down on public demonstrations and publications. Many of the city's leading scientists were active in the campaigns for greater democratic rights.[54]

An important model for Bowditch when he was in France was François Raspail, "an excellent chemist and also . . . a Republican." Raspail was perpetually in prison for his open engagement in republican demonstrations. Bowditch saw in him a model for an engaged intellectual: a famous chemist but also an activist. Bowditch wrote about Raspail's death, "À l'heure mon héros!"[55] Soon Bowditch was attending political gatherings, rallies, and writing home criticisms of the French government.[56] He found Paris liberating, "my years residence in Paris had liberalized my mind. Free speech and free thought were my delight."[57]

Bowditch's second year in Paris involved him in even more deeply in French politics.[58] He attended the funeral of the radical republican deputy Duleny, where Bowditch joined "the republicans with naked arms and bonnets rouge."[59] In 1833 Bowditch wrote home to his father that, "I want to see everything more free than it is now . . . that is what is done here and what ought to be done in America." He went on to argue, "my grand aim shall be to give to everybody the opportunity of study, and in this way repay to humanity at large the immense debt of gratitude that I owe to France."[60] In a letter to his mother Bowditch noted that he was "far more liberal now than I was before visiting Europe."[61] By the time Bowditch left Paris for home he was a convinced French radical in his view of both medicine and politics.

Not only politics and medicine caught Bowditch's fancy while he was in Paris. In his second year Bowditch moved from the Place de l'Odéon to a room in a *pension bourgeoise* at No. 1 Rue d'Aubenton closer to Louis's hospital, La Pitié. A seventeen-year-old English woman in Paris to complete her education was also staying in the *pension* with her elderly aunt. The young woman was Olivia Yardley, and Bowditch fell in love. In March he proposed, and then, while on a four-month tour of Italy, he wrote his parents of his intention. This was the first his parents had ever heard of Olivia; they were not pleased. Nathaniel Bowditch, who was paying for Bowditch's studies in France, wrote to his son of his displeasure. Fearing that he had unduly offended his parents and not wanting to jeopardize his studies abroad, Bowditch asked Olivia if they could put their plans on hold for a year. They agreed to break off all communication for a year, and then, if they still felt the same toward each other, they agreed to appeal again to Bowditch's parents for approval of their marriage.[62]

Bowditch finished his studies in Paris and returned to Boston, where he threw himself into building a practice. Developing a successful medical practice in the nineteenth century was no easy matter. Doctors with extensive training, such as Bowditch, had to compete for patients with others who had little or no training. Patients looking for a physician had little way of distinguishing one form of training from another. Without a common curriculum or course of study, doctors' knowledge and practices varied widely. The patient walking in off the street knew little about what to expect from her or his physician. And even a well-trained physician such as Bowditch had little to offer patients. To build up a practice doctors looked to referrals by word of mouth, reputation in the community, and other doctors, particularly other members of the Massachusetts Medical Society.

Young Henry Bowditch had been away from the city for over two years. Few knew him, and few understood the nuances of the new clinical approach to medicine over the older methods. Purges and bleeding with a lancet were still common practice in 1830s Boston.[63] Bowditch did not help himself by maintaining self-defeating principles of freedom. "So desirous was I of being free, that for a time, I declined to join the Massachusetts Medical Society for fear of being bound by any pledges which I might want to disregard, but I soon found that I was carrying principle too far and really losing good influences of exchange and thought with honorable peers."[64]

By 1838 the Bowditch family was thoroughly reconciled to Olivia Yardley and Bowditch's love for her. On July 17, 1838, only two days after Olivia arrived in America, she and Henry were married.[65] By this time Bowditch's practice was also well established. In 1846 he was appointed to the medical staff at Massachusetts General Hospital along with Oliver Wendell Holmes. They joined Jacob Bigelow, Enoch Hale, and J. B. S. Jackson, three of the most prestigious doctors in New England.[66]

The newlywed couple moved into their home at 8 Otis Place, at the foot of Beacon Hill.[67] Later, as his practice improved, they purchased a house in the Back Bay at 324 Boylston Street. There Bowditch began serious research into the causes and pathology of tuberculosis and other respiratory diseases.[68] He combined his study of disease causation with a growing load of patients. Olivia helped in the practice by maintaining the financial records and running the house and drew illustrations of his microscopic observations for his scientific presentations and publications.[69]

Practicing medicine and doing medical research did not occupy all Bowditch's intellectual interests. On June 26, 1849, he joined Harvard professor Louis Agassiz, Boston's leading naturalist, in a scientific excursion in Buzzards Bay off Martha's Vineyard. It was a grand time for Bowditch: "my whole being harmonized with nature. Perfect health, a clear . . . atmosphere, a pure scientific voyage into a new wonder of the almighty and all in companionship with such a man as Agassiz."[70]

Although suspicious of religious orthodoxy, Bowditch saw science and nature's wonders as confirming the existence of a divine force. Yet even in college he had demonstrated a surprising ecumenicalism and skepticism about religious dogma. Those tendencies were reinforced during his years in France, where anti-clericalism pervaded the intellectual community. Upon returning home, Bowditch continued to hold to religious skepticism.[71] In an 1835 letter to his former minister in Salem, he noted that he "signs no creeds . . . observes no ceremonies. I am neither a Unitarian nor a Trinitarian."[72] Yet he never totally left behind the strong religious beliefs of his "sainted mother."[73]

After returning from Paris, Bowditch began talking to the Unitarian minister William Channing about God and faith to see whether he could reconcile his skepticism with a desire for a belief in a benevolent divinity. Although he felt uneasy about the religious doctrines popular at the time in Boston, he respected Channing. Yet Channing could not convince him: "I don't want to offend all my friends . . . yet I cannot but feel that the church as a church is false and faithless and therefore I ought not to attend it."[74] When his friends urged him to go to church, he responded, "how absurd. . . . I have avoided the ceremonies of Christians because they seemed to me unholy. . . . The everyday actions of life, the constant endeavor to school [oneself] to the dictates of duty"—these were the measures of religiosity for Bowditch. And he believed that the sooner mankind "endeavored to do justly and to have mercy the sooner we shall do the world and ourselves good."[75]

Ultimately Bowditch found religious meaning in nature, his wife and children, and striving for justice.[76] His brother William claimed that Bowditch "did not believe in the creeds of men" and looked instead to values that expressed a common good and humanity whether those values were "Catholic, Protestant, or Agnostic."[77] William claimed that Bowditch did believe in God and the immortality of the soul, which William thought was all nonsense. Henry centered his belief in noble and pure action. He did not doubt a divine existence, but he doubted what religious leaders had to say about the matter. Bowditch felt that he was "by nature and partly by education from Father, a Quaker in spirit . . . [believing] each person being his or her own priest."[78]

Bowditch once told C. F. Folsom that his microscope was "the noblest cathedral for the highest religious thought."[79] He may have been "indifferent" to churches, but he had a strong belief in action to bring about a better world. He claimed he identified more closely with the "Associationists" than with any religion. "My confidence is in the idea of cooperation which is brought forward by the socialists. A dawn of a new empire is seen in that beautiful thought. And could I not believe in the main doctrines of the Associationists, I should feel that this world is a god forsaken spot."[80]

Action to do justly and love mercy defined morality for Bowditch and spurred him to found the Warren Street Chapel, a proto-settlement house, with his college classmate Charles F. Barnard and John Emmons, another Boston acquaintance. The Chapel was located on what is today Warrenton Street, south of Eliot Street between Tremont and Charles Streets in a neighborhood of poor artisans and day laborers. The Chapel was to be a place free from the normal constraints of religious dogma and received opinion. Bowditch noted that the Chapel was not a religious but an educational institution. "As far as I was concerned I never alluded to religion or the bible."[81] It was a center devoted to the "general improvement of the young of the poor."[82] The Chapel ran programs for the poor staffed by volunteers.[83] Bowditch taught classes, instructed children in crafts, provided medical services to the Chapel's poor neighbors, and organized cricket practices and matches and other outdoor excursions.[84] Soon other well-off Bostonians, such as Horace Mann, were offering their services to the Warren Street Chapel.[85]

The Chapel initially met all Bowditch's hopes. It was a center for open discussion without any formal religious institutional link. "No place seemed to me half so sacred."[86] Visiting the homes of the Chapel's participants convinced Bowditch that more than just education and play in the fresh air was necessary. He "was determined that something ought to be done about improving the tenements of the poor." He organized Chapel meetings to discuss the problem and formed a committee to "do something about housing for the poor."[87] Decent housing for the city's poor of both races remained a concern for Bowditch for the rest of his life.

But the Chapel's very success created conflict for Bowditch. As more of Boston's elites came to see the Chapel as a fitting place for their charity, the directors became ever more anxious not to offend. Bowditch, by contrast, "liberalized [in his] mind" and with "free speech and free thought" his "delight," believed that the Chapel should be not just a place of charity but also a forum for discussions about justice and oppression, particularly slavery. At a meeting of the directors Bowditch noted that he had told the children about Halley's Comet, but had failed to mention the more momentous event of the West Indian Emancipation, when "800,000 human beings were made men and women."[88] Bowditch felt "the stings of remorse" over the Chapel's silence on the issue of slavery and believed that it was time to "clear my conscience." Given that the Chapel allowed temperance meetings, Bowditch believed it should also sponsor anti-slavery lectures. The "institution should take some interest" and take "an open stand." The board of directors expressed concern that if abolitionists spoke at the Chapel some of "our friends" would demand their gifts back. Several board members said the Chapel should remain neutral, to which Bowditch replied that if he "saw an indecency in the community—violating justice and everything else—I certainly should be disposed however much the institution was for general purposes to cry aloud."

This was not Bowditch's first conflict with the board of directors. Earlier when a black child had attempted to join one of the Chapel's groups and white children objected, the board had initially wanted to create a segregated group for black children. Indignant over the suggested segregation, Bowditch threatened to resign and the board relented. But on the subject of anti-slavery lectures, the board did not relent.[89] Bowditch argued that the Chapel was becoming more concerned for "order" than for "love." John Emmons disagreed. He was concerned that if the Chapel became a forum for unpopular ideas such as anti-slavery, its wealthy backers would withdraw their support.

Bowditch saw no problem with the wealthy withdrawing their support, for in his vision he saw the Chapel as an ideal, not as an institution. Barnard sided with Emmons. Painfully, Bowditch severed his ties with the Chapel.

Agonizing about his decision, Bowditch visited William Channing, hoping to win an ally in his campaign to force the Chapel to embrace social justice. Channing, "a good man," nonetheless failed Bowditch, further convincing him that "the true leaders of philanthropy were outside the church."[90] Bowditch then complained to Lydia Maria Child, one of Boston's radical abolitionists, about the Chapel's position. She told him that he had outgrown the Chapel anyway and that it was time he focused his attention on a more pressing issue.

Although opposed to slavery, Bowditch was initially reluctant to join an abolitionist organization for fear that membership would restrict his liberty and freedom of thought.[91] Convinced, however, by fellow radical thinker Charles Follen (who taught German at Harvard until he was dismissed for his abolitionist ideas) that opposing slavery required one to act and to act in concert with others, Bowditch joined the Massachusetts Anti-Slavery Society (MASS) in 1836.[92] He explained to Maria Weston Chapman his realization that "man is social and very many great ends never can be accomplished save by united action." Follen, Bowditch claimed, told him that he could "not find it in my conscience to keep away from these who were united for the sole purpose of abolishing slavery."[93] Once active in MASS, Bowditch found that, although he disagreed with many of the members on a number of issues, particularly the issues of political involvement and disunion, his membership did not limit his freedom and did increase his ability to be effective. It also supplied a community of fellowship. As Bowditch noted in reflection many years later, "antislavery knit honest people together more firmly than any other tie."[94]

Howe's and Bowditch's anti-slavery work did more than just link them into a community of radical reformers. Abolitionist work taught them how to organize to effect a political end, whether that end was freeing a fugitive slave, helping stage a social fair to raise money and build community links, or getting issues addressed in public arenas. Abolitionist work also helped crystallize their thoughts about political ideas, particularly the ideal of natural rights. Although Bowditch came to abolitionism already politicized by his years in France, he sharpened his political teeth in the abolitionist campaign. As he reported in an autobiographical note, "my antislavery views . . . have been of infinite service to me, and I believe to many others in that they have made one look deeper than mere dogmas or personal opinions." Others accused the abolitionists of being intolerant, but Bowditch felt his anti-slavery work taught him how to work with others to reach a common goal, even those whose "whole opinions I wholly dispute, [but who had] evidences of hearty character and purity of life. I feel I have found of late that I had a real zest for the company of those with whom I disagree . . . I believe that I am almost alone on the Board of Managers of the Antislavery Society who does not go for disunion," but "we embrace at the same time that we fight, for we have learned to tolerate difference of opinion." Of course the toleration Bowditch spoke of was restricted to accepting differences of ideas within the larger community of radicals. Toleration could flourish atop a shared "foundation" in the struggle for freedom.[95]

Bowditch's radicalism, like Howe's, did not stop at abolitionism. He championed tenement house reform and women's suffrage. He was a leading advocate for women's equal rights in medicine and used his position in the Massachusetts Medical Society and the American Medical Association to get women admitted as equal members. It was to his role as the first chairman of the Massachusetts State Board of Health that Bowditch brought the lessons from his years of struggle against slavery as well as his call to "go forth for justice of the oppressed."[96] Bowditch argued that the state had a responsibility to protect the rights to life, liberty, and the pursuit of happiness. For citizens to pursue happiness and enjoy liberty they needed a clean and healthy environment and safe living conditions, and he felt the state should guarantee these conditions. As he told the Harvard graduating class of 1863, "public authorities" had a responsibility for alleviating the miserable conditions and "terrible life-long toil," for "surely the [conditions] which the poor live and love and have their being ought . . . like the schools . . . be cared for by the public; if not for humanity's sake, then for the sake of public health."[97]

Bowditch and Howe were not the only abolitionists who carried their struggle "on the side of right and justice" beyond the issue of slavery. Abolitionist Elizabeth Buffum Chace noted, "in the process of overthrowing one great wrong, there is always laid bare some other wrong. . . . In the progress of the Anti-slavery movement experience revealed [other] great injustice. . . . And these experiences were to the abolitionists, in this as in other directions a liberal education."[98]

Chapter 2

"With Other Good Souls"

Abolitionism "aroused his public spirit . . . formed his character, and . . . shaped his life work."

—Henry Ingersoll Bowditch

When confronted on that evening of October 21, 1835, with the mob attacking William Lloyd Garrison, Bowditch, who prided himself on his love of "free speech and free thought," was appalled. Here in Boston, just down the street from the spot where "Attucks and his comrades fell in the earliest days of the revolution," a crowd was trying to stop abolitionists from speaking out.[1] Seeing Samuel Eliot at the edge of the crowd, Bowditch urged him to join in fighting the mob in defense of free speech. Eliot's response was not what Bowditch expected. "I was surprised at his apparent coolness," Bowditch remembered, "instead of sustaining the idea of free speech he . . . rather intimated that the authorities, while not wishing for a mob rather sympathized with its object which was to forcibly suppress the abolitionists."[2]

The New England symbols of the American Revolution were part of Bowditch's life. Moreover, he felt that his experience in France had brought him closer to the American ideal of freedom. Although he loved and cherished France and his radical French friends, he also honored the New England tradition of protest and principled defense of liberty. The mob's attack on Garrison and Thompson and the failure of others to rush to their defense sickened Bowditch, for it seemed to give the lie to that Revolutionary tradition. "I am an Abolitionist from this very moment," he declared.[3]

What Bowditch observed that October evening was a "broadcloth mob" breaking up a gathering of the Boston Female Anti-Slavery Society. The BFASS had invited the charismatic radical English abolitionist George Thompson to address its meeting. It was not an easy thing to do. Earlier that year, after denying abolitionists the use of Faneuil Hall, Boston's establishment themselves used the Hall to convene an August

21 meeting to attack abolitionism. Boston of the 1830s was still dominated by the merchant class. These leaders made their money in trade,
much of it with the South and the slave plantations of the Caribbean. By
the end of the 1820s and increasingly in the 1830s, the cotton textile industry was adding wealth to the region, and merchants and traders were
investing heavily in the mills that depended on slave-produced cotton.

Concerned that abolitionist activity might threaten their trading and
political links to the South, New England political and economic elites
(led by Harrison Gray Otis and Peleg Sprague and presided over by
Mayor Theodore Lyman) called for the suppression of abolitionist agitation. A mob in Haverhill stoned the stage to prevent Samuel May
from talking on slavery, and John Whittier found himself covered with
rotten eggs tossed by an anti-abolitionist crowd. William Lloyd Garrison
faced continuous threats including a gallows erected at his front door
on Brighton Street. Despite the violence and threats, the Boston Female Anti-Slavery Society announced that Thompson would address its
first anniversary meeting. Public outcry closed off most of the city's venues to the meeting. Under the firm leadership of Maria Weston Chapman, the organization decided to go ahead with the meeting at its
headquarters at 46 Washington Street. After announcing their intention to have speakers talk on the "cause of human rights," the women,
fearing for Thompson's life, decided to have Garrison speak.

Not realizing Thompson was not the speaker, anti-abolitionists distributed handbills on Boston's streets urging citizens to gather at the
BFASS headquarters to get Thompson. Offers to pay $100 to those who
tarred and feathered the man circulated. When Garrison arrived at the
hall to speak, a huge crowd was there as well. Inside, a few dozen brave
women, led by Chapman, two of her sisters, Deborah and Caroline,
Susan Paul, an influential black schoolteacher, and Mary Parker, waited
as the crowd began pushing and screaming to get in. Garrison, realizing he could not go on, retreated into a back office. Faced with impend-
ing violence, Mayor Lyman demanded that the women leave for their
own safety. Chapman then accused Lyman of complicity to mob violence. The mayor dismissed the idea, repeating his concern for safety.

Walking arm in arm, the black and white women of the BFASS
marched out of the hall and sought to reconvene at the Chapman
home on West Street in fashionable Chauncy Place (two blocks east of
the Park Street Church and the north end of the Commons). With the
women gone, the crowd grabbed Garrison and called for his lynching.
Daniel and Buff Cooley, two large teamsters, pulled Garrison from the
crowd and hurried him to City Hall and Mayor Lyman. Not wanting to
confront the crowd, Lyman protected Garrison by arresting him.[4]

The riot offended Bowditch's sense of justice and right. It also offended his sense of history. Bowditch saw Faneuil Hall as a symbol of revolutionary commitment to freedom, the place where great patriotic leaders such as Samuel Adams had defended free speech and liberty against arbitrary power. For a mob of Bostonians to attack a man for speaking out for freedom was for Bowditch a violation of history and sacred tradition that could only be put right if people of conscience stepped forward and acted in defense of the oppressed.[5]

Failing to convince his social peers to rally to Garrison's defense, Bowditch proclaimed his solidarity with the besieged abolitionist. The following morning he went to the office of the *Liberator* at 25 Corn Street (north of Tremont Street and Boston Common and around the corner from Faneuil Hall) and subscribed. And he proclaimed to all who would hear him his commitment to the cause of anti-slavery. He soon found, however, that his outspoken position of slavery was not popular in Boston. Doctors to whom Bowditch expressed his newfound commitment warned him that his views would destroy his career. Rather than appreciate the warning, Bowditch attacked: "you who would repress free speech upon slavery, are men wholly recreant to the principles for which our fathers fought and died at Bunker Hill."[6] Given the reality of slavery Bowditch came to feel, "do what you will, destroy my life, my reputation which is more than life, my property, but I will never prove false to that holy cause of humanity."[7]

What Bowditch did not realize that October evening was that the brave women who marched out of 46 Washington Street, arm and arm, black and white together, to Maria Weston Chapman's home would soon become as close to him and as much a part of his life as the Putnam children of his youth or his Paris friend James Jackson. They would fill the social void left by the ostracism of Boston Society. If to the mob threatening them these women and their male supporters were crazy agitators, to each other they were friends, companions, and lovers. In an 1843 letter to Maria Weston Chapman, Bowditch wrote that when he first heard the abolitionists, he was put off by their "ungracious manner," and "vehement language," but he came to realize that what he was really afraid of was what others of his social set would think of him if he were identified with the abolitionists. "In keeping aloof from the anti-slavery society I was making myself a slave of public opinion and really judging the abolitionists not by their own deeds and writings but by the standard of a corrupted public sentiment."[8]

The movement Bowditch joined was dedicated to fundamental change in society, not just ending slavery but achieving racial equality. Abolitionists were shrewd organizers and calculating political operatives who understood that Boston's elites viewed them as "revolutionary, lawless, and not respectable."[9] To be successful they needed to win popular support and discredit their opponents, to popularize their message yet hold true to their fundamental principles. They also needed to build networks of friendship and comradeship to hold together in face of a hostile community.[10]

This was a formidable challenge. The fundamental principle to which these abolitionists committed themselves was revolutionary. Just two years earlier, at the founding convention of the American Anti-Slavery Society (AASS), the delegates had pledged themselves not just to end slavery but "to secure to the colored population of the United States all the rights and privileges which belong to them as men and as Americans." The members of the AASS understood that they held that pledge "come what may to our persons, our interests, or our reputations—whether we live to witness the triumph of Justice, Liberty and Humanity, or perish."[11] In a nation that daily drank deeply the bitter wine of racism, these abolitionists were proclaiming a commitment to absolute equality.[12] They made that claim on the basis of both divine revelation and the Declaration of Independence.

These were men and women Henry Ingersoll Bowditch embraced as he had once embraced "the republicans with naked arms and bonnets rouge" in France. They shared his historical memory. At the founding of the American Anti-Slavery Society in Philadelphia in 1833, the delegates noted that fifty-seven years earlier "a band of patriots" had met in Philadelphia to end the yoke of foreign oppression. Now these delegates hoped to complete that work. They also shared a commitment to "free speech and free thought" and a call to go "forth for justice of the oppressed." To do so involved commitment to a movement and a community.

Henry Ingersoll Bowditch was not the only Boston Brahmin who felt the attack on Garrison was an offense against the region's history. On that October day Wendell Phillips of the wealthy Phillips family, student of history, lawyer, and one of Harvard's golden boys, looked out his law office window to see the mob gathered outside the Boston Female Anti-Slavery Society.[13] At the time Phillips had no interest in abolitionism. He shared his family's conservative commitment to order, discipline, and paternalism. His father, a wealthy lawyer, had been a Federalist mayor of Boston in 1821.[14] Although his college friend Charles Sumner, later to become the radical militant senator for Massachusetts, was moving more into reform circles, including abolitionism, Phillips saw abolitionists as disrupters of social peace. He accepted the rationalization by his southern friends from Harvard of slavery in a context of social control and order.[15] His classmates noted that he was "the least likely to give his labor and enthusiasm" in "defense of popular rights."[16] Yet at that moment in October it was the mob attacking the abolitionists that seemed to violate order.[17]

The crowd of anti-abolitionists offended Phillips, but in his words he "did not understand anti-slavery then."[18] What led him to understand it was love. Shortly after the incident at 46 Washington Street, Charles Sumner arranged for Phillips to join him and a few friends on an outing. The morning of the event, Sumner slept in, and Phillips found himself paired with the young Ann Greene for the carriage ride to the outing.[19] Although Greene's family had been wealthy merchants, she was now an orphan living with her cousins the Chapmans. And like Maria Weston Chapman, Ann was an active abolitionist and member of the Boston Female Anti-Slavery Society. Striking up a conversation, Phillips mentioned his displeasure with the handling of the anti-abolition riot at Washington Street.

Ann knew well the event; she had been there. She was not one to hold her tongue. She described how she "talked abolition to him all the time up and all the time there."[20] As a son of a wealthy Boston Brahmin family and Harvard's star graduate, Phillips was one of the city's most eligible bachelors, yet none of the region's young women had yet caught his eye. Ann Greene was something else. She was bright, opinionated, articulate, and self-assured. By the time the carriage returned the couple to Boston, Phillips was enchanted and began to seriously court the young Miss Greene. But Ann was not to be courted in traditional Boston Society fashion. She insisted that if Phillips wanted to be with her, it would be at abolitionist affairs. Through Ann, Phillips spent time with the Chapmans, where he met the tough and resourceful Maria Weston and the financially successful Henry Chapman, who provided much of the money for abolitionist activity. The Chapmans opened their home to the Boston abolitionist community. There on any given evening would be the shoemaker-printer Garrison and his wife Helen, the Brahmin abolitionist lawyer Ellis Gary Loring, and of course Maria's sisters Caroline and Anne, who ran a racially integrated school in Boston. Visiting from Lynn might be James Buffum, or up from New Bedford Maria's sister (Ann's cousin) Deborah.

Despite this deep immersion in the abolitionist community, Phillips held back. In a visit to New Bedford he stayed with Deborah Weston. Deborah liked Phillips and believed him a good match for Ann, though she felt Phillips "slightly Whiggery and rather conservative." But she "talked considerable abolitionism" to him and felt he was coming around.[21] He came around enough that Ann agreed to marry him, and they exchanged their vows within the community of abolitionists, a community to which Wendell's mother was openly hostile.

Ann taught Wendell the language of egalitarianism and particularly anti-racism. Phillips wrote in a letter to the Irish abolitionist Richard Webb, "my wife made an out and out abolitionist of me, and she always preceded me in adoption of the various causes I advocated."[22] Ann brought Wendell into the community of abolitionists, but the event that publicly linked him to their cause was the killing of Elijah Lovejoy, a printer who published an abolitionist paper in Alton, Illinois. On November 7, 1837, anti-abolitionist mobs murdered Lovejoy as he attempted to defend his press from destruction. Outraged Boston moderates called for a meeting at Faneuil Hall to protest the murder.

Before the meeting could come to a resolution on the Lovejoy affair, state attorney general James T. Austin rose and denounced Lovejoy and the abolitionists for threatening southerners with immediate abolition and the prospect of thousands of uncontrolled freed ex-slaves overrunning their region. Austin argued that the crowd that killed Lovejoy acted in self-protection in the spirit of the revolutionaries of 1776. He fed the crowd the standard racist fare of nineteenth-century America: blacks were uncontrollable beasts that slavery held in bounds, abolitionists were stirring up slaves and sectional conflict and harming trade, and they deserved to be put down for the sake of harmony, order, and white supremacy.

Phillips had come to the event in support of Ann and anger at Lovejoy's murder. Hearing Austin defend the murder as the act of patriots in the mode of 1776 was more than he could take. He leaped onto the lecture platform and denounced Austin with an eloquence that stunned the Hall. Using his sweeping knowledge of American history Phillips argued that patriots defended liberty and free speech, not terror and murder, and that it was the abolitionists and Lovejoy who were upholding the traditions of Revolutionary Boston.[23]

With his Faneuil Hall speech Phillips realized his calling and commitment. Within a year he quit his law practice and was elected president of the Boston Anti-Slavery Society and general agent of the Massachusetts Anti-Slavery Society. He brought to abolitionism a sweeping knowledge of history and the best oratorical skills in New England. What he learned in abolitionism and in the bosom of his new home was the language of social justice and egalitarianism.

Many came to see the slave as an equal and slavery as an unacceptable evil through religious belief and appealed to Christians to oppose slavery as a moral wrong; for Phillips, Bowditch, Nathaniel Rogers, and Bowditch's brother William, slavery was not only a moral evil but also a civil one. Bowditch and Phillips saw in slavery a repudiation of the ideals of the nation as expressed in the Declaration of Independence and a smear on the nation's revolutionary ideals. They argued that slavery should be understood politically as a fundamental violation of natural rights. Slavery represented uncontrolled power of one human being over another; it was the ultimate oppression.[24] Slavery denied the slave the inherent natural right of liberty. Phillips and the Bowditches criticized slavery as a violation of the republican ideal because it was a tyranny over the individual that corrupted civil society. Even the word "slaveholding" obscured the nature of the situation. Bowditch felt that it

glossed over the defect by saying it was rather the fault of the age than of the man . . . but now we can give but partially the truth when using the epithet "man-thief." Every slaveholding man and woman of the South is a "man-thief" for he or she not [only steals] a man from the first moment of his existence and deprives him of the right to his own muscles' property, the right of going in and out at his own pleasure, the right to his own wife and child all of which things are too enough to make the epithet "man-thief" so shallow and unexpressive to my mind now that I long to find something more pungent something more true.[25]

As the examples of Phillips and Bowditch indicate, there were many avenues that brought abolitionists into the cause. For William Lloyd Garrison, Amos Phelps, George Benson, James Wright, Samuel May, Samuel Johnson, and Lydia Maria Child, intense religious belief and a hope of perfecting society brought them to their uncompromising belief that slavery had immediately to be abolished.[26] Others, like Julia Ward Howe, found their way into the community and language of social justice, egalitarianism, natural rights, and anti-racism through their links of friendship and love of other people.[27]

Thomas Wentworth Higginson, like Wendell Phillips, graduated from Harvard with great expectations: his father was the college steward and Higginson was the class star. But this did not mean Higginson had a clear vision of his future life. He thought he might study literature. His mother, feeling that a rather vague calling, tried to persuade him to choose a career. Higginson resisted and felt that a career would inhibit his freedom. Instead, he wrote his mother that he had to have "my whole time" to pursue his thinking.[28] Yet he was not thinking particularly about the burning social issues of the day. In a letter to Frank Parker after going south to visit an uncle, Higginson accused Frank of being prejudiced against the slaveholding South. Higginson argued that slavery was not as oppressive as northerners made out.[29]

While thinking, Higginson spent considerable time socializing with friends, the aspiring poet James Russell Lowell, and Maria White and the communitarian Brook Farm group. He regularly visited Brook Farm, mostly for the social interaction.[30] He also visited the Channing sisters, Mary and Barbara, whose social set included abolitionists. Mary and Barbara were daughters of abolitionist Dr. Walter Channing; Mary encouraged Higginson to come with her when she visited Brook Farm.

The sisters attended Theodore Parker's free church and also abolition-ist James Freeman Clarke's services, and they insisted that if Higginson wanted to spend time with them, he must come to hear Parker's and Clarke's sermons.[31] Higginson's infatuation with Mary grew. He realized that if he wanted her to take his proposal for marriage seriously, he would have to become more serious about life and about slavery. Yet in 1842, although Mary had agreed to his proposal, Higginson was still un-sure about his future or his involvement in abolitionism.[32] To Mary's pressure was added that of Higginson's friend and fellow writer James Russell Lowell. Lowell had married Maria White, who along with her brother William White, also a friend and schoolmate of Higginson, was a fervent abolitionist. Under the influence of Maria and William, Low-ell joined the cause.[33]

Higginson's social world increasingly became interlocked with aboli-tionism. Within six years of his marriage to Mary, Higginson found a ca-reer. After a rocky beginning where he entered and then left Harvard Divinity School, he finally completed his studies and was ordained a Unitarian minister. The model of the radical free-thinking Unitarian minister Theodore Parker finally convinced Higginson he could com-bine his desire for freedom with a career. He found himself with an ap-pointment to a congregation in Newburyport and quickly established his reputation as an abolitionist.[34] He organized Lyceum lectures on slavery, and in 1848 ran for office on the Free Soil ticket. His anti-slavery activity soon alienated his wealthy parishioners, and after two and a half years he was forced to resign his position.[35] In 1852 the radical free con-gregation of Worcester asked him to become their minister. Higginson described the church in Worcester to his mother as "the new free church resembling Mr. Parker's in Boston. This is a very thriving and active place . . . there is as much radicalism here as at Lynn."[36] In a letter to his wife he claimed that they could be happy at the church and in Worcester, "there are 600 come-outers and a very thriving city [with] a clear Free Soil majority."[37]

In Newburyport and later in Worcester, abolitionists made up the Higginsons' social community. John Whittier, the famous abolitionist Quaker poet, became their closest friend.[38] Although friendship, love, and community moved Higginson from his position that northerners were prejudiced against the South to active abolitionism, once there Higginson embraced the ideal that slavery was a fundamental violation of the "unalienable rights" of the slave.[39]

Like Higginson, Samuel Gridley Howe, Julia's husband, also came to abolitionism slowly. Howe was New England's own version of Lord Byron.[40] Born with the turn of the new century, November 10, 1801, he was the son of an owner of a ropewalk who was an ardent Democrat in a Federalist town. Howe's father's objection to Harvard's Federalist influence sent Howe to Brown College, where Horace Mann, soon to be one of Howe's closest friends, was a tutor. Upon graduating, Howe, like Bowditch, entered Harvard Medical School out of a lack of the appeal of alternative careers. He earned his degree as Doctor of Medicine at the age of 23.[41]

At Brown and in medical school, Howe drank deeply of the wine of romanticism. He read the romantic poets and yearned to make his mark in the world. Byron's "The Isles of Greece, the Isles of Greece" were calling young men to battle for Greek independence. Howe determined to add his hand as surgeon and swordsman to the cause. Despite his father's disapproval Howe set sail for Greece, arriving shortly before the death of his hero, Lord Byron.

The excitement of the Greek independence movement enthralled Howe. In a letter to his friend Mann, he wrote, "I liked the excitement immensely; the dangers gave zest to it, and I was as happy as youth, health, a good cause, and tolerably clean conscience could make me."[42] In 1830 Howe left Greece (except for a year back in America to raise funds, he had been there since January 1825). Before returning to Boston, Howe went to France, arriving just in time for the "Three Days" Revolution that put the "citizen king" Louis Philippe on the throne.

Howe did not know what he wanted to do with his life once he returned to America; he did know that he did not want to practice medicine, but "follow a path as yet untrodden."[43] That path proved to be the New England Asylum for the Blind. Accepting the position as director, Howe immediately set sail for Europe to research European institutions and engage teachers. In France the Marquis de La Fayette sent him on a secret mission to Poland in aid of the Polish Revolution. On that mission Howe was captured by the Prussians and thrown in jail for five weeks, then shipped out of the country.[44]

Back in Boston Howe proceeded to build up the Institution for the Blind. Soon, thanks to a gift from Thomas H. Perkins, Howe's school had a home, grounds, students, and a new name—Perkins Institution. He taught his students to read by feeling letters, and printed books using a raised modified alphabet. In 1837 Howe brought the deaf and blind Laura Bridgman to the institution. His success in teaching Laura to read and write soon became world-renowned. Howe was now not only Boston's Byronic hero, known by his friends as the "Chevalier," but the savior of society's most unfortunate.

When not working at the Institution, Howe spent his time with his closest friends, Henry Wadsworth Longfellow, Charles Sumner, Cornelius Felton, George Hillard, and Horace Mann. Abolitionism was not something of particular interest. Early in the Institution's history,

Garrison accused Howe of turning away a black child because of race. Howe denied the charge and accused Garrison and the Boston abolitionists of being unrealistic fanatics. But he did argue that if the slaves rose up in rebellion he would "strike with them for the rights of man."[45] In 1843 Henry Ingersoll Bowditch wrote to Howe and asked him to join in an anti-slavery action. He declined, believing his "presence would [not] be of any service." He also wrote that he did not believe anti-slavery activity effective, and that slaveholders were open to the arguments of the North as long as northerners acted as friends not enemies.[46]

Rather than attend abolitionist gatherings, Howe enjoyed spending evenings with his friends, particularly Longfellow and Sumner. Longfellow and Sumner initially had their eyes on the celebrated "three Graces of Bond Street," New York, who regularly visited friends in Boston. In the summer of 1841 Julia Ward spent the summer in Boston, and Longfellow and Sumner made a habit of visiting. One visit led to an outing to the Perkins Institution to see Laura Bridgman and her famous romantic teacher, an event that led to Julia's marriage to Howe. Following their return from an extended but not particularly romantic honeymoon in Europe, the Howes set up house at the Perkins Institution. There Julia struggled to maintain the household in face of continual criticism from Samuel. Struggling with a depressing marriage, Julia spent more and more time with the Parkers, whom she met with her husband in Italy.[47]

Although Maria Chapman felt that Theodore Parker lacked moral courage to come out strongly for abolitionism in the early 1840s, by mid-decade he clearly identified himself with the abolitionists. Parker believed in equality.[48] He felt that slavery was the ultimate form of oppression, and as people in New England divided in opposing by direct action, or supporting it by inaction, he joined with those in opposition.[49] His home in the old South End, within a few minutes walk of the Phillips home, quickly became a center for anti-slavery activity, planning, and discussions. Into that home came Garrison, Phillips, Bowditch, the Weston sisters, Abby Kelley Foster and her husband Stephan, and Julia Ward Howe and her husband. Within the company of the Parkers, the Howes, particularly Julia, became closer to the radical abolitionists.[50]

One evening at the Parkers, before the Howes had identified themselves with abolitionism, Julia was seated next to Wendell Phillips. She was reluctant to talk to a man identified by many of her society friends as "outside the pale of good society in Boston," but she was becoming "a member of a community that was still forming," even if she thought Phillips a bit quixotic in his commitment to equal rights for blacks and women. Julia remembered that through her time spent at the Parker home, she increasingly became free from older ways and restraints. As she socialized with Phillips at the Parker home she came to feel he "brought with him the breath of that freer air, the power of that larger world," and her "strongest imaginary dislikes vanished as though it had never been."[51] The more she listened to Phillips the more she came to respect him and ultimately embrace his views.[52] Julia began to attend anti-slavery meetings, where she came to know and admire Maria Chapman, who reminded her it was time for anti-slavery people to "stand by each other."[53]

While Parker was introducing Julia to the Garrisonian abolitionists, Samuel's closest friends, Sumner and Longfellow, were also becoming more active in abolitionist activity. Sumner and Howe got involved in political activity in support of their friend Horace Mann's campaign to reform Massachusetts schools.[54] Once involved, Sumner chose to become active in anti-slavery politics. In 1845 he led a revolt against what he called the "Cotton Whigs." With the outbreak of the Mexican-American War, his attacks against the regular Whigs grew more virulent.[55]

Sumner argued that slavery not only corrupted the nation's political health, but also violated fundamental human rights. Isolated from his former social circle, he spent more and more time with those who shared his opposition to slavery, particularly Longfellow and Richard Dana. Increasingly Sumner came to see beyond slavery as a wrong and to understand that any form of racial discrimination was a violation of fundamental human rights. In 1849 he argued before the Massachusetts courts that the racial distinctions used in maintaining Boston's segregated schools were an unconstitutional violation of civil equality and the natural rights promised in the Declaration of Independence. Samuel Gridley Howe, already influenced by Parker, moved now with his closest friends into the abolitionist camp.[56] With Richard Dana, Howe and Sumner left the Whig Party and joined the Free Soil Party.[57] Although he declined Bowditch's invitation to join the abolitionist campaign in the early 1840s, by the end of 1846 Howe wrote Bowditch that "resistance to slavery was paramount to every other consideration of politics."[58]

Henry Ingersoll Bowditch's younger brother William also felt several forces tugging him into the abolitionist community. He subscribed to the *Liberator* and encouraged William to read it as well. By 1843 the Massachusetts Anti-Slavery Society had elected Henry a counselor to the organization along with Phillips, Maria Chapman, Edmund Jackson, and Edmund Quincy. Henry urged his brother to come to abolitionist events and hear Phillips's eloquent attacks against slavery. Phillips's abolitionist wife Ann had been Bowditch's sister Mary's closest friend. The Bowditch family home was a short distance from the

Chapmans with whom Ann stayed, and she and Mary were inseparable. Ann's anti-slavery views became well known at the Bowditch home. Her marriage to Phillips and his speaking out against slavery, along with Henry's constant pressure, roused William's interest. Hearing Phillips, also a lawyer, finally swayed the young Bowditch.[59] He joined and became active in the Massachusetts Anti-Slavery Society. There he met and fell in love with Sarah Higginson, sister to Thomas Wentworth Higginson. William was not drawn to abolitionism because of religious beliefs; he defined himself as a nonbeliever.[60] But he was deeply committed to the idea of natural rights and human dignity. It was that aspect of Phillips's rhetoric that appealed to Bowditch.[61]

Once committed to the cause, William gave it his all. After being appointed justice of the peace in 1846, he resigned because he could not take an oath to the Constitution that endorsed slavery, particularly article 4, section 2, which dealt with returning fugitives.[62] His older brother Nathaniel called him "a damn fool" for resigning.[63] William believed his public repudiation of the Constitution cost him professionally, yet it was an act strongly supported by his wife and friends within the abolitionist community.

William felt that those in the community "desired to feel for those in bonds as bound with them and our aim was to speak and act accordingly as if we ourselves were slaves." To act "as if we ourselves were slaves" meant to reject "namby pambyism in speech or action."[64] He and his wife ran a station on the Underground Railroad at their house at Linden Place, Brookline Village, although this was a risky venture. Armed slave-catchers promised violence to those who hid slaves.[65] Unlike Henry, who "would not give up the right to vote against slavery," William "was a non-voter and therefore excluded from politics."[66] In autobiographical notes William wrote that both he and Phillips were "non-voting abolitionists." Yet they believed their radical position would push elected anti-slavery people to "go as far as they could against slavery." Despite his non-voting position, William was a close friend of both Sumner and Richard Dana. Once elected to office, Sumner regularly asked his advice of issues relating to slavery and the law.[67] And although he admired Garrison's strong stands and harsh words against slavery, William was never a Garrisonian nonresister. Instead, like his brother Henry, he accepted violence as a means of fighting slavery.[68]

Abolitionists were a contentious lot. Conflict mingled with love, admiration, friendship, and fellowship. Bowditch was not particularly fond of Garrison, who did "good anti-slavery work but was essentially an unlovable man. He was utterly intolerant even of the smallest dissent from his views."[69] Yet even while disagreeing with him "even in matters of right and wrong," Bowditch still believed "it is true he was harsh as truth. . . . No slave that I have ever heard of has ever found fault with his language even when he was uttering his harshest denunciations . . . a revolution [in public opinion] was what [Garrison] sought to accomplish."[70]

Despite the conflict and disagreements a social movement was forged. For some the disagreements became too great to bridge and bitter political feuds broke out, leading at times to splits and personal antagonism. Although Horace Mann and Wendell Phillips shared many friends and a common commitment to abolishing slavery, Phillips roundly attacked Mann when he was a Free Soil Representative to Congress, accusing him of indirectly supporting the Fugitive Slave Law when taking his oath of office. In a long series of newspaper attacks and counter-attacks Mann and Phillips sparred throughout the summer of 1853. Friends of both tried to intervene. Parker wrote to Phillips that the conflict would "harm and weaken both of them," while Sumner begged Phillips to go easy on their common friend.[71] But despite Sumner's call for a truce between fellow soldiers in the cause of anti-slavery, Mann and Phillips were not friends. Although he had tried to put the issue behind him, Mann had long resented Phillips's attack when in 1846 Mann had failed to support desegregation of the Boston schools. Phillips believed Mann needed to be pushed by the Garrisonians to keep him from abandoning the principle of immediate emancipation. The conflict between them never healed, yet despite their personal animosity, they understood that they both had a role to play in the larger campaign. For others moral and political conflict became divisive.

By the late 1830s New England abolitionists increasingly embraced an egalitarian, equal rights vision of anti-slavery and increasingly saw their female members as some of their best advocates. Abolitionist women went door-to-door gathering signatures and confronting prejudices. Almost everyone recognized that Maria Weston Chapman was the effective leader of the New Englanders. If Garrison and Phillips were the spokesmen of the movement, Chapman and her sisters were the generals and strategists. Chapman responded to claims that women were out of their sphere by claiming women have a right to be heard, "we feel ourselves called in common with men, to toil and suffer, as all must, who effectively defend the truth."[72]

A young Quaker woman from a farming family near Worcester, Abigail Kelley became one of the most successful anti-slavery lecturers. Kelley began teaching at a Quaker school in Lynn, Massachusetts, in the 1830s and became active in social reform. While teaching in Lynn, Abby heard Garrison lecture on anti-slavery, and she soon joined the Lynn Female Anti-Slavery Society. In 1837 she represented the Lynn society at the first American Female Anti-Slavery Convention, where she met fellow Quakers the Grimke sisters, Lucretia Mott, and Bostonian Lydia Maria Child.

In 1838 twenty-seven-year-old Abby attended her second Female Anti-Slavery Convention, this time in Philadelphia, where anti-abolitionists attacked the hall and burned it down. Kelley joined with the other women in linking arms with the black female delegates and marching through the hostile crowd. At the Philadelphia meeting Abby became friends with Sarah Mapps Douglass, a black Quaker abolitionist, and soon realized the power of her own voice.[73] Within a few years Kelley grew to be one of New England's most effective speakers and organizers. Soon she, the Grimke sisters, and her protégée Lucy Stone became legendary. Crowds of men and women, promiscuous crowds they were called at the time, filled halls to hear these dynamic speakers.

Not all members of the movement looked positively toward the prospect of equal participation of women. Although the Massachusetts Anti-Slavery Society and the New England Anti-Slavery Society recognized women as voting members, the American Anti-Slavery Society had never formally decided the issue.[74] In 1839 Massachusetts sent both male and female members to the AASS as voting delegates. Questions of female equal participation dominated the meeting. The New York group pushed for male voting members only. Equal female participation won the contest, but the issue did not die.

Back in Massachusetts, conservative anti-slavery ministers, who were already angry with Garrison and his supporters for their increasingly critical view of the clergy's failure to attack slavery publicly, began organizing against the Massachusetts Anti-Slavery Society. The conservatives attacked the egalitarian role of women in the MASS and formed a competing organization, the Massachusetts Abolition Society. Despite the support of several important ministers, particularly Amos Phelps, Henry Stanton, and Charles Torrey, the Massachusetts Abolition Society failed to win wide support. Black abolitionists supported MASS, as did most of the state's female and male members.

Although those supporting woman's rights won this battle, it did leave scars. During the conflict, Maria Weston Chapman demanded that her friend John Whittier openly denounce Phelps and Stanton. Whittier supported Garrison but publicly remained neutral. In response Chapman accused Whittier of being "either a fool or a knave." The conflict between Whittier and Chapman bothered other members of the abolitionist community. Edmund Quincy wrote to Chapman that "it's very unpleasant to have controversies among friends," and he hoped that they would "die of their own accord."[75] Whittier and Chapman both continued as active members of the movement and had many common friends, but to each other neither spoke again.[76]

Failing in Massachusetts, the conservatives looked to the 1840 national American Anti-Slavery Society Convention as a vehicle for redirecting the movement. The conservatives had much stronger support outside New England, particularly in New York, where the wealthy Lewis and Arthur Tappan carried significant influence. When New Englanders proposed Abby Kelley to the executive committee the conservatives objected, and only following a close vote was Abby elected to the committee. Thereupon the conservatives refused to meet in a "promiscuous" fashion and withdrew to form the separate American and Foreign Anti-Slavery Society. Without the conservatives, the AASS added Maria Weston Chapman, Lydia Maria Child, and Lucretia Mott to the executive committee.

Although outside New England the defections of the religious orthodox significantly cut into the unity of the abolitionist campaign, in New England for the most part, the movement survived. It built links between people with differences, between the non-voters and the political activists, the nonresisters and the resisters. It survived because of these links and because the movement was built on the solid ground of a core belief in the absolute human rights of the slaves as people. People put their personal animosities aside. Or, as with William Bowditch's evaluation of Garrison, they overlooked the differences for the sake of "good anti-slavery work."[77]

When Abby Foster was away organizing in Ohio, she wrote to William Sewell that she longed to be with them at their gathering in Framingham. Foster missed her friends who had gathered to celebrate the Fourth of July and the comradeship, support, and nurturing those friends provided. Fellowship between abolitionists was an important part of the movement.[78] It was consciously nurtured and maintained, even if at times strained by personal conflict and tension. At Helen Benson Garrison's funeral in 1876, Wendell Phillips remembered "the large and loving group that lived and worked together; the joy of companionship, sympathy with each other—almost our only joy—the world's dislike of what we aimed at, the social frown, obliged us to be all the world to each other; and yet it was a full life. A life worth living; the labor was its own reward, we lacked nothing."[79]

Like all social movements, abolitionism combined the social with the personal and political. Elizabeth Buffum Chace, daughter of the first New England Anti-Slavery Society president, remembered that her family's abolitionist activity alienated them from their friends. But she found that her "labor for the cause of the slave" brought her into a new community of fellowship so that she had little concern for the "lost friendships."[80] The Buffums and Chaces were Quakers, but when they began their radical abolitionist work they were shunned by the Society of Friends. Elizabeth left her Quaker meeting because of the disapproval she received for her uncompromising views. But although excluded from the conservative Quaker community, the Buffums and Chaces nurtured a new community of abolitionists.

Seldom was Elizabeth's Fall River and then Rhode Island home without a visiting abolitionist. Garrison, Phillips, Parker Pillsbury, Stephan Foster, Abby Kelley, Henry Wright, Lucy Stone, Lydia Child, William Wells Brown, and black abolitionists Charles Lenox Remond and Frederick Douglass regularly stopped at the Chaces' on their journeys. Abolitionists speaking in Fall River or Providence invariably stayed with the Chaces.

Once the Chaces moved to Valley Falls, their home became a summer gathering place where abolitionists could talk abolitionism and also relax. The Garrisons regularly came for extended visits. Garrison's daughter Fanny's closest friend was Lillie Chace, Elizabeth's daughter. Abolitionists came down from Boston and in from New Bedford, Fall River, and Providence for evenings of conversation and singing. This community included blacks as well as whites.

Although abolitionists disagreed among themselves, Elizabeth Buffum Chace's experience was one of unity in face of disagreements. She and her husband were non-voters like William Bowditch and Phillips, but her parents were Liberty Party advocates. Into her home came a variety of abolitionists with different views about the tactics to end slavery. Their common commitment to basic human rights and equality offered them a welcoming hearth. And the movement provided more than fellowship. Elizabeth and her sister regularly hid runaway slaves. Doing so was against the law. Not only was there the potential danger of armed slave-catchers bursting into their home, but there was also the constant risk of arrest. By arrangement fellow abolitionists stood ready to assume responsibility for the children and household should Elizabeth and her husband be hauled off to jail.

Elizabeth Buffum Chace's concern for community and fellowship was not unique among abolitionists. Many found that their anti-slavery activity, commitment to equality, and radical rhetoric put them outside their previous circle of friends. Even some of those who became part of the abolitionist community initially found the militancy of the abolitionists too much to accept. Caroline Dall remembers her first meeting as an unpleasant affair where she was "not at all edified but rather disgusted by the violence with which they spoke of all those who did not coincide with them in their opinions." Yet at another time Dall was "much aroused by some of the remarks I heard."[81]

Abolitionists found themselves isolated from people with whom they had gone to school or canoed rivers or broken bread. Sumner's increasing militancy isolated him from his former social circle. Although it was anticipated that he would be appointed to fill Joseph Story's chair at Harvard, the university, deciding he had become too radical, passed him over. Sumner found he was no longer a welcome guest at homes he had previously frequented. George Ticknor excluded him from his Park Street literary gatherings. G. S. Hillard, Sumner's old law partner, and C. C. Felton, close friends and part of the "Five of Clubs," refused to speak to him. Felton carried on a vicious public attack on Sumner's abolitionist position in the press and in letters to mutual friends.[82]

In face of hostility these activists, like Elizabeth Buffum Chace, forged new friendships and community networks that, as Henry Ingersoll Bowditch claimed, "knit honest people together." But knitting, as any wielder of needles knows, requires work and effort.

In May 1834 abolitionists gathered for the New England Anti-Slavery Convention. Eloquence, unity, and devotion to the cause dominated the gathering. Those attending the convention felt it to have been a great success. It drew a huge audience. But following this success the momentum and energy seemed to dissipate. The optimism that the abolitionist campaign would surge forward turned to disappointment. The initiative behind the petition drives to end slavery that had previously brought people, particularly women, into the movement and given them an activity was gone. The drives continued in the face of a congressional gag rule that tabled all anti-slavery petitions without debate. Although John Quincy Adams continued to attempt to bring the issue forward, the failure of the petitions to receive a hearing undermined their effectiveness as an organizing tool. A group of female abolitionists realized that the movement needed a new activity to hold people together and give them direction.[83] Conventions were all well and good, Maria Weston Chapman noted, but without something tangible to do between conventions the movement could not mobilize people for action to replace the petition drives.

Chapman, Louisa Loring, Lydia Maria Child, Maria's sister Anne Weston, Henrietta and Catherine Sargent, and black abolitionist Susan Paul decided to hold a fund-raising Christmas fair. They felt that by asking people to make things, or organize to get things, for the fair, they could tie people to a task linked to abolitionism. In December people could come to the fair, socialize, see each other's contributions, buy Christmas gifts, and feel connected to the larger movement. Working on producing and gathering up things for the fair would keep people active between conventions, and activities such as sewing caps or knitting mittens would be a way to ease people into identifying with the movement without initially forcing them to challenge society or traditional roles.

The fair would also produce much needed funds to sustain the abolitionist newspapers.[84]

The first fair, in December 1834, was a one-day affair held in a home that raised $360. The following year the mob attack on the Boston Female Anti-Slavery Society meeting caused the women to retreat to the Chapman house, which was also attacked. Amid this crisis, Maria Weston Chapman decided that the Boston Female Anti-Slavery Society should hold annual fairs. That year's Christmas fair was extended to a two-day event held at Chapman's parents' Beacon Hill home.[85] By the third year the fair had outgrown individual homes and was held at the Artist's Gallery Hall. Women began forming sewing circles and knitting groups early in the year to make plenty of goods to sell, and communities around the state began competing to see how much they could produce for the fair. The Christmas fair became an important community event lasting several days. Abolitionists from Boston and the surrounding areas came to meet friends and buy gifts. By 1838 over $1,100 was raised.[86]

The financial success of the fairs guaranteed that the conflict between the orthodox ministers led by Phelps, who complained of the anti-clericalism of the Garrisonians, and the female equality group of Garrison, Chapman, and her supporters, would have an impact on the fair. Female members of Phelps's Congregational church and Nathaniel Colver's conservative but anti-slavery Baptist church, who were also members of the Boston Female Anti-Slavery Society, believed that the Chapman faction was pushing its "woman's rights question," on an organization that should focus solely on slavery.[87] The anti-woman's rights group turned out in force and voted that the fair's funds should be kept away from the Massachusetts Anti-Slavery Society.[88] Chapman responded by organizing a separate October fair that garnered significant funds while the Phelps-backed fair failed.[89]

By 1840 those opposed to the Chapman wing of the BFASS had withdrawn and the fair was once again organized around Christmas. Soon it became an annual part of the Christmas ritual for New England residents. Exhibits and goods came in from around the region. Eventually the fair was transformed into a racially integrated festival lasting several days and involving food and goods.[90]

By the 1840s the fair was not only an organizing tool but an extremely successful fund-raiser. To keep people interested and to bring in more money, the Massachusetts women tapped their links in Europe to gather more exotic items for sale. Anti-slavery friends in Glasgow, London, and Dublin sent boxes full of goods. Hoping that French goods would add to the excitement, Chapman wrote to Bowditch and Fanny Longfellow asking them to use their contacts in Paris to get goods from there.[91] Fair organizers put together a souvenir pamphlet, the *Liberty Bell*, that offered stories and tracts by anti-slavery's leading intellectuals. Supporters took out advertisements (called subscriptions) in the *Liberty Bell* as a further fund-raising strategy.[92]

The fair's popularity expanded each year. By the tenth fair it lasted over a week. Samuel May wrote to the English abolitionist Mary Carpenter, who had donated several drawings to the event, that the "fair [was] held in a very large [hall] and was tastefully dressed with evergreen and hung with portraits and anti-slavery banners with appropriate mottoes. Some of the articles from England did not arrive till after the fair was opened. Among them was a handsome variety of Sturbridge dinnerware, paper folders, work-boxes, [and] tea caddies."[93] Gifts from Europe poured in, including paintings, works of poetry, novels, books, sewing works, china, and glassware. Famous writers and poets such as Harriet Martineau sent signed original works written specifically for the event.[94] Each fall a representative of the organization had to make several trips to the customs house to clear the gifts from European friends.[95] Financially the fair was a phenomenal success. By the end of the 1840s it was raising almost $5,000 each year.[96]

The organizers planned the event to emphasize its social side as well as its fund-raising. In 1840 the Fair Committee began organizing evening soirées to accompany the fairs. These events of fun and conversation helped cement friendships, particularly among those who came from outside Boston for the fair. The organizers also put on evening lectures by leading female and male abolitionists.[97] Henry Bowditch, whose wife Olivia was active on the Fair Committee in the early 1840s, came up with the idea, as May wrote to Carpenter, to have a gigantic "Christmas Tree—a German idea . . . well filled with candles and the boughs . . . hung with little articles of all sorts suitable for children's gifts for it is for children almost exclusively that this exhibit was got up."[98]

By the mid-1840s the fair's success in Boston burgeoned into similar smaller fairs in communities around the state. Goods that were not sold at the Boston fair were sent out to the smaller fairs held at different times of year.[99] Boston's event became more of a bazaar than a simple fair. By the 1850s it had been transformed into a festival held in Faneuil Hall, where anti-slavery activists gathered for fun and social interaction. The festival ended in a gigantic integrated banquet, organized as a buffet so that no one would be serving anyone else.[100]

The gifts and items that flowed into Boston from Europe for the annual bazaar were not the only transatlantic links New England abolitionists sought to maintain. Abolitionists regularly traveled to England to lecture on the anti-slavery circuit there and raise money for the campaign back home. On these trips they stayed with English, Scottish, and Irish anti-slavery activists. Irish abolitionist Richard Webb was in constant communication with abolitionists on the western side of the Atlantic. When American activists traveled to Europe a visit with Webb was usually on the itinerary.[101] When Samuel May wrote to Webb encouraging him to visit Boston, he reminded him that "many is the American abolitionist who has found rest and food and fire under your roof and such of them as can will be very happy to have the opportunity of opening their doors to you."[102] Elizabeth Pease's English home was always open to visiting abolitionists, and her funds helped maintain the American Anti-Slavery Society. George Thompson, whose anti-slavery reputation crossed the Atlantic and earned him a riotous reception in New England, was always willing to receive visiting American abolitionists at his home and sent boxes of items to the Boston fair. When New Hampshire radical Parker Pillsbury toured Europe as an agent of the AASS, he got off the ship in Liverpool and proceeded directly to Dublin to stay with Webb for several weeks. He then traveled to Bristol to stay with an English abolitionist family, the Estlins.[103]

New England abolitionists understood that it was difficult for people to stand alone through the long struggle. Another means of forging community was mutual visiting. Young female abolitionists regularly spent summers in the homes of other abolitionists. Abby May, an abolitionist activist and daughter of an abolitionist family and sister to Samuel May, spent summers (May 30–October 26) with Julia Ward Howe in her isolated home in Dorchester Heights south of Boston.[104] James Freeman Clarke's daughter Sarah regularly stayed with the Higginsons for extended periods of time.[105]

Lecturing abolitionists on the road stayed with other abolitionists exchanging information, gossip and enjoying good fellowship.[106] In a letter to his mother, Higginson noted that he went to Boston to lecture at Theodore Parker's church. While in Boston Higginson visited Phillips at his home at 26 Essex Street in the old South End, stayed with the Parkers at their home around the corner from Phillips, took tea with Sarah and William Bowditch in Brookline, and walked the long way back to have dinner with the younger abolitionist Channing at his Essex Street home, which was down the street from Phillips and Parker and only a few blocks from the Chapmans'.[107] Family events were also abolitionist events. William and Sarah Bowditch's home became a place for Thanksgiving family gatherings. Thomas Wentworth Higginson and Mary were there, as were others involved in the struggle against slavery.[108] At other times the Bowditches would travel to Worcester to stay with the Higginsons, where family gossip and anti-slavery activity would merge.[109] When Franklin Sanborn, a young senior at Harvard, became interested in anti-slavery work, he stayed with Higginson to talk abolitionism and discuss what a "young man of the day" should do.[110]

Maria Weston Chapman's home in fashionable Chancey Place (a few minutes walk from the homes of most of the inner circle of Garrisonian abolitionists) became a particularly popular gathering place for abolitionists.[111] An occasion might involve simply tea and cake or a more formal evening entertainment such as an abolitionist play.[112] People dropped in to talk strategy and just to chat.[113] In a letter to her sister Deborah, Caroline Weston wrote that Henry Ingersoll Bowditch was coming down to spend an evening with the Westons in Hingham to visit and organize.[114] When conventions occurred in Boston, anti-slavery people from out of town filled the homes of those living in the area. Maria Weston Chapman noted to her sister Deborah, "it is all the abolition there is in the western counties and by course deserves a nights lodging of us."[115] Edmund Quincy noted the "custom of abolitionists of entertaining each other at their houses [was] very common arising from the closeness of the connection in the days of persecution."[116]

Abolitionists also organized "anti-slavery tea-parties." At one such party organized in Worcester, Garrison came to talk with others involved in the cause. Henry David Thoreau and his brother and sister (Thoreau's mother and sister were active abolitionists) were there, along with the political abolitionist Free Soiler George Hoar.[117]

The social world of abolitionism also had its lighter side. In 1844 New England abolitionists gathered in Hingham for meetings and "a grand time," enjoying the seaside and country air.[118] A large contingent took the boat down from Boston. On the way home the boat ran onto a sandbar and remained stranded until the tide rose to lift it off. It was a hot evening, and water and food on the boat were in short supply. Fearing that tempers were soon to fray, Frederick Douglass began a discussion about what to do about food and water as if it were a serious abolitionist meeting. Douglass parodied parliamentary procedure and soon others picked up the game. By the time the tide finally freed the boat, everyone was laughing uproariously and had long forgotten heat and thirst.[119]

Samuel Gridley Howe and Julia got up "a fishing party to Cohasset" of abolitionists and invited the Parkers to join them. Parker tried to beg off, claiming that he did not care for fishing, but Howe persisted. "We don't want you to fish nor even to see a fish caught only to eat fish." Howe continued that the point of the trip was to "eat, drink and be merry."[120]

Conflicts could lead to splits within the abolitionist community, as in the conflict between the pro-clerical group and the Garrisonians. Bitter personal feuds disrupted friendships, as when Maria Weston Chapman attacked Whittier. Yet social links among people on different sides of particular issues helped to hold the movement and its members together.[121] Maria Weston Chapman and Edmund Quincy both plotted to defeat Loring and Bowditch's attempt to get the Massachusetts Anti-Slavery Society behind the Liberty Party, yet at other times both were welcome guests at the Weston and Chapman homes and social events.[122]

There were limits to this social mixing. Maria Weston Chapman sent a nasty letter to Miss Ball complaining that Abby Southwick had invited people to the Chapmans' house assuming they were abolitionists. Chapman did not feel the guests were abolitionists and was annoyed with Abby for inviting them. "I consider them at present as not occupying the position of members of the cause. My sense of . . . consistency . . . constrained me to rebuke my friend Mrs. Southwick for her course in this thing."[123] Maria did not rebuke Southwick for inviting strangers to the Chapman house; the informal social community of abolitionists expected such behavior. What disturbed her was that the other parties were not "members of the cause."

Abolitionists of various persuasions met together in a variety of venues. The fair brought political abolitionists who supported anti-slavery political party activity together with those such as Garrison and the Chapmans who were opposed to party politics as corrupting. Political activists not only found fellowship and tea at the homes of those who adamantly refused to participate in politics, they also mingled in the churches of Boston's anti-slavery ministers. John Andrew, a leading radical political abolitionist and future governor of Massachusetts, and Julia Ward Howe belonged to James Freeman Clarke's Church, as did many non-voting moral suasionists. Clarke was more than just Andrew's pastor; he and Andrew were close friends.[124] Still other political abolitionists mingled with moral suasionists at Theodore Parker's free church.[125]

Because politics involved a particular form of organizing, political abolitionists also had their own social centers. Bowditch, John Whittier, Charles Sumner, Richard Dana, Samuel Sewall, George Bradburn, Horace Mann, and John Andrew struggled to get anti-slavery issues before the voting public as candidates in the Liberty or later Free Soil Party.[126] Higginson's close friend John Whittier, at whose house Higginson spent many an evening, roped him into party politics by maneuvering to put his name on to the ballot as a Free Soil Party candidate for office. Francis Bird, an abolitionist from Walpole, began gathering about him other politically active abolitionists. By 1850 Bird hosted a regular weekly dinner group with his friends at George Young's Hotel in Boston. Bird and regulars such as Sumner, Howe, Andrew, and George Stearns encouraged friends to join them at the dinners there or at

Theodore Parker's home. The gathering grew to some 100 regulars and became the basis for a significant political organization known as the Bird Club, which took control of Massachusetts politics in 1860.[127]

Yearly conferences, fairs, and festivals were forums the abolitionists used to build a sense of common purpose between people united in the opposition to slavery but divided on strategy or personality. Abolitionists also used events to create abolitionist demonstrations. When the old abolitionist fighter Charles Torrey died while being held in a Baltimore jail for anti-slavery work, New England rallied to its fallen son. Although Torrey had been a central figure in the clerical revolt against women's equal role in the movement, and had left the American Anti-Slavery Society, he was still an abolitionist. Bowditch and other members of the Massachusetts Anti-Slavery Society staged a major public funeral for Torrey when his body returned to Boston, carrying it in a procession from Park Street to the Tremont Temple.[128]

Black abolitionists William Cooper Nell, a close associate of Garrison, and Charles Lenox Remond organized a special Commemorative Festival in 1858 to recognize the role of blacks in the American Revolution, particularly the symbolic importance of Crispus Attucks, killed at the Boston Massacre. With posters and documents of black Revolutionary soldiers and Remond's opening speech before the large interracial crowd, the festival linked the ideals of the American Revolution with the struggle against slavery and "revolution of the present."[129] It was a message both white and black abolitionists wanted New England, so proud of its revolutionary past, to hear.

Boston's white abolitionists depended on and recognized the importance of their black fellow activists. William Lloyd Garrison gave recognition to the important role of David Walker's militant tract, *Appeal in Four Articles, Together with a Preamble, to the Coloured Citizens of the World*, in helping Garrison move to the immediacy of abolition.[130] In his attack against the racial assumptions of the American Colonization Society and Thomas Jefferson's depiction of blacks in his *Notes on Virginia*, Walker mobilized Boston's black community. He helped found the Massachusetts General Colored Association (MGCA) in 1826 along with William G. Nell, father of William Cooper Nell.

Boston's black community was small, but it was a vital presence in the struggle against slavery. When Garrison began publishing the *Liberator* there were 1,875 African Americans living in the city—3 percent of the city's population—mostly in the West End, on the north side of Beacon Hill. MGCA, black leaders such as William Cooper Nell, John Hilton, leader of the MGCA and grand master of the Prince Hall Masonic Lodge, Charles Remond, Joel Lewis, John Rock, and James Barbadoes challenged segregation in the region, particularly in the public schools.

In 1850 the militant Lewis Hayden and his activist wife Harriet moved to Boston and became vital in the campaign for fugitive slaves along with Robert Morris, Boston's first black lawyer. Boston's black community organized rallies, protest meetings, petition drives, and disobedience campaigns against segregated institutions. Although maintaining its own organizations and leadership, the community was also deeply intertwined with the city's white abolitionists. Black women, particularly Susan Paul and Sarah Parker Remond, were important voices in the Boston Female Anti-Slavery Society and part of the crowd of women who marched together through the mob on the night of the anti-Garrison riot in 1835. Without subscriptions from the region's black population, the *Liberator* would never have survived. Blacks held leadership positions in the MASS and were particularly active in the vigilance committees. Although white abolitionists were involved in the Underground Railroad, blacks were the key to its success.

Building a movement also meant nurturing the next generation. In 1836 Lucia Weston and Sarah Southwick decide to "form a juvenile society" for "the children of Boston," to be a place where young people concerned about slavery, mostly the children of abolitionists, could gather, play, and "do great things."[131] Massachusetts abolitionists also produced didactic books and plays directed to a young audience that stressed the evils of slavery and racial prejudice. In *The Young Abolitionists, or Conversations About Slavery*, by Elizabeth Jones and produced by the Boston Anti-Slavery Office, the message focused not only on the evils of slavery, but on how abolitionists including children "must have themselves set the example of treating the colored man as an equal."[132]

Abolitionists created a tight-knit community. In a time when people spent more time visiting than is common today, women had regular visiting hours and people were expected to drop in. One of the griefs of Julia Ward Howe was her husband's insistence that they live in South Boston away from most of her friends. It was a considerable project for Julia to see her friends in Boston and Brookline, and few people dropped in on her. Julia dealt with this isolation by regularly venturing out to see friends, particularly the Parkers, and then increasingly in the 1850s those involved with the *Atlantic Monthly*. The *Atlantic Monthly* crowd held regular dinners that Julia attended, with others including abolitionists Thomas Wentworth Higginson, Edmund Quincy, James Russell Lowell, John Whittier, and non-abolitionists such as Oliver Wendell Holmes and, somewhat sympathetic to abolitionism, James Fields.[133] Higginson introduced the young author Harriet Prescott to the Boston literary community by first taking her to Wendell Phillips's house, where she met Wendell and Ann Greene Phillips. The abolitionist poet John Whittier was also there. From the Phillips house Higginson and Whittier took Prescott to the home of Harriet Beecher Stowe, where Lowell, Longfellow, Quincy, and Charles Whipple, a friend of Garrison who helped edit the *Liberator*, had gathered for dinner. Julia Ward Howe, a regular at these dinner gatherings, was expected but detained.[134]

Julia Ward Howe was not only smart, but loved social and intellectual events, and she turned her considerable energy into making sure they happened. Her husband once complained that if Julia were marooned on a desert island with a fugitive slave she would find a reason to have a party.[135]

In the prewar years, as Phillips noted, abolitionists dwelt in a hostile world, so they had to be "all the world to each other." Despite differences in strategy and personality that drove them apart, their friendships and social links helped maintain the movement. Their position of opposition to the dominant society also functioned as a bond to hold people to the cause and to each other. This community of friends also provided the context for politicalization of those involved.

Chapter 3

"All the Great Men and Men of Respectability Stood Aloof"

Looking back sixty years, Thomas Wentworth Higginson remembered a time in Boston when "the anti-slavery movement drew a line of cleavage through all Boston Society, leaving most of the more powerful and wealthy families on the conservative side."[1] Higginson, if not a Brahmin, certainly came from the upper part of New England society.[2] His father's position as steward of Harvard College meant that the Higginsons mingled with the region's elites.[3] Thomas Wentworth's early memories were that the dominant class "who then ruled Boston opinion" believed that abolition of slavery would lead to chaos and insurrection and that abolitionists "ought to be hung."[4] Higginson also remembered abolitionist gatherings where "among the devout women . . . and fiery orators brought together from different fields of action where they had been alternately starved, frozen or mobbed . . . [would be] a few city delegates, the most high-bred men and women in appearance to be found in Boston, such as Wendell Phillips, Edmund Quincy and Mrs. Chapman."[5]

Higginson's memory did not mislead him. New England abolitionism did cleave the city, and most of the wealthy and powerful members of the region did tend to fall on the side opposed to abolition. Most of Boston's leading families were tied to either merchant trading or the newly emerging textile industry. Both depended heavily on trade with the South. Boston's shipping merchants regularly shipped food—dried cod, salted pork and beef, wheat and rye flour—and manufactured items, shoes, and tools to the South and cotton from southern ports to England and back home to the growing textile cities of New England. New England textile mills depended on slave-grown cotton to feed their machines. Many, including Higginson, had family and friendship ties to slaveholders in the South. They personally may have disliked the idea of slavery, but they did not feel it polite or politic to attack the South's peculiar institution. They instead rallied to the compromising position of the regular Whigs. Typical of this position was

Dr. Oliver Wendell Holmes, Bowditch's fellow student in Paris, on the faculty at Harvard Medical School and a leading member of Boston's intellectual circles. Although not wealthy, Holmes was related to several of Boston's leading merchant and manufacturing families, the Lees, Cabots, Jacksons, and Bradstreets. He shared membership with abolitionists Lowell, Longfellow, and Dana in the Saturday Club and was a founding member of the *Atlantic Monthly*, most of whose other members and writers were abolitionists.

Holmes may have shared intellectual circles with abolitionists, but he had no time for their politics and persuasions. In a public talk he called them "ultra melanophiles" and traitors to both the union and the white race.[6] Holmes's distaste for the abolitionists was not unusual for a person of his social standing; what was unusual was that he was still willing to attend functions and interact with those committed to abolition. More typical was George Ticknor, who not only snubbed radical abolitionist Bowditch but wrote to Richard Dana, an old personal friend, that since Dana was now identified with the abolitionists, Ticknor would no longer consider seeing or meeting him.

Higginson's remembrance was also the product of a conscious construction by the abolitionists that defined themselves as of the people and their opponents as the wealthy elites. By constructing their opponents in this way, the abolitionists were framing their struggle against slavery in a traditional American trope of the common people against the powers of privilege. It was the language of republicanism that went back to the days of the revolution.

Abolitionists began their campaign against slavery by denouncing the institution as morally reprehensible and a violation of God's law. But slavery, unlike adultery, involved more than personal behavior. Beyond the individual stood an institution sustained by an elaborate political-state apparatus. For many abolitionists it became clear that slavery had to be attacked as an institution. That meant undermining the economic and political structures that sustained it. They may have hoped that they could convince slave owners of the sinfulness of slavery and have them voluntarily end the institution, but they also came to the idea that they had to undermine slavery as a social and political institution. That meant building a popular movement against slavery. William Lloyd Garrison and the other members of the moral suasionist wing rejected party politics, but even they did not reject the idea of building a broad movement against slavery.[7] In the articles of the constitution of the American Anti-Slavery Society, the members claimed to "convince all our fellow-citizens, by arguments addressed to their understanding and consciences, that slave-holding is a heinous crime in the sight of God, and that the duty, safety and best interests of all concerned, require its immediate abandonment, without expatriation." The society at the same time took as its task "to influence Congress to put an end to the domestic slave-trade, and to abolish slavery in all those portions of our country . . . and likewise to prevent the extension of it to any State that may be hereafter admitted to the Union." The society also pledged to remove public prejudice and create a condition of "equality with whites, of civil and religious privileges."[8] They worked to make sure that Article Four, section two of the Constitution, which allowed for the return of a "person held in service or labor in one state under the laws thereof," would not be enforced in northern states.

The campaign against the institution of slavery and for racial equality engendered opposition not only in the South but in the North as well. That opposition took many forms, some violent. Mob attacks such as those against Garrison and Thompson were common experiences for anti-slavery speakers.[9] Angelina Grimke and Theodore Weld celebrated their 1838 wedding by holding an abolitionist meeting in Philadelphia that had a mob of thousands smashing the windows of the hall. The crowd returned the following day and burned the hall to the ground. A stone-throwing crowd broke up an anti-slavery talk by Samuel May in 1835. When anti-slavery lecturers Lucy Stone and Parker Pillsbury attempted to speak on slavery in 1848, they had a variety of objects hurled at their heads, including one that almost knocked Stone unconscious. A couple of months later a large crowd attacked Pillsbury, Foster, and William Brown when they spoke in Harwich, Massachusetts, throwing the three off the platform and then kicking and beating them.[10]

The conservative press in Boston called for a boycott of abolitionists. The *Boston Advertiser* attacked abolitionists as "this pack of Reverends and lay detractors of the good name of the merchants," and that "a decent self-respect in those who are thus assailed [merchants] demands that confidential relations with [abolitionists] should cease."[11] The *Boston Courier* advised its readers that abolitionists should not be turned to for services. "They are untrustworthy practitioners of their professions, who spent so much time on their outside activities that they could not give enough attention to their clients."[12] The *Courier* singled out Bowditch as a person to be shunned: "if a physician is eagerly running about town to help break the laws; if we hear of his offering money to a jailor to let one of his prisoners go free; if he is secretary of noisy political meetings; if he makes speeches in the streets, we do not ask him to come and see us when we are sick."[13]

Abolitionists were aware that their demands not only for the immediate end to slavery but also for equal rights for blacks put them at odds with the majority of Americans. Their opponents were plenty and ubiquitous. Abolitionists worked in a society that only occasionally recognized Bowditch's maxim: "all men are equal, born free and equal."[14] To realize this goal of freedom and equality they had to bind themselves together closely to build a mass movement. The emotions of righteousness provided some of the social glue. Abolitionists viewed themselves as members of a community of self-sacrificing moral activists. By contrast they defined their opponents as self-seeking, self-interested privileged profiteers who gained by supporting slavery. Although abolitionists readily admitted the power of racism in American society to mobilize large numbers of people, they focused their anger and rhetoric against those they accused of profiting from slavery. Abolitionists also believed that these powerful wealthy interests were behind much of the violence directed against their movement. As Abby Folsom liked to remind her fellows, "it's the capitalists!"[15]

Franklin Sanborn remembered that it was the "wealthy and commercial classes of Boston" who supported slavery and the Fugitive Slave Bill against the "plain people of the North."[16] Sanborn believed that the "broadcloth" gentlemen who wanted to protect their "trade with South Carolina" used their influence as men of "property and standing" to incite the mobs who attacked abolitionists.[17] Phillips claimed that it was the "lords of the loom" who were inflaming opposition to the abolitionists.[18] Charles Francis Adams felt that, as more manufacturing development occurred in Massachusetts, the superficial anti-slavery sentiment, exemplified by the American Colonization Society, that had been fashionable among some New Englanders gave way to a commonality of interests between the cotton manufacturers of the North and the cotton producers of the South. Charles Sumner named that community of interest as the link between "the lords of the loom and the lords of the lash."[19] In a letter to Samuel Gridley Howe, James Freeman Clarke reminded Howe that the fight was against the "combined influence of power and money."[20] Both Bowditch and Julia Ward Howe came from elite society, yet both felt that the region's aristocracy supported slavery while the common man was more likely to oppose it. "All the great men of respectability stood aloof," Bowditch remembered.[21] Julia Ward Howe recalled a city divided with the "class of wealthy conservatives and their followers" supporting slavery. Slavery, she felt, was "upheld by the immense money power of the North."[22]

Abolitionists took strength from the idea that they were of the people defending the liberty of the weakest members of the community. Then, as the attacks on abolitionists increased, they saw themselves as defending the principle of liberty itself.[23] When Thomas Wentworth Higginson looked back on his early abolitionist days, he remembered that, unlike the civil service reform, which was mostly a movement of the upper class, the anti-slavery movement "was predominately *a people's movement*, based on the simplest human instincts and far stronger for a time in the factories and shoe shops than in the pulpits or colleges" (emphasis original). He noted that it was a common saying about abolitionists that "radicalism went with the smell of leather."[24] Clarke called the struggle a movement "of the people," against those with "force and money."[25] Bowditch believed the city's aristocracy was either indifferent to slavery or supported it, while the common folk opposed it.[26]

The claims of the abolitionists contained an element of truth but also ignored another reality of their time. The 1830s, 1840s, and 1850s were a time of significant economic and social upheaval in New England. The agricultural decline that had begun in the 1820s accelerated over the next several decades. Farm families lost their children to Boston and the surrounding mill towns. Boston expanded and prospered as a commercial hub, but as more people flooded into the city from the rural countryside and from Europe, particularly from Ireland after the potato famine, competition intensified for housing and low-skilled day work. Many unskilled whites saw the city's black population as competition for limited resources and turned against the abolitionists who called for equality in all things.[27] Yet, although Higginson, Clarke, and Bowditch may have exaggerated the extent to which the abolitionist movement was a movement of the people, it did draw in recruits from across the social classes. The remembrance of the movement as a people's movement was also partly the product of a purposeful political construction on the part of the abolitionists.

In their political struggle against the institutions of slavery, the abolitionists adopted the common practice of American political discourse. They gave their enemies a derisive term: "Hunkers."[28] Samuel Gridley Howe, for example, claimed that Boston was under "Hunker" control and that people had abandoned natural law for "the temporary considerations of profit and loss."[29] The origins of the term Hunker are unclear. By the mid-1840s it came to be identified with political conservatives from the idea of a post that would not move or that of a covetous person. By the late 1840s it had become a common derisive term of New England abolitionists to refer to their opponents.

Such labeling fit well with their equalitarian political campaigns. Theodore Parker made this class point again and again in his sermons. He preached to his congregation that "in America the controlling class is divided into two great parties: one is the slave power in the states of the South, the other is the money power in the cities of the North . . . both in general are hostile to the great Idea of America [liberty]."[30] Parker argued that in America "money is power." "National legislation almost invariably favors capital and not the laboring hand."[31]

As the abolitionists constructed the conflict, the wealthy privileged classes defended slavery for their self-interest and profit against the poor slaves and those in support of liberty.[32] Parker reminded Bostonians in 1854, "have you forgotten the 1500 gentlemen of property and standing who volunteered to conduct Mr. Sims to slavery? . . . The men of property and standing all over New England" supported the Fugitive Slave Law. Parker believed that the enemies of freedom and justice were the "wealthy capitalists."[33] "Large numbers of crafty, rich, designing and respectable men supported slavery," he argued, although he did allow that "some of the richest men were strongly in favor of freedom, but alas not many and for the most part they were silent."[34] Parker saw the opposition to slavery as rooted among the middle and laboring people of the region.

Because abolitionists argued that the struggle against slavery pitted them against society elites, people such as Julia Ward Howe and Henry Ingersoll Bowditch found themselves alienated from their old friends. Bowditch noted that once he embraced abolitionism he was "degraded in the eyes of ladies in Park and Beacon Street," "disowned by the Ticknors and Goodwins and other good friends of my father and myself," and excluded from the homes of other respectable Boston families.[35] As he walked the streets of Boston, old acquaintances passed him without recognition or openly mocked him.[36] Julia Ward Howe wrote to her sister about Boston, "how the old Whigs do hate us! They will hardly speak to Sumner, or invite him to their homes."[37] Even families found themselves in conflict. The eldest Bowditch brother, Nathaniel Ingersoll Bowditch, was annoyed at the younger brothers because of their involvement in abolitionism.[38]

It is unclear how much of the separation Bowditch and Howe felt from their former friends was a product of the old friends no longer welcoming them, or of their increasing discomfort in the homes of those they now felt to be on the other side of a huge political divide. These activists believed they were right and members of a morally superior community. It is very likely that family, neighbors, and friends found these committed activists, with their constant drumbeats about the evils of slavery, difficult companions at best. Bowditch saw those who opposed his abolitionist activity as "adversaries and opponents [to whom he] turned a deaf ear when I thought of the slave whips."[39] Bowditch noted that when he walked down the street with Frederick Douglass his old acquaintances turned away in disgust. Yet in purposely walking arm in arm with Douglass in the streets of Boston, Bowditch was making a statement to that disapproving community, a statement he expected to be received with hostility.[40]

For Howe and Bowditch how one responded to slavery was increasingly not an abstract question of politics but went to the very core of the person. In explaining why he did not believe that Emerson was with the abolitionists, Bowditch explained that "to be an abolitionist and a supporter or an open defender of the doctrine of immediate emancipation meant ostracism and contempt—ostracism from some of the so-called elite circles of society for us Bostonians. [Family friends] shut their doors upon us refused to speak to us. . . . Mob law led by men of property and standing broke up meetings of abolitionists; death by the gun, or Bowie knife or by prison suffering was the lot of not a few men for their actions. These were the abolitionists with whom I have said Mr. Emerson did not sympathize." Bowditch felt that Emerson may have been an "anti-slavery man in belief but kept aloof from immediate abolitionists when they were acting as a body for the definite purpose of helping the slave or threatening the slave hunter while he was grasping his victim."[41]

Bowditch cared less for sympathy than for action; it was in the sphere of action that Emerson failed. "He was never with us in *action*. . . . He never came to us to help us when in the thickest of the fight and when his presence and his winning eloquence would have been to us worth a thousand men" (emphasis original).[42] The abolitionist movement demanded commitment and sacrifice. Those who did not act were not part of that movement. As Bowditch replied to a defender of Emerson, "I judged Mr. Emerson by his acts as I judge other people. Whenever there was an anti-slavery case in Boston, Emerson was not among the abolitionists as Frances Jackson and the other well-known abolitionists were."[43] Bowditch's strongest criticisms were directed at those he saw as opposing the campaign to end slavery. He called Daniel Webster "intellectually white," a derisive term to describe Webster's failure to see blacks as equals. Bowditch felt Webster was "morally reprehensive in all the common relations of life."[44]

Maria Weston Chapman's feelings toward the grand old man of Boston's religious community, Dr. Channing, were also pointed and unforgiving because he failed to step forward for abolition. Although she thought of Channing as a "tender hearted fatherly sort of man," she nevertheless felt he "had neither might for right, moral courage nor firmness and he just was as deficient as himself."[45] She never forgave Theodore Parker, who became one of the most ardent abolitionists, because in 1842 he did not open his pulpit to Bowditch, Cabot, and William Channing to gather petitions for a fugitive slave. Parker suggested they circulate the petitions outside the church.

Although Julia Ward Howe could and did criticize those within the abolitionist community, for those outside the community she had nothing but contempt: "I do shame the woman who has a word to say in defense of slavery."[46] Howe's world was divided over slavery: "the anti-slavery people attacked it with might and main, while the class of wealthy conservatives and their followers strongly deprecated all opposition to its enactments."[47] In that divided world she "cast [her] lot with those who protested against new assumptions of the slave power." Even in her old age Julia held to her feelings that she would not socialize with those outside the movement. In 1884 Julia told her daughter how she ran into the elderly Samuel Eliot (who as a member of Congress voted for the Fugitive Slave Law) on the street, but she would not "stop to talk to him" because of his positions on slavery and other reforms.[48]

By imagining themselves as of the people and their political enemies as privileged wealthy, the abolitionists defined the conflict as a moral conflict that extended outward, as James Freeman Clarke wrote to Howe, to a "real struggle for human rights."[49] They understood the conflict against slavery to be part of a larger struggle for justice, and that "justice [was] the common interest of all men." "The wealthy capitalists," he repeated, were the enemies of freedom and justice."[50] Yet, Parker reminded Boston, the "money of Boston [was] against [the abolitionists]."[51] Parker argued that the basic principle of New England ought to be the opposition to tyranny and slavery.[52] He argued that those principles were incorporated into "the truths of the Declaration [of Independence which had] . . . wide reaching consequences, so beneficial to mankind."[53]

In its formal principles America was the ultimate Lockean nation. Jefferson freely plagiarized the Declaration of Independence from Locke's Second Treatise on Government. Property law rested solidly on Locke's understanding of the origin of property.[54] And as students of history, abolitionists believed legitimate governments were instituted among men to protect basic rights. There was little disagreement among Americans about these basic principles; what they meant, however, varied widely. For southern planters, slaves were property, and it was a function of government, as Locke noted, to protect property. Northern abolitionists took from Locke's theory of rights and the government the idea that humans were born with certain "inalienable rights" that slavery denied to those held in bondage.[55]

In the heat of the abolitionist struggle Parker proclaimed that "the people of Massachusetts still believe that all men are *born free and equal and have natural, essential, and unalienable rights*" (my emphasis).[56] In 1858 Bowditch paid James Deane, a recently deceased abolitionist and doctor friend from Greenfield, Massachusetts, the ultimate compliment by proclaiming, "Dr. Deane was throughout his life, a consistent and fearless defender of the *rights of man*" (my emphasis).[57] For many abolitionists the South's use of the state to sustain slavery was a perversion of its legitimate role as articulated by Locke. The state should uphold freedom and protect the weak from the powerful rather than be an instrument of power for holding humans in slavery.

The abolitionists confronted the southern argument that slaves were property by denying the legitimacy of human property.[58] They argued that it was not just a question of the "protection of the Negro." They also "sought," Phillips noted, "to establish a principle, the rights of human nature."[59]

The problem was not state power but how it was exercised and for whom.[60] Since the wealthy privileged were using state power to undermine popular will and human rights, many abolitionists came to believe it was the responsibility of the people to seize that power. Parker called on the people of Boston for "action and organization for the defense of personal liberty and the state rights of the North."[61] For those who became identified as the radical political abolitionists that meant involvement in political parties. In 1842 Bowditch claimed that history and the Declaration of Independence taught that "a tyrant . . . [would not] lift, unless forced by blood, his heel from the neck of his slave."[62] Thus, most abolitionists saw the cause as a struggle for human rights and a contest for power till "every yoke is broken."[63]

His brother William and his friends Phillips, Garrison, and the Chapmans believed that party politics were so compromised by slavery that the movement should focus its action outside the electoral system. Initially they believed that abolition would come with the conversion of the nation to the moral evil of slavery and a popular cry for its immediate abolition. As the South burned abolitionist tracts, censored the mails, and cut off debate in Congress, many of these moral suasionists came to believe that ultimately it would take an insurrection to end slavery.

Henry Ingersoll Bowditch felt that one should not abandon any avenue of opposition. After its initial feeble beginnings, and despite Garrison's, Chapman's, and Quincy's opposition, by the mid-1840s the Liberty Party was winning adherents from among active abolitionists. Bowditch became involved with the party early in its history and attempted to convince other New England Anti-Slavery Society members to join.[64] The Liberty Party nominated him as its candidate for representative to the General Court and then to the Massachusetts State Senate.[65]

Beginning in 1845 with the debate over the admission of Texas to the union, the war with Mexico, and the nomination of a slave owner, Zachary Taylor, for the presidency, the New England Whig Party began to splinter. Worcester Whig activist Charles Allen called for the dissolution of the party.[66] In Boston Bowditch's college classmate Richard Dana, John Albion Andrew, Charles Sumner, Charles Francis Adams, and Samuel Gridley Howe organized a group of "conscience Whigs" to leave the party and join the new Free Soil Party.[67] Liberty Party activists, although concerned that the Free Soil Party was not abolitionist enough, nonetheless joined the new party. Whittier became an active party organizer in Essex County and eventually convinced his close friend Thomas Wentworth Higginson to run as the Free Soil Party candidate for the House of Representatives.[68] The party nominated Bowditch to run for the Senate, but, fearing that it might actually win the election, he withdrew his name. He believed enough in party politics to run for office to raise anti-slavery issues, but did not actually want to give up his medical practice for political office. For that he wanted someone else, someone like Charles Sumner.[69]

By 1850 the Free Soil Party in Massachusetts had gained a significant mass following. Although there was still hostility to the radical racially egalitarian abolitionists, the party focused its attention on the growing northern anxiety about the expansion of slavery and the seemingly unstoppable southern power in Washington. Even New Englanders unsympathetic to the radical abolitionists found the Free Soil Party's position one they could support, while political party active abolitionists began to fear that the party might not adhere to "the uncompromising anti-slavery tone which was the strength of the Liberty Party."[70]

Political party active abolitionists hoped access to elected office would give them both a forum to denounce slavery and a vehicle to stop its expansion. Some disagreed with the Garrisonians that the constitution protected slavery and argued that it was constitutionally possible to abolish the institution.[71] But winning political office involved the nitty-gritty and compromise of politicking. In January 1850 Higginson was asked by Free Soiler John Palfrey to take over the anti-slavery newspaper, the *Commonwealth*. Higginson decided against the position because he felt the paper was too uncritical of Free Soil senators.[72] Shortly afterward Samuel Gridley Howe took over the paper during a time that "politically things look to me very dark on all sides. . . . Slavery exulting while none but the Garrisonians are up to doing anything for the grand cause. We need stern prophets to raise their voices."[73] In these dark times, Julia Ward Howe took over writing articles on philosophy and literature while Samuel wrote editorials attacking slavery and compromising politicians.[74]

In 1851 the Free Soil Party flirted with an open coalition with the Massachusetts Democrats. Despite support of the idea from Sumner, Horace Mann, Henry Wilson, and other Free Soil Party Boston members, Higginison, Whittier, and the other Essex County Free Soilers fought against it for fear it would mute the party's anti-slavery position.[75] When in 1854 a wing of the Free Soil Party led by Wilson joined the Know-Nothings (the anti-immigrant, anti-Catholic party that rose up overnight in response to increased Irish immigration into the region following the potato famine) to gain office in Massachusetts, Sumner, Dana, and Howe opposed the nativists.[76]

In the highly politicized world of Boston in the decades leading up to the Civil War, it was not just Hunkers and wealthy capitalists who were cast as the enemies of justice and human rights. Because they saw slavery as a sin and a fundamental denial of human rights, abolitionists expected religious leaders to come forward. And many did. But most of the religious leaders who actively joined the abolitionist community came from the radical fringe of Boston's theocratic community. Parker and Clarke, for example, were involved in the free-church movement, open to a variety of social reforms. Parker's habit of opening his church to female speakers, and even offering his pulpit to the radical minister Antoinette Brown Blackwell, put him well outside the mainstream of the Unitarian community. Clarke was also known for his radical views on any number of reform subjects. Beginning his professional career as a Congregational minister, Parker Pillsbury's involvement in abolitionism moved him to radical free-thinking. Henry Wright and Stephan Foster rejected their Congregational training for itinerant agitating and farming. Thomas Wentworth Higginson, after being removed from his ministry in Newburyport for his radical ideas, took over a "free church" (one without charges for pews and that accepted all within its community) in Worcester already made up of dedicated "come-outers."[77] Established church leaders were far more cautious on the issue of slavery, if not hostile to abolitionism.

Abolitionists increasingly turned their ire against established churches and their leaders. Higginson claimed that "the pulpit [has] become a refuge for scoundrels."[78] Radicals such as Foster and Pillsbury actually denounced churches as corrupt and disrupted church services, demanding the members "come out" of the corrupt institution. This growing radical anti-clericalism, along with women's rights, among New England abolitionists contributed to the conflicts and split of the 1830s.[79]

Henry Ingersoll Bowditch was no stranger to anti-clericalism. Despite his mother's insistence on a traditional religious upbringing, his time in France nurtured an anti-clerical seed in his thinking.[80] This sentiment grew as he saw the clergy avoiding the issue of slavery. At one point he noted that the majority of churches were a hindrance to humanity; the true leaders of philanthropy were outside the church. The church "was faithless to humanity."[81] He believed that slavery and money corrupted the church, "no preacher dared open his mouth [against slavery] but the fingers of money holders were thrust over it."[82]

In this highly conflicted world, justice became the overarching issue. More than just wanting to end slavery, these abolitionists, despite personal limitations and the patronizing attitudes of many of them, were committed to racial equality. When William Cooper Nell and a number of black parents spoke out against segregated schools in Boston, it was the abolitionists who joined them and made ending school segregation a major campaign. Among themselves, they framed their struggle with more than the image of slavery. Bowditch reminded Garrison's son that "all of us professed a desire to feel for those in bonds as bound with them and our aim was to speak and act accordingly I.E. as if we ourselves were slaves."[83] Abolitionists may have felt bound to the slave, but most northerners viewed slavery as a distant abstraction. But the union of justice with the struggle against slavery became far more immediate when these issues presented themselves in Boston itself.

Chapter 4

"To Do Battle for Justice and the Oppressed"

There has been a man stolen in this city of our fathers!
—Theodore Parker

On July 30, 1836, a ship dropped anchor in Boston harbor carrying among its passengers two African Americans, Eliza Small and Polly Ann Bates. Matthew Turner, an agent of a wealthy slaveholder in Baltimore, boarded the ship and claimed the two women as fugitive slaves. He requested that Captain Eldridge hold the women until Turner could get a warrant for their arrest. News of the event quickly spread to Boston's black community, and soon black and white abolitionists gained a writ of habeas corpus from Chief Justice Shaw to have the women released until their hearing. The following Monday, with the courtroom filled with African Americans and white abolitionists, the lawyer for Eldridge and Turner argued that under the Fugitive Slave Law of 1793 the women should be returned to Baltimore. Samuel Sewall, a young abolitionist lawyer, argued from Locke that all human beings were freeborn and had a natural right to the enjoyment of their liberties. This led to a burst of cheering and applause from those gathered in the courtroom.

Judge Shaw took the narrow view that the captain did not have the right to convert his ship into a prison and that the women were free. With Shaw's ruling, Turner announced he would get a warrant in the court and have the women arrested there. Before Turner could move, word spread throughout the mixed race crowd, and abolitionists quickly grabbed the two women, threw the court officer to the ground, and dashed out the door. Abolitionists in a waiting carriage scooped up the women and rushed out of town with a posse in pursuit. Bates and Small disappeared into the underground network of New England abolitionists.

The Boston establishment was outraged. The very people who turned away when a mob attacked Garrison now called for tough measures against the "abolitionist riot[ers]."[1] Despite the clamor for arrests by Boston's leading citizens and newspapers, however, no arrests were made and the young women were never captured. Samuel Sewall did not escape totally unscathed. Four weeks later a naval officer from Baltimore and a relative of the slave owner entered Sewall's office, shouted threats and epithets at him about interfering with southern property rights, and beat him with the butt end of his horsewhip.

Despite Sewall's beating, Boston quickly forgot the dramatic slave rescue. The Garrisonians publicly deplored the violence involved, but most in the abolitionist movement found comfort in the fact that the state's leading justice, Lemuel Shaw, had supported the writ of habeas corpus and released the women, and in the successful interracial direct action of the rescuers. Their comfort lasted only six years.

On a chilly fall morning in 1842, Boston abolitionists again confronted the horror of slavery in their own back yard. On October 9 Constable Stratton, with a Police Court warrant on the request of Norfolk merchant James Gray, arrested George Latimer. Anticipating a rescue attempt by a mostly black crowd of some 300 who gathered at the Court House, Latimer was lodged in the fortified jail whose jailer was also a paid agent of Gray. Samuel Sewell attempted to get Latimer released on writ of habeas corpus from Chief Justice Shaw. This time Shaw, basing his decision on the 1793 Fugitive Slave Law, dismissed the writ and ordered Latimer returned to custody. A large crowd attempted but failed to rescue Latimer on his way back to the jail. Eight, all black, were arrested in the attempt. Latimer was held in the Boston jail as the personal custody of Gray until the court decided his fate under the Fugitive Slave Law.

Henry Bowditch, Sewall, Francis Jackson, Phillips, and Frederick Douglass began organizing a protest meeting at Faneuil Hall for October 30.[2] Six days before the mass meeting, Sewall and Amos Merrill argued for Latimer's release under the state's personal liberty law of 1837, basing their argument on natural rights. Shaw ruled against Latimer, declaring that "an appeal to natural rights and the paramount law of liberty was not pertinent. . . . By the Constitution, the duty of returning run-away slaves was made imperative on the free states and the act of Congress . . . was in accordance with the spirit of that instrument."[3] At the Faneuil Hall gathering Douglass, Sewall, and Jackson denounced Shaw and the proceedings against Latimer, while Phillips cursed the Constitution itself.[4] Garrison called Shaw a traitor to the honor of Massachusetts.[5]

Following the mass meeting, Bowditch began publishing an anti-slavery journal, the *Latimer Journal and North Star*. The tri-weekly paper, edited by Bowditch, William Channing, and Frederick Cabot, sent over 20,000 copies of each issue around the state denouncing Shaw's ruling and calling on the citizens to assert natural law over constitutional law. Bowditch, Channing, and Sumner circulated a petition demanding Latimer be released from a public jail. Faced with the possibility that his escaped slave would be rescued if released from the jail, Gray offered to sell Latimer to Bostonians for $400. Bowditch arranged for the money to be collected, but asserted that the people of Massachusetts "do not recognize the right of James Gray to the possession of said Latimer, but we are desirous of freeing our city from disturbance."[6]

The enthusiasm over Latimer's freedom spurred Bowditch and his compatriots to push to limit the Fugitive Slave Law. Abolitionists gathered 51,862 Massachusetts signatures in a petition the size of a barrel that John Quincy Adams was prevented from presenting to Congress because of the "gag law."[7] Back in Massachusetts, Bowditch directed a petition campaign that produced over 65,000 names. In 1843 six men carried a petition to the Massachusetts State House demanding a law preventing state institutions from being used to hold fugitive slaves.[8] Under the then passed Latimer Law, no state official or state judge could assist in or issue certificates of rendition (the term used to refer to sending fugitive slaves back into slavery), nor could state jails be used to confine fugitives.[9] Without state law officials to arrest and hold the fugitives and without jails in which to put them, fugitives could easily be "rescued" by local action. Soon other New England states picked up on Bowditch's initiative and similar laws were passed in Connecticut and Vermont.[10]

Although abolitionists were bothered about their complicity in the institution of slavery with the purchase of Latimer, his freedom was still celebrated. In his famous poem, "Massachusetts to Virginia," John Whittier announced "no fetters in the Bay State, no slave upon our land." Massachusetts abolitionists may have been successful in preventing the "fetters" of slavery from entangling the Bay State, but the attempt to render blacks from Massachusetts into slavery increased the intensity of the debate about slavery even among those who previously had remained aloof. Conservative textile manufacturer Amos Lawrence noted, "we went to bed one night old fashioned, conservative, Compromise Union Whigs and w[oke] up stark mad abolitionists."[11] For all their words and moral suasion, slavery was not declining but increasing, and its tentacles were now spreading into the very heart of New England. Even with the passage of the Latimer Laws it soon became clear to Boston abolitionists that more needed to be done to guarantee "no fetters in the Bay State." In the fall of 1846 the "outrage" of a kidnapping of a slave in Boston Harbor led Bowditch to call a group of "friends to meet . . . and consult," about what to do to prevent a recapture in Boston.[12] Out of those discussions came a call for a Faneuil Hall meeting and the formation of a Vigilance Committee designed to protect "all persons who may be in danger of abduction from the Commonwealth."[13]

The formation of the Vigilance Committee convinced Howe that he should no longer sit on the sidelines. He wrote to Bowditch, "I should not despair even of seeing the day when, high and noble interests being at stake, the truly great and noble spirits of the land would start forward to take the lead; men who will not now enter into the political strife when such paltry watchwords are inscribed upon the party banners. Under such men I should delight humbly to serve; and to forward such measures as they would propose, I should willingly spend and be spent."[14] He joined the Committee and, as a recognized man of action, joined Bowditch, John Andrew, and William Channing on the executive committee.[15]

The Vigilance group acted as a committee of the Massachusetts Anti-Slavery Society. It paid boatmen to move slaves to Canada, defrayed the costs of slaves staying in homes on the way north, and paid for medical expenses and clothing. It also gave slaves letters of introduction as they moved north to Canada. Through the 1840s the Committee operated without much urgency or secrecy. It documented what it paid out with receipts, notes, and minutes of meetings.[16] This open atmosphere changed dramatically with the passage of the Fugitive Slave Law of 1850.

The Fugitive Slave Law was designed to undermine the Latimer Law. While the Latimer Law prevented slave owners from using individual state police power to aid in the return of fugitive slaves, the Fugitive Slave Law empowered federal officials to capture fugitive slaves. New England Cotton Whigs rallied to the new law and its supporter Daniel Webster. They fired cannons on Boston Common to celebrate the "Compromise of 1850." Opponents of the law called a meeting at Faneuil Hall and revived the Vigilance Committee of 1846.[17] Renamed the Committee of Vigilance and Safety, it enrolled more than 50 (soon to grow to more than 200) active members, both black and white, sworn to take whatever action necessary to protect fugitives from the abominable law. Thirty lawyers, including John Andrew, Charles Sumner, Samuel Sewall, Charles Davis, Charles List, Ellis Morris, Ellis Loring, Richard Dana, John G. King, and Robert Morris, the first African American admitted to the Massachusetts Bar, formed a subcommittee to handle legal challenges and raise money to fight the law and aid fugitives. Eight people were elected to the executive committee to organize and direct actions. This committee, which included Lewis Hayden, a militant leader of Boston's black community, Henry and William Bowditch, and Samuel Gridley Howe, chose Parker as head.[18]

Within a month of its formation the committee sprang into action when slave-hunters arrived in Boston looking for Ellen and William Craft. After a dramatic escape from Georgia with Ellen masquerading as an elderly white man and William as her servant, the Crafts settled in Boston. Believing they were safe, they did not hide. William Craft ran a successful cabinet making shop and acted as vice president of a meeting of Boston's black community to protest the Fugitive Slave Law.[19] For a time Ellen and William stayed with Lewis Hayden at 66 Southac Street (now West Cedar Street) on the back side of Beacon Hill. Hayden and his wife Harriet regularly took in fugitive slaves, at one time hosting 13 in their home.[20]

Willis Hughes, the leader of the slave-catching group that arrived in Boston, had difficulty finding a judge in the city who would issue a warrant for the Crafts' arrest as stipulated by the Fugitive Slave Law. Finally Judge George Ticknor Curtis of the U.S. District Court issued the warrant. Another of Boston's Union Whigs and a relative of George Tichnor, Curtis came from the height of Boston's social set. Hughes then took his warrant to U.S. marshal Charles Devens to execute. Meanwhile abolitionist lawyers for the Vigilance Committee harassed Hughes, having him arrested for attempted kidnapping.[21] When Devens attempted to deliver the warrant to William Craft, Craft, armed with two revolvers supplied by the Vigilance Committee, refused to submit. Devens, who had no interest in being an agent for a slave-catcher and had been warned by Vigilance Committee lawyers that they would take action against him if he exceeded his authority in any fashion, decided he had done enough and returned to his office empty-handed.[22] Hughes promised to get reinforcements and take the Crafts by force. An armed group of the Committee of Vigilance led by Parker and including Samuel Gridley Howe tracked down the slave-hunters at their hotel. Bowditch, armed with his own revolver and resolved to shoot to kill if the slave-catchers attempted to take the Crafts, hurried them out of Boston hidden in his carriage to his brother's Brookline safe house.[23] Meanwhile the Vigilance Committee found the slave-catchers in their hotel. While a large crowd waited threateningly below, Parker and Howe burst into the slave-catchers' room. Parker offered them safe passage through the crowd if and only if they would agree to leave town and not return. Hughes and his compatriots fled Boston.[24] The Crafts then sailed for England, where they found sanctuary among English abolitionists.[25]

After the Crafts' escape it was clear to Boston abolitionists that the community had to be constantly vigilant at home if it hoped to provide any security to the region's black residents. The Vigilance Committee became more secretive. Austin Bearse remembers that meetings were now closed. He would go around to the homes and workplaces of members to tell them about meetings so that no one but members would be there, and stand at the door to bar nonmembers from coming in.[26]

The Committee indeed needed to be more vigilant, for on February 15, 1851, shortly after the Crafts were rescued, John Caphart, a "hired kidnapper," arrived with documents claiming that a waiter at a local coffee house was a fugitive slave. Curtis, as commissioner of the United States Circuit Court, issued an arrest warrant for Frederick Wilkins, known in Boston as Shadrach Minkins. This time Devens conveniently was called out of town and his assistant, Deputy Marshal Patrick Riley, arrested Minkins and whisked him into the Federal Court House before anyone was aware of what was happening. News of the arrest spread quickly through the abolitionist and black communities. Vigilance Committee lawyers rushed to the Court House to begin legal defense for Shadrach Minkins. After much legal maneuvering Judge Curtis called for the proceedings against the fugitive to continue the following Tuesday.

Sympathy for the fugitive slave as well as curiosity drew a huge interracial crowd outside the Court House. As the door opened to let out the legal defense team, a large crowd of black activists led by Lewis Hayden and including white abolitionist editor Elizur Wright rushed into the building and grabbed Minkins, lifted him up, and carried him out of the building. Hayden moved him first to a hiding place in the black section of Boston just north of Beacon Hill, then to a Vigilance Committee member's home in Cambridge and on into the abolitionists' underground network that moved him to Canada.[27]

The rescue electrified Boston's abolitionist movement. John Andrew wrote to James Freedman Clarke "the rescue of Shadrack [sic] was a noble thing and nobly done."[28] Boston abolitionists celebrated the act as worthy of their revolutionary ancestors, black and white (these were the people who celebrated Crispus Attucks and John Hancock and Sam Adams). Andrew told Clarke, "I would less regret the death of a 100 men defending successfully the sacred rights of human nature . . . than I should the return to bondage a single fugitive."[29] Henry Bowditch marked the day of the rescue on his calendar as a "holy day" of celebration.[30] Parker called it the most "noble deed done in Boston since the destruction of tea in 1773."[31] Boston's abolitionist community, Parker noted, "rejoiced that Boston was innocent of the great transgression of her sister-cities [New York and Philadelphia] and thought of the proud days of old."[32]

Boston's establishment was much less enthusiastic about the rescue. The Whig press and politicians demanded arrests and retribution. They saw the rescue as a flaunting of law and order and were concerned how it would be seen in the South. And the South did follow the fugitive cases in Massachusetts. Both southerners and northern appeasers were particularly outraged that it was blacks with white help that carried out the rescue. The inter-racial rescue played into their worst racial fears. President Fillmore and his cabinet member Daniel Webster both promised federal troops would be available in the future to prevent such actions as occurred in Boston. Immediately federal marshals began arresting black activists and charging them with crimes around the rescue. Among the ten blacks arrested were John Noye, a truckman, James Scott, a clothing merchant, Lewis Hayden, and attorney Robert Morris; also arrested were white lawyer Charles Davis, Vigilance Committee member Joseph Hayes, and editor Elizur Wright.[33] Richard Dana immediately came forward with a team of abolitionist lawyers to defend the accused.

Charles Davis came to trial first, before Benjamin Curtis, brother to George Ticknor Curtis who issued the original warrant. The case against Davis was weak and he was found innocent. The cases against Hayden and Morris were stronger, and being black did not make their situation any easier. Yet despite significant pressure they were both found innocent, much to Dana's surprise.[34] Years later Dana ran into a member of the jury, Francis Bigelow, a blacksmith, and Dana noted that he was surprised that they found for the accused. Bigelow then admitted that, although he had taken an oath of impartiality, he was also the person who drove Shadrach Minkins from Concord to Sudbury on his way out of the state.[35]

Once Morris and Hayden were found innocent, the other cases were dropped. But Boston's black community had little to celebrate. The president and leading state politicians promised to use federal troops to enforce the Fugitive Slave Law. And despite the verdicts, the sight of leading members of the black community being swept up in arrests, some with clearly no connection to the rescue, was not reassuring.

And there was reason to be concerned. On April 3, 1851, only two months after Minkins's dramatic rescue, Thomas Sims, a fugitive from Georgia, was arrested in Boston. This time federal authorities made a show of their authority and determination to enforce the Fugitive Slave Law. Theodore Parker believed that New England's call for open defiance of the law encouraged Fillmore and Webster to use Boston as a showcase for enforcement of the law.[36] The Court House was surrounded by a "chain . . . drawn around it, and numerous police officers were behind it besides several hired agents."[37] The Vigilance Committee called a meeting to decide what to do. Bowditch came "determined to be there and whatever happened to act according to my best judgment."[38] Higginson got word in Newburyport and rushed down for the meeting. Unfortunately Boston's abolitionist movement was not ready for the new resolve of its opponents. Unlike in earlier cases, federal officials frustrated the abolitionists' legal maneuvers and moved quickly to send Sims back to Georgia. They also prepared for a violent confrontation. More than a hundred armed police were stationed around the Court House with another hundred anti-abolitionist volunteers. Only authorized persons under guard by Deputy Marshal Riley were allowed in the Court House.[39]

At the Tremont Temple meeting Wendell Phillips, with "fire in his eyes" and "revolution" in his rhetoric, called on Bostonians to rush the Court House and free Sims.[40] Although Phillips excited the crowd to action other speakers urged caution. Higginson claimed that Garrison and the nonresisters were afraid of violence, while many of the political abolitionists were afraid direct action would hurt their political chances. Hayden and Higginson argued that the black community would join any action, but privately Hayden admitted that following the Shadrach Minkins prosecutions the black community was scattered and many of its most militant members in hiding.[41]

That night the Vigilance Committee met secretly with everyone present identified. It was assumed by all that plans would be developed "that involved risking one's life and reputation-activity against laws, state and nation."[42] Yet because of internal conflicts, fear, and caution the meeting failed to develop a plan of action. Bowditch, Higginson, Phillips, and Lewis were disgusted.[43] Still, many in Boston did not believe that Sims would actually be returned to slavery. Phillips called on the people of the city to fill the streets and prevent the Sims removal.[44] Higginson, Hayden, and William Bowditch were behind a plan to free Sims through a window of the Court House. Bowditch got a ladder and stored it in his office, but before they could put their plan into action, court officials had bars put on the windows.[45]

On April 12, 1851, Boston awoke to find the street leading to the Long Wharf, where the ship *Acorn* waited to take Sims back to slavery, lined with armed police. Crowds began to gather along the route. Bowditch rushed from his home to the Court House to be part of any rescue attempt. He quickly realized any effort would be futile. Police now numbering close to 300 armed with swords and clubs represented a formidable force; any rush to free Sims would lead to significant loss of life. Bowditch, Parker, Channing, and other abolitionists were now surrounded by hundreds of previously noninvolved Bostonians outraged at the sight of armed troops escorting a young black man back to slavery.[46]

As the armed guard marched Sims past the spot where "the British soldiers slew Christopher [sic] Attucks in 1770," the crowd shouted "shame and infamy."[47] Bowditch claimed that "the minions of slavery" were desecrating the "holy spot" where Attucks, "the martyr of the revolution," had died.[48] At the wharf a huge crowd gathered. Henry Bowditch spoke for the Vigilance Committee and denounced the city officials, the marshals, and the wealthy of Boston for their complicity in the tragedy.[49] But despite their shouts and screams, no rush to grab Sims occurred, and he was led out onto the *Acorn* and set sail for Georgia.[50] Boston abolitionists and particularly the Vigilance Committee felt failure and blamed themselves.[51] Although it was "a wrong against . . . all of us," committed by "those who worship money," Theodore Parker reminded Boston, "on the people's part it was a great defeat; your defeat and mine."[52]

On the anniversary of Sims's kidnapping, Parker shared his feelings of shame that in 1770 when Attucks and others were "massacre[d] the people of Boston massed and forced the troops out of the city. But the people in this case did no such thing."[53] Boston failed its revolutionary tradition and the honor of those who had earlier fought for liberty and justice. Wendell Phillips reminded a crowd on July 4, in Framingham, that "here under the blue sky of New England, we teach the doctrine that whenever you find a man down-trodden he is your brother, whenever you find an unjust law you are bound to be its enemy; that Massachusetts was planted as the furnace of perpetual insurrection against tyrants."[54] Theodore Parker felt that Bostonians of 1851 fared badly when compared to their eighteenth century grandparents. When the Fugitive Slave Law was passed "by those who faithfully represent money," there was no opposition.[55] The people should have "come together in a great mass meeting and decree as their fathers had often done, that so unjust a law should not be kept in the old Bay State."[56] "How different had Massachusetts met the Acts of Trade and the Stamp Act. How are the mighty fallen."[57] Boston was the home of the "bones of Adams and Hancock, dangerous relics in any soil; they ought to have been sent back at the passage of the Fugitive Slave Law and Faneuil Hall demolished."[58]

The story of Crispus Attucks and the Boston Massacre was a repeated motif in the abolitionist rhetoric after Sims's return to slavery. The comparison of the successful rescue of Minkins by black abolitionists with the help and aid of white supporters, the idealized interracial unity of the revolutionary crowd in 1770, and the total failure of white abolitionists to free Sims played heavily on the minds of New England abolitionists. They noted the fact that Sims was marched over the "spot where 81 years before the ground had drunk in the African blood of Christopher

Attucks, shed by white men on the fifth March; brother's blood which did not cry in vain."[59] Boston's abolitionists noted the irony that April 19, the day Sims landed at Savannah and entered the block to be whipped, was the day of the Battle of Lexington, "sacred to liberty and the rights of mankind."[60]

In his sermons Parker reminded the congregation of New England's sacred trust, commitment to liberty, and resistance to tyranny. "In New England the one issue above all else is our freedom of our men and women."[61] But he also preached that the region had failed its tradition, "Oh Boston! . . . thou art dishonored now; thou hast taken to they arms the enemies of men. Thou hast betrayed the slave; thy brother's blood cries out against thee from the ground. Thou art a stealer of mankind. In thy borders for long year, the cradle of Liberty has been placed. . . . O Massachusetts, noble state, the mother that bore us all; parent of goodly institutions and of noble men, whose great ideas have blessed the land! How art thou defiled, dishonored. . . . I conjure thee by all thy battlefields, by the remembrance of the great men born of thee who battled for right . . . to forbid forever all such deeds as this [returning Sims] and wipe away thy deep disgrace."[62]

Abolitionists felt responsible but did not know what to do. Radicals from Lynn and Newburyport as well as the western part of the state believed that the Boston Vigilance Committee should have done something "to deliver the man."[63] Parker admitted to this, but argued that, although "the country [rural Massachusetts and towns outside Boston] has never forgiven the Committee for not doing it; I am chairman of the executive committee of the Vigilance Committee . . . believe me when I say the Vigilance Committee did all it could."[64] Samuel Gridley Howe felt that he had somehow personally failed. Like Bowditch, Howe had started out to do something for Sims. But at the moment when he felt he should have rushed forward he held back, feeling ill and concerned about his children.[65]

The failure to rescue Sims shook the confidence of these abolitionists. Was it enough just to stand firm in face of hostility and violence for principle? The Crafts and Minkins had been saved, but the Vigilance Committee had failed to protect Sims, a man who came to Boston, as, Parker noted, "the cradle of Liberty and hoped here to enjoy the liberty of a man."[66] Male abolitionists particularly saw the failure to rescue Sims as their failure to live up to the traditions of their forefathers and their failure to be men. Parker reminded Boston that the city "once was full of manly men that rocked the cradle of liberty," but no more.[67] "I rated you too high! Pardon me, town of Boston, that I thought your citizens men!"[68]

Abolitionists shared with most Americans a belief in the importance

of courage and honor. For the men and women who took to the abolitionist stage and were attacked bodily, courage was exemplified by their
steadfastness in face of danger, hostility, and bodily harm. Being
knocked from the stage, punched, beaten, and having their lives threatened were not only regular occurrences for abolitionists; they were af-
firmations of their fearless commitment. Courage was something both
male and female abolitionists demonstrated regularly. Yet, increasingly,
even though male abolitionists regularly saw females facing as much
risk and threats as their male counterparts, male abolitionists saw that
courage as a reflection of manliness.[69] Bowditch believed that James
Deane, a western Massachusetts physician and abolitionist, proved he
was "a man" by his commitment to the cause and his willingness to express opposition to slavery even if it was likely to "diminish his personal
reputation or his monied receipts.[70] Of himself, Bowditch said, "by my
antislavery acts I had been made in reality a man."[71] Nathaniel Rogers
encouraged Parker Pillsbury to become a lecturer for the Anti-Slavery
Society, by arguing that it was a "manly activity."[72]

The risk both men and women took with involvement in the Underground Railroad proved the commitment and integrity of those involved. But, with the passage of the Fugitive Slave Act and the
reactivation of the Vigilance Committee, gender divisions among abolitionists emerged. Unlike the Massachusetts Anti-Slavery Society and its
traveling lecturers, which included both men and women, including
the officer positions after 1840, the Vigilance Committee was all male.
Male abolitionists particularly saw standing up to the Craft kidnappers
and sending them out of town as an example of courageous manly action on the part of the committee that reflected Boston's proud revolutionary tradition of defense of liberty. The interracial cooperation of
the Shadrach Minkins rescue affirmed for abolitionists their honor and
courage. Bowditch felt that his home was "ennobled" by being the hiding place of one of the rescuers of Minkins willing to die for the "cause
of liberty."[73]

Slavery came home to Boston with Sims's return to Georgia. And
male abolitionists came to see that reality as requiring more of themselves. Higginson returned to Newburyport convinced that Boston abolitionists lacked the backbone and resolve necessary truly to fight
slavery. Parker called on Bostonians not just to discuss slavery but to act
in a manly fashion. "Is there no male or manly virtue left?"[74] Boston's
abolitionist community began to divide along gender lines. It was certainly not the first gender division within the community, but it was a
subtler division that would come to be more pronounced as the struggle became more physical and violent.[75]

It was in this context of feelings of failure that Boston faced another crisis when, on May 24, U.S. deputy marshal Asa Butman and five other agents for a Southern slaveholder seized Anthony Burns on his way home from work in a clothing shop. With the excuse that he had stolen goods from a jeweler's shop, Burns was hauled into the Federal Court House (under the Latimer Law neither state nor local jails could be used to hold fugitive slaves) and charged with being a runaway slave. He was held without access to counsel and pressed to admit he was a fugitive slave. The following morning, surrounded by 70 armed guards, Burns came before Judge Loring. Two local lawyers representing a Virginia slave owner presented documentation claiming Burns was a fugitive slave belonging to the Virginian. At that point Richard Dana, Charles Ellis, and William Bowditch from the lawyers' committee of the Committee of Vigilance came forward to defend Burns.[76]

Meanwhile the Committee on Vigilance sent word to its members throughout the state. Samuel May sent word to Thomas Wentworth Higginson (who took his position with the Worcester Free Church because of the strong core of militant abolitionists in Worcester) to come to Boston with as many Worcester radicals as possible.[77] The committee called a protest meeting at Faneuil Hall, and the executives met to formulate a plan of action. But once again these leaders could not decide what to do. The lack of resolve on the part of Boston abolitionists outraged Henry and William Bowditch, Higginson, and the Worcester group.[78] Henry noted that the Worcester group "sneered at the cowardness of Boston" and came to Boston for the "purpose of doing what Boston could not or would not."[79] Accusing the Boston abolitionists of lacking "a trace of manly feelings," Higginson met with his 200 "manly" Worcester "men" and with the support of some radical Bostonians planned an action to free Burns. The group purchased axes to break down the Court House doors and stored them in William Bowditch's office. It was decided that Higginson and the Worcester group along with the more dependable Bostonians, including several black abolitionists, would charge the Court House at the same time as the meeting at Faneuil Hall. As the radicals attempted to seize the Court House, the Faneuil Hall protest meeting would be signaled and the crowd told of the rush on the Court House. It was assumed that the crowd would join those attacking the Court House and provide the numbers needed to overcome the armed guard and police reinforcements.[80]

As the "largest gathering . . . ever [seen] in that hall" listened to the speakers at Faneuil Hall, Higginson and some of the Worcester group along with Lewis Hayden and some of the (mostly black) Boston abolitionists rushed the Court House.[81] They broke through the first door and confronted a well-armed group of guards. In the confusion the guards were able to block the remaining doors and prevent others from pouring into the Court House. Inside guards armed with sabers, clubs, and pistols began pushing the abolitionists back out. At one point Higginson was isolated and a group of guards went in for the kill. A saber blade cut him badly. Hayden, seeing Higginson's danger, pulled out a revolver and shot dead James Batchelder, the guard closest to Higginson. As Marshal Watson Freeman rushed forward, Hayden shot at him but missed. In the confusion Higginson escaped, but the guards secured the doors against the crowd.[82]

Meanwhile the signal never got through to the Vigilance Committee members at the Faneuil Hall mass meeting. Confusion about who was supposed to signal whom reigned, and when word reached the Hall some of the speakers urged caution and attempted to keep the crowd at the meeting. Henry Bowditch was at the Faneuil Hall meeting, unaware of the plan to free Burns, despite his brother's involvement. When he heard about the attack from the person who was trying to pass the signal to the speakers, Bowditch rushed out of the Hall. In the confusion on the street Bowditch saw some abolitionists attempting to restrain the crowd while others wanted to join the attack on the Court House.[83] Without effective planning and with mixed messages from the leadership, the crowd in Court Square failed to provide effective support for those battling within. Bowditch ran for the Court House, but failed to get in. Meanwhile police reinforcements arrived and began breaking up the crowd led by Samuel Gridley Howe and William Channing. Bronson Alcott, arriving late to the Court House, asked Higginson, "why are we not within?" Higginson replied, "because these people will not stand by us."[84]

The rescue attempt failed. Higginson was wounded and a guard lay dead. More than a thousand federal troops, including a detachment of U.S. Marines and an attachment of cavalry arrived in Boston to reinforce the guards holding Burns. The mayor called out local militia "under the pretence of preserving the peace."[85] In the days following, moderate Bostonians tried a variety of peaceful means to free Burns. An attempt was made to buy him, but the agent for his owner, interested more in making a point than a profit, refused to sell. The failure to rescue Burns haunted Bowditch. Higginson's attempt on the Court House was the model of "noble" action. "When Massachusetts is filled with such [noble men] then slave hunting will be impossible. I felt I was really unworthy of them when I passed."[86]

On the morning of June 2, 1854, huge crowds filled the streets of Boston in anticipation of the ruling by Slave Law commissioner Edward Loring on Burns's fate. Well-armed federal troops took over Court Square. State militia mustered on State Street. Store merchants, disgusted by the idea that southern slavery was reaching into the heart of

New England or cynically wanting to appear sympathetic to what had clearly become the majority feeling in the city, hung black banners in their windows and from balconies. Flags were hung at half mast or upside down. More than 50,000 people gathered in protest, with thousands coming in on special trains from the surrounding countryside.[87]

At 1:00 Loring ruled that Burns was to be sent to slavery. The crowd hissed and hooted. The mayor issued the order to clear the streets. As Bowditch joined the crowd in denouncing the ruling, marshal Francis Tukey threatened him with a warning that "you had better be careful what you say, every word you scream has been taken down, and it may be hard for you." Bowditch refused to be cowed and "continued jeering at all and any officials."[88] Troops rushed at the crowd with bayonets, and the police swung their clubs to force people off State Street, knocking to the ground, among others. Anthony Burns's lawyer Richard Dana. At one point the cavalry charged, swinging their swords. As Burns approached the spot of the Boston Massacre, a cry of shame rose from thousands of throats.[89] Burns left Boston Harbor under heavy guard.

The affair left a bitter taste in the mouths of the people of Boston. Those who had never before joined with the abolitionists felt outraged that the city had become an export market for slaves. Captain Joseph Hayes of the police resigned from his commission. Bowditch noted in his journal "the people now are more ripe than ever for revolution . . . no slave hunting in Massachusetts is the muttered oath under everyone's lips."[90] Theodore Parker claimed "all Massachusetts is incensed, the wrath of Massachusetts is slow but she has wrath and has courage."[91]

Bostonians were soon to feel the brunt of federal anger over the Burns affair. On hearing that he was identified as one of the rescuers, Lewis Hayden went into hiding, first at William Bowditch's house and then out of town.[92] Initially two white and two black abolitionists were arrested and charged with the murder of Batchelder.[93] The wounded Higginson was clearly a target.

Higginson returned to Worcester to a hero's welcome. Through his house streamed a flow of neighbors and fellow abolitionists pledging support and solidarity.[94] Soon word reached Worcester of the issuance of a warrant for the arrest of Higginson and Martin Stowell for inciting a riot. Higginson was brought into Boston on the morning train, where he was met by Richard Dana, whose head was still bandaged from the beating during one of the police charges the day Burns was returned. Bail was quickly raised by William Bowditch, and Higginson returned to Worcester again to a celebratory welcome.

Following his arrest Higginson, went off to Pigeon Cove on the north shore of Boston.[95] The Clarkes came up to stay with the Higginsons and show support, followed by a parade of abolitionists. Although there were conflicting feelings about the wisdom of the attempted rescue, abolitionists rallied around Higginson.[96] Garrison, who thought the attack was wrong-headed and ill-conceived, nonetheless offered Higginson his support. Whittier, the old Quaker pacifist, was a constant companion.[97]

After vacationing in Pigeon Cove, Thomas and Mary Higginson returned to Worcester to wait for his trial. At a rally Higginson praised Worcester men for their manly behavior and proclaimed Worcester a safe haven for fugitives.[98] Slavery, he told a crowd in August, would be ended not by reform but by "revolution," and he declared himself a "revolutionist."[99]

In October deputy U.S. marshal Asa Butman, the man responsible for the arrest of Sims and Burns, came to Worcester in search of another fugitive slave. Word of his arrival spread quickly through the community. A crowd gathered outside his hotel and threatened to do him harm if he did not leave town. At one point Butman emerged from the hotel, drew his gun, and threatened to shoot. The local marshal then arrested him for carrying a concealed weapon and threw him in jail. When he appeared in court the crowd rushed him. The mayor arrived and promised that Butman would be sent from town on the next train. At that point Higginson, Martin Stowell (one of those charged in the Burns attack), Stephan Foster, Thomas Drew, and George Hoar joined the mayor in calling for calm and the quick removal of Butman. The mayor refused him police protection. The abolitionists then stepped forward and escorted him through the crowd and out of town, with Foster imploring the crowd to let him pass. Despite the efforts of Higginson, Foster, Hoar, Drew, and Stowell to protect Butman, six Worcester abolitionists, three whites and three blacks, were arrested for inciting a riot. Among those arrested was Stephan Foster, who refused bail and scandalized established society by demanding that his wife Abby be his defense counsel.

Ultimately the charges for inciting a riot were dropped.[100] But the federal government continued to press charges against those involved in the attempt to free Burns. The state grand jury found that the evidence did not point to any particular person for murder.[101] The federal district attorney then charged the group, which now included Theodore Parker, with inciting to riot.[102] The first grand jury, many sympathetic to the abolitionists, refused to indict. A second grand jury did indict, but the district judges threw out the indictments.

The government success in the rendition of Burns stirred resentment and anger. New England abolitionists had developed a radical natural rights critique of slavery and tried to live a life free of "colorphobia." They had struggled to end segregation in the region and built a movement and a community to oppose slavery. But slavery seemed as strong as ever and even pushed its tentacles into the very heart of New England. It was clear to all the elements of the abolitionist community that more needed to be done. What exactly was not so clear.

Whatever the particulars of the failure to rescue Burns, most abolitionists agreed that New England had to be better prepared if it wanted to prevent another person from being sent into slavery. New Englanders also became more sophisticated in their Underground Railroad work. Bowditch and a group of friends, including his brother William, Higginson, May, and other radicals, bought a pleasure yacht ostensibly for cruises up and down the coast, but in fact as a cover for moving slaves into Canada. Austin Bearse captained the yacht.[103]

When Higginson was arrested, William Channing offered to take over Higginson's pulpit and preach action, not peace; "the next thing to do is a guerilla war at every chance."[104] Bowditch also became convinced that New England had to engage in "physical resistance to slavery as we saw it in the North."[105]

On August 10, 1854, Bowditch called a secret meeting of radicals willing to engage in violent illegal action to stop the capture of fugitive slaves in New England.[106] Out of the meeting came the Anti-Man Hunting League. The league called meetings, gathered weapons, and began military training. Members had to be recommended and elected to the "secret" society pledged to make "impossible the coming or remaining of man hunters among us."[107] The league set up cells or lodges (24 in all with 469 members) around New England and used codes to communicate between members and cells.[108] With the exception of leaders, even cell members were unaware of members in other cells.[109] The leagues trained to kidnap "slave hunters" and hold them prisoner until any fugitive slaves were released.[110]

New England abolitionists moved increasingly toward militancy. In a sermon after the charge on the Court House, Higginson told New Englanders "the body also has a part to do in resistance."[111] The world of conflict was also becoming an increasingly male world. Higginson admired and respected women like Lucy Stone (who had married in her famous feminist wedding) and Abby Kelley Foster for their intelligence and courage, but after 1854 he had little time for activity that did not address "our proper manly life on earth." In a letter to one of the Weston sisters, who had risked life and limb facing hostile crowds in the 1830s and 1840s, Higginson agreed to speak before a group of women abolitionists, but only under protest. "To speak at fairs," he wrote sarcastically, "seems to me the only real martyrdom of the nineteenth century for who can be inspired among pin cushions? But I think one is bound to do this and I yield implicitly to your commands."[112]

Male and female abolitionists had struggled together since the end of the 1830s. The movement in New England had embraced the ideal of gender as well as racial equality, yet the same people who embraced equality were increasingly finding that there was something special in male action. James Fowler, the abolitionist minister wrote to his friend Higginson, "I think we need a *man's movement*" (emphasis his).[113]

The path to action cut through different terrains. For Bowditch it led to setting up secret paramilitary cells; for others it involved more intense political activism. Massachusetts had a history of sending active anti-slavery people to Congress, including John Quincy Adams. Abolitionists John Palfrey and Charles Allen were elected to Congress in 1846, and two years later moderate abolitionist Horace Mann was sent to fill Adams's seat. Palfrey voted against fellow Massachusetts Whig Representative Robert Winthrop for Speaker of the House because of Winthrop's support of the war with Mexico. Two years later both Palfrey and Allen voted against Winthrop.

In 1851, anger over the Cotton Whigs' and Senator Daniel Webster's support for the Fugitive Slave Law led to a rebellion against the state's political establishment. In those years the Massachusetts legislature, like those throughout the nation, chose U.S. senators. When Daniel Webster entered President Fillmore's administration, Robert Winthrop, a supporter of Webster and the Fugitive Slave Law, was appointed to fill Webster's seat until the state legislature could vote. The Whig establishment then put Winthrop forward for legislative election. Free Soilers in the state legislature countered by supporting the fiery Charles Sumner.[114] Although it appeared to Edmund Quincy that Sumner did not stand a chance, with the support of Howe and some clever trading with Democrats, Sumner won and in 1851 took Webster's seat in the Senate as a Free Soiler.[115]

The news of the passage of the Kansas-Nebraska Act in 1854 swept over Massachusetts with waves of frustration and despair. The new law shattered the thirty-five-year Missouri Compromise by opening formerly forbidden territories to the possibility of slavery. Convinced that the southern slave powers would settle Kansas with pro-slavery forces, tip the balance in the Senate in favor of the slave states, and use that wedge to open the whole nation to slavery, northern abolitionists became obsessed with settling Kansas with Free Soilers.[116] Getting settlers to Kansas who would vote against slavery and providing them with arms was difficult and dangerous work. Settlers needed to be recruited and financed in the more densely populated areas of the northeast and sent west by train and wagon. It required extensive organization and money. New Englanders organized the Emigrant Aid Society to raise money for the settlers and took money wherever they could find it, even from the "lords of the loom." Both Eli Thayer and Amos Lawrence contributed to the cause.

Once in Kansas, Free Soilers were subjected to attacks by pro-slave "ruffians" from Missouri as well as the normal sod-busting hardships of settling on the open treeless prairie. Conflict between free settlers and pro-slavery Missourians led to what Higginson called "the English Crimean War on a small scale in Kansas."[117]

Thayer and Lawrence were not the only New Englanders financing the settlement of Kansas as a free territory. Howe raised money for emigrants and to get Sharp's rifles to the settlers. He was joined not only by Higginson, who also transported the supplies west to the settlers, but also by a recent graduate of Harvard, Franklin Sanborn.[118] Like Higginson and Phillips, Sanborn was the star of his Harvard class: bright, articulate, energetic, and handsome. The young graduate idolized Higginson and Howe and went to Higginson for guidance on what to do with his life. Higginson advised action for the general good and sent him to Howe, who immediately got the young man involved in raising money for John Brown's work in Kansas.[119] By the fall of 1856 Sanborn and Howe were moving weapons to Kansas.[120]

For some, the frustrations of the 1850s encouraged a more radical, revolutionary position. Distressed with the presidency and Senate dominated by southerners, and a Constitution that implicitly endorsed slavery with the 3/5 clause that gave southern whites voting power well beyond their numbers, Phillips, Garrison, and several of their supporters began to argue in the 1840s that the free North should leave the union. Garrison argued that, since the South would not voluntarily give up slaves, the North must break away in order to protect itself from complicity with the sin of slavery. With the passage of the Fugitive Slave Law in 1850 more and more abolitionists came to the idea of disunion. Initially the political abolitionists rejected disunion as a politically naive abandonment of the nation and of slaves in the South. The combination of the passage of the Kansas-Nebraska bill and the 1857 Dred Scott decision convinced even some political abolitionists that New England needed to leave the union before it too was subjected to the degradation of slavery.

In the larger realm of national politics, the Free Soil Party merged with the newly created Republican Party in 1855. New England abolitionists greeted the union with mixed feelings. Higginson had worked for years with the Free Soil Party, but by the end of 1856 the situation in Kansas and the nation finally pushed him to embrace the politics of division.[121] Higginson, Abby Foster, and the Worcester radicals were not the only Free Soil Republicans leaning toward disunion. F. W. Bird, the powerful political figure behind the Bird Club, was sending money to support a state convention for disunion. New Englanders who had recently joined the Republican Party were already talking about pushing the party to endorse disunion.[122] At the 1857 Abolitionist Festival, Higginson found that even prominent anti-slavery politicians admitted that the time was approaching when "political action was exhausted [and] disunion . . . our duty."[123] Worcester abolitionists led by Abby Kelley Foster and Higginson drafted a statement calling for radical action: "the anti-slavery cause now seems to be [calling for] political action which shall be avowedly and actually revolutionary. There are men enough already prepared to use their political power for the overthrow of slavery."[124]

Disunion was never an idea that interested Bowditch. He joined the Republican Party and, except for his work with the Anti-Man Hunting League, the years after the Burns's capture were quiet ones for him. He published a number of scientific and medical papers during these years and was appointed Jackson Professor of Clinical Medicine at Harvard. He made a canoe trip down the Penobscot River in Maine from the headwaters to Bangor, took his son on an extended vacation to the Isles of Shoals, and went to England and France to visit old friends. But soon the chariots of war would disrupt this quiet. For Boston abolitionists the Civil War followed a long path of frustrations, alarms, and the confusions of politics. Yet in time it transformed the lives of everyone. For abolitionists the war's importance lay in its role in ending slavery.

Chapter 5

"The Issue Is Universal Justice"

Let us . . . stand claiming for the Negro justice not privileges; rights, not alms.

—*William Lloyd Garrison*

Justice will sustain us even in this our last step forward in civilization.

—*Memorial to Nathaniel Bowditch*

The war's ending did not end the grief of lovers, families, and friends who lost loved ones, but for abolitionists it did bring to focus the purpose of all those years of conflict. Abolitionists struggled to respond to the new world with, in the words of Abraham Lincoln, its "new birth of freedom," in a fashion that held to their principles while at the same time appreciating the reality of a nation without slavery. Central to their response was their continued commitment to racial justice.

In 1861 Francis Jackson died at age seventy-three. Jackson was a founding member and long-standing president of the New England Anti-Slavery Society as well as a close friend of both Garrison and Phillips. He had been a member of the Vigilance Committee and an agent on the Underground Railroad. In his will Jackson established two trusts to provide funds for the causes closest to his heart, abolitionism and women's rights. It took several years for Jackson's wishes on these matters to be resolved as heirs contested his will.[1] Family members challenged the section that left money to women's suffrage. The courts sided with the family members and gave that money to Jackson's children. Eventually some of the heirs who supported the original intent of the will gave money to set up a trust for women's rights.[2] Jackson also bequeathed an unspecified amount to be used "to create public sentiment" against slavery, and named a board of trustees that included his old friends Phillips, Garrison, Quincy, May, Maria Weston Chapman, Lydia Child, Charles Whipple, Edward Jackson (Francis's brother), and William Bowditch.[3]

When the money finally became available, in 1867, the Constitution itself prohibited slavery. Garrison, supported by May and Quincy, argued that the money should be used for the education of the newly freed slaves. Child and Chapman had left the board. Phillips, supported by Bowditch, Whipple, and Jackson, argued that the money should be used to push for black enfranchisement.[4] Bowditch argued that if the money was not used for advancement of equal rights for blacks it should be given to the women's rights campaign.[5]

Initially the board members compromised on splitting the fund, $5,000 for Garrison's idea of giving the money to the Freedman's Union Commission and $4,200 to the *Anti-Slavery Standard* campaign for suffrage. Before the compromise could be acted upon the Fifteenth Amendment was passed, giving black males the suffrage. Garrison then argued that all the money should go to the Freedman's Union Commission; Phillips replied that political and social inequality remained and the money should be used for continued agitation for complete racial equality. In the ensuing bitter feud, the board split, with the majority— Bowditch, Jackson, Whipple, and Phillips—refusing to give all the money to the Freedman's Union Commission. Garrison and his supporters went to court, which ordered the board to release all the money to the Commission. The board majority refused. The court then removed Bowditch, Phillips, Whipple, and Jackson from the board and had the others appoint new members who proceeded to release the money.[6]

The battle over the money split friendships. Garrison became alienated from Bowditch and from Wendell Phillips, his closest friend.[7] Quincy also no longer spoke to Phillips. Higginson remembered Quincy and Phillips: "having worked side by side together through storm and through calm, having been denounced, threatened and even mobbed side by side, the two men had yet separated in bitterness on the interpretation of a will made by a fellow laborer, Francis Jackson."[8]

Personal conflict was conflated with principle, with each side charging the other with "perversion of a sacred trust" and "violations of the very vital spirit and principle of our great cause of freedom."[9] In a letter to Bowditch, Garrison wrote that Bowditch's claim to be more in the spirit of Jackson was "offensive," and "mutual esteem and confidence must here terminate. For he who declares or insinuates that I am false to a sacred trust and recreant to a cause to which nearly forty years of my life have been devoted, can not consistently keep me upon his list of friends nor . . . have a place upon my list."[10]

The conflict over the Jackson fund was not just about friendships. It was also about differing abolitionist goals and how to achieve them.[11] Friendships helped abolitionists survive differences over strategies and tactics and helped hold people together when their principles led them to be isolated from others. But conflicts over principles could also produce so much strain on personal relationships that friendships failed to overcome differences.

Long before the Civil War, abolitionists committed themselves to a radical vision of racial equality. The original declaration of sentiments of the American Anti-Slavery Society bound abolitionists to end not only slavery but white racism as well. Within their organizations black and white abolitionists worked together. When the Fall River Female Anti-Slavery Society was formed it opened its membership to blacks and whites on equal terms.[12] As early as 1839, female abolitionists from Lynn, Massachusetts, organized a petition drive directed at the Massachusetts legislature demanding the repeal of all racial discrimination in the state. Although black males could vote in Massachusetts, before the 1850s most of the state's schools were segregated, as were most transportation facilities, and interracial marriage was outlawed.[13] These practices called forth a campaign by both black and white abolitionists that lasted for the fifteen years before formal discriminatory practices were made illegal.

It has been well noted that many white abolitionists patronized their black fellows.[14] Certainly in a racist society it would have been unusual if a mass movement, even one to end slavery, did not include some who had racist views about blacks. What should not be forgotten is the extent to which the abolitionists fought that racism within themselves, their movement, and society in general. Samuel May, who attacked "colorphobia," also believed that racial prejudice was so deep-seated in society that it required not only collective but individual struggle.[15] "We are prejudiced against the blacks; and our prejudices are indurate . . . by the secret, vague consciousness of the wrong we are doing."[16] To combat the "ignoble prejudice" in themselves, abolitionists urged each other to "receive [blacks] as we do our white fellow citizens," not only in the public sphere but in the private sphere as well.[17] Abolitionists invited blacks into their homes and community while most other white Americans practiced private and public exclusion.

White abolitionists not only struggled against their private prejudices, they also protested public manifestations of racial distinctions. They made a point of riding in the "Negro cars," and supported the actions of black abolitionists such as Charles Remond, William Nell, David Ruggles, and Frederick Douglass when they insisted on riding in the "white cars."[18]

When in 1846 black parents pulled their children out of the Boston public schools to protest segregation, Henry Bowditch and Edmund Jackson, who were members of the School Committee, demanded an end to separate schools and resigned when it refused to end segregated schooling. When their friend Horace Mann, at the time secretary of the Massachusetts Board of Education, failed to come forward and publicly endorse integration of the Boston public schools, Phillips and Garrison viciously attacked him. Massachusetts abolitionists both black and white continued to fight for school integration until 1855, when, under the leadership of Charles Sumner and John Andrew, the state passed statewide desegregation legislation.[19]

As a consulting physician at Massachusetts General Hospital, Henry Bowditch made a point of admitting black patients on an equal basis with whites. When the hospital board privately objected to Bowditch about the number of black patients he was admitting, he insisted he would continue to admit blacks on an equal basis. The hospital responded by enacting a provision prohibiting the admission of blacks. Bowditch resigned in a public demonstration of outrage. Faced with the resignation of one of its most prestigious physicians, the hospital rescinded its prohibition and asked Bowditch to withdraw his resignation. Having gained the principle of equality he agreed.[20]

When the New Bedford Lyceum segregated blacks from whites in its programs, abolitionists organized a separate lyceum based on the principle of racial equality. Abolitionists argued that the issue was not a local or personal one but "a struggle for the welfare and rights of mankind."[21] Both Ellis Loring and Samuel Sewall accepted blacks as apprentices in their law practices.[22] Higginson, in the midst of the battles in Kansas, argued that opposing separate laws for blacks and whites was as important as stopping slavery in Kansas. It was "not merely freedom or slavery but is the American principle strong enough to cover more than one race? . . . Every law about a colored school, or restricting the seats in cars or the marriages of races is as important a battle as any in Kansas."[23]

Elizabeth Buffum Chace noted that much of the objection among whites to full equal rights was rooted in a racist fear of interracial contact. "They did not want their daughters to marry Negroes."[24] Yet in face of this the white abolitionists continued to insist on full and absolute equality. Higginson argued in 1856 that any marriage law that did not give full equality to blacks and whites, including the right to intermarry, would be a sham. He argued that the issue of "amalgamation" was already settled in the South, where the large numbers of mulattos indicated that the mixing of the races was a fact. The point was that black women in the South were not protected from white men, so society clearly was really concerned not about race mixing but only about holding blacks down. Higginson believed that only equality under the law would protect black women.

The white abolitionists readily faced down the "prejudice against color."[25] Henry Wright proclaimed, "I am a Negro. I feel that I am in heart and soul. The scorn and hate cast on him, are cast on me."[26] Frederick Douglass noted that when he came to Boston few would have him to their homes as an equal; the exceptions were the radical abolitionists like Henry Ingersoll Bowditch and Wendell Phillips.[27]

Although there was considerable disagreement about how to achieve their goals once the war began, New England abolitionists did not abandon their commitment to racial equality.[28] They were suspicious of Lincoln's commitment to ending slavery, but after the firing on Fort Sumter they supported his military efforts against the South while continuing to demand that the war be about emancipation.[29] Radicals in New England formed the Emancipation League and pushed for Lincoln to declare the war one against slavery. They also agitated for enlistment of blacks in the army and that they be paid on a par with white soldiers.[30] Governor Andrew appointed Frederick Douglass and George Stearns to recruit two black military regiments from the state. Henry Bowditch felt that until emancipation was made the central purpose of the war, it went badly for the North. "Once the war moved to the issue of freedom with Lincoln issuing the emancipation proclamation and Governor Andrew ordering up the Massachusetts 54th and 55th black regiments and with their heroic actions at Fort Wagner, the North took to the cause of liberty."[31] Phillips, Pillsbury, and Foster, believing that Lincoln would not move beyond emancipation and support full equality, campaigned for the more radical John Fremont to replace Lincoln as the Republican candidate for the presidency.

What emancipation would mean for the freed slaves haunted the abolitionist community as the war drew to a close. In 1864 Phillips argued that the Massachusetts Anti-Slavery Society was committed not only to ending slavery but also to complete equality. That equality, he claimed, was rooted in the natural rights of men, and it was the responsibility of government to protect those rights. Phillips proposed that the society endorse land distribution, black suffrage, compulsory education, and an amendment against discrimination.[32] Garrison believed that with the coming end of slavery the more important task for abolitionists was to provide immediate help to those now faced with freedom; continued agitation for equality and suffrage would divert attention from the pressing needs of newly freed slaves. He argued that the aim of the society was to end slavery and aid the freedmen, not to guarantee absolute political and social equality. Garrison, the old crusader, leader of New England abolitionists for thirty years, was defeated 3 to 1 as New England abolitionists stood by Phillips's radical notion of complete political, social, and economic equality guaranteed by the state.

Later, at the 1865 American Anti-Slavery Society meeting, Garrison reargued the issue, claiming that the members should focus on aiding the freedmen primarily by starting and funding schools and providing financial assistance, and proposed that the society be dissolved. Phillips countered that the organization was founded on the principle of complete equality between the races and an end to white racism; as such, the society should not disband until there was "absolute equality before the law—absolute civil equality for the freedman."[33] In speaking against Garrison's attempt to dissolve the society, Phillips argued, "Let us . . . stand claiming for the Negro justice not privileges; rights, not alms."[34] Frederick Douglass spoke in support of maintaining the organization, that it should not disband until "The black man of the South and the black man of the North shall have been admitted fully and completely into the body politic of America."[35] Again, Garrison, grand old man of the abolitionist movement, was defeated, 118 to 48. Phillips became the society's president. Garrison, Chapman, Quincy, and May resigned. Supporting Phillips were John Whittier, Parker Pillsbury, Richard Wright, Abby and Stephan Foster, Frederick Douglass, Charles Remond, and most of the other black members, as well as most of the feminist abolitionists.

The division was one of emphasis rather than principle. Certainly few would accuse Garrison of not being committed to racial equality. Elizabeth Buffum Chace remembered that "the long-tried abolitionists saw the necessity of all removal of race prejudice and the establishment of the principle of a common humanity."[36] How to achieve that equality was what divided these old friends.

Once slavery ended, the moral argument against slavery ended, but the larger claims that slavery was a form of oppression that denied basic human rights did not. Higginson reminded Massachusetts residents that the issue was "about life, liberty, and pursuit of happiness." Where blacks faced separate laws or separate conditions, those laws undermined the basic "principle of liberty and legal rights."[37]

Because governments were instituted to protect basic rights, including life, liberty, and the pursuit of happiness, abolitionists believed that the state needed to guarantee black equality. In practice this meant the right to property and the franchise. Julia Ward Howe stated to a black audience shortly after the civil war, "the issue is universal justice." Blacks needed to "stand fast in the liberty university," and people of "all color [had] to hold forth freedom."[38] Although Garrison, Maria Weston Chapman and her sisters, Quincy, and others saw the end of slavery as the end of the struggle, for the majority of AASS abolitionists the struggle was a struggle for human rights, and it would not be over until blacks had complete equality.[39]

Although Garrison was not opposed to black enfranchisement, he saw the path to equal rights as leading through education. He believed that without education white prejudices would be reinforced and blacks would be pushed down into another form of servitude. Education would put the freedman in a position of equality with whites.[40]

For Phillips, equality was a natural condition; what was needed was government action to guarantee that equality. The government needed first to pass legislation immediately giving blacks access to the vote so that they would not be forced down into subordination. He believed that the power of the state resting upon universal suffrage should enforce social justice and equality: "from the possession of political rights a man gets the means to clutch equal opportunities of education and a fair space to work."[41] But he believed that racial justice also depended upon the state guaranteeing equality.[42]

From the perspective of Massachusetts, the years immediately following the Civil War held great promise for significant social change. Abolitionists' conversation never drifted far from the question of the rights of the freedmen and how best to secure the truly egalitarian society promised by both the Declaration of Independence and thirty years of abolitionist struggle. Phillips felt "these are no times for ordinary politics; these are formative hours. We radicals have all the elements of national education in our hands."[43] For Garrison that meant working to educate the newly freed slaves. Hundreds of New England abolitionists went south to open schools and libraries, including Sarah Clarke, daughter of James Freeman Clarke and close friend of Julia Ward Howe and Thomas Wentworth Higginson.[44] For Phillips and the other radicals it meant more. When the renowned English reformer Samuel Augustus Barnett toured America in 1867, he was amazed and appalled at the deep-seated commitment to racial equality of New England abolitionists. Barnett felt they were "rather fanatical in . . . opinions. [Their] starting point being that every man has a right to vote."[45] Barnett called the abolitionists "Negro worshippers" because they wanted blacks to be elected to Congress.

The radical abolitionists had reason to believe that such an egalitarian world was within their reach. In Massachusetts the state house and governor's office had been in the hands of the radicals for several years. (John Andrew, governor in 1860–1866, had been a radical abolitionist and was a member of the Vigilance Committee.) The Bird Club, made up of radical, militant abolitionists, dominated the state Republican Party. Radical Republican egalitarian Charles Sumner represented Massachusetts in the Senate, while Benjamin Franklin Butler represented the state in the House, before becoming the state's Democratic governor. Massachusetts had outlawed most forms of discrimination. At the national level, abolitionist-minded politicians had turned back the southern attempt to come back into the union unreconstructed. The Thirteenth Amendment had been passed and ratified. The Fourteenth with its sweeping first section soon followed, and in 1869 Congress passed and sent to the states the Fifteenth Amendment prohibiting denial of the suffrage on the basis of race, color, or previous servitude. The impeachment of anti-Reconstruction president Andrew Johnson was being considered. If Johnson were removed from office, radical abolitionist Benjamin Franklin Wade would become president. With Wade waiting in the wings, it looked very much as if the South could be radically reconstructed as the egalitarian society the abolitionists first envisioned.

Johnson escaped by one vote the two-thirds vote necessary to remove him from office, but the abolitionists continued their campaign for racial equality. In 1870 Sumner introduced his Civil Rights Bill to give all persons equal rights in public places, including railroads, steamboats, hotels, restaurants, theaters, schools, incorporated churches, and cemetery associations. Violators would be tried in federal courts. Although Sumner failed to get his bill passed in 1870, he continued pushing until, on his deathbed on March 11, 1874, he said, "My bill, the civil-rights bill,—don't let it fail."[46] A weakened bill finally was signed into law one year later.

Although the English reformer Barnett saw New England abolitionists as fanatics, they were in fact not as clear about what the future should bring as the rhetoric of their more public figures suggested. The radicals argued for egalitarianism and rights-based state action, but Christian paternalism also vied for their allegiance. Henry Ingersoll Bowditch, who in the 1840s proclaimed so forthrightly the absolute equality of all men, was unsure how this equality might play out in the postwar South. He worried about the "propriety of letting all the ignorant blacks of the South have all the rights of citizens. Universal suffrage and the universal right to hold office by the uneducated as well as the educated seemed to me a delusion. [Yet it] has been given and been well received by the blacks. . . . At any rate four million of men most of them entirely ignorant have been raised in the twinkling of an eye so to speak from bondage to citizenship. This is the great fact of the hour. The noblest of historic events."[47]

In 1863 Samuel Gridley Howe was appointed by Secretary Stanton to the American Freedmen's Inquiry Commission, along with Robert Dale Owen and James McKaye, to look into what to do for the freed slaves. Howe consulted America's most renowned natural scientist, his friend Harvard professor Louis Agassiz. It was an unfortunate choice. Agassiz's reputation as a brilliant thinker awed Howe. Scientific racism, however, was becoming the rage among natural scientists in Europe and America. The vogue had infected Agassiz's thinking and he in turn tried to influence Howe, arguing that blacks were an inferior race and any political policy that ignored that fact was doomed to fail. Howe agreed that before any political principles should be settled, it was important to understand the physiological and ethnological issues at stake. But he held to the principle of "entire freedom, equal rights and privileges and open competition for social distinction."[48]

Parker Pillsbury, a militant defender of absolute black equality through the 1850s and war years, came by the end of the 1860s to argue that the condition of freed slaves proved the fallacy of black suffrage. Thomas Wentworth Higginson, whose own position on African Americans and equality was all over the map, attacked Pillsbury for trying to "prove [freedmen's] unworthiness of freedom."[49]

New England abolitionists defended black equality at home, but the issue before the nation was what to do for the millions of ex-slaves in the South. Phillips believed that land redistribution, universal suffrage (the first salvo being the push for black male suffrage), and open and free public institutions such as schools and libraries would expand social and economic equality. Along with many abolitionists, he assumed that once ex-slaves had gained the franchise and basic civil rights and established themselves economically, they and poor whites would come together into newly reformed state governments and carry out public policy for the good of all.[50] Under these conditions Phillips believed the South would be reconstructed in a more egalitarian form. This new society would destroy the power and privilege of the old planter class and open opportunities for both blacks and whites. He imagined that racial animosity and discrimination would eventually melt away.[51]

But Reconstruction in the South did not follow the script Phillips laid out. Southern opposition was more intransigent than abolitionists imagined, and the willingness of the North to follow through on promises, either overt or implied, proved weak. Johnson's impeachment failed to remove him from office. Republicans failed to pass land redistribution legislation. Even the limited land experiments in turning over confiscated land to ex-slaves were reversed. In several Southern states, most spectacularly in Louisiana, armed vigilantes intimidated black voters, attacked Republicans, killed dozens, and drove Reconstruction governments from office with violence. Except for abolitionists, northerners were reluctant to use federal troops to protect the Reconstruction governments. In 1873 the Supreme Court ruled in the *Slaughter-House* decision that the Fourteenth Amendment applied only to national citizenship rights and privileges, not to state or private actions.

Although most abolitionists held to their calls for absolute equality and suffrage for freedmen, how to respond to what was actually happening in the South was less clear. At times Higginson, a man of action and literature never constrained by consistency, demanded absolute social equality; at others he believed equality would only come slowly.[52] In 1878 he visited the South and, while still proclaiming his belief in racial equality, came away believing that black suffrage had been a failure and that once blacks achieved economic self-sufficiency and advancement they would slowly be integrated into southern society. In the meantime he supported Booker T. Washington and accepted the idea that southern whites would not take advantage of southern blacks if just left alone by northerners.[53]

Julia Ward Howe was less impressed with Washington's approach to race relations in the South. In a speech before a convention of African Americans, she attacked Washington's approach to race relations. She argued that blacks must demand equal education to protect their freedom, and that they must have not just basic education but education to the highest levels, producing "experts in the various professions. You need lawyers and ministers so that you may know your rights and be able to get representation." Unlike Washington, who ridiculed blacks who learned Latin and Greek, Howe urged her audience to excel in Latin and Greek. "Education is honor, get it and keep it."[54]

Higginson's early hope that blacks would eventually find equality in the South was not shared by many old abolitionists. Indeed, Higginson himself came to reject this early optimism. By the end of the century he realized that left to its own the South did not open up to a more equal society. He came to see that the "half-freedom as has been given him—a freedom tempered by chain-gangs, lynching, and the lash," was not producing true freedom and equality.[55] William Bowditch decried the setbacks on the road to equality: "As a rule the South gives little or nothing to the education of the Negroes. Peonage actually exists, and a vagrant Negro may even now be put on the auction block and sold to a master for a term of time."[56] His brother Henry denounced both Congress and others whose racist attitudes toward blacks undermined progress toward racial equality.[57]

In the messy racial politics in the second half of the nineteenth century these old abolitionists tried to hold to the principles that gave them their sense of who they were as people. Central to those principles were the ideas that blacks were "human with all of human's faults," and that as humans they had all the natural rights of humans including life, liberty, and pursuit of happiness.[58] Julia Ward Howe in an address to a predominately black audience reminded them of the importance of their struggle for all Americans: "Your deliverance was our deliverance." She also called attention to the ongoing nature of the struggle for equality: "be not entangled again to any bondage. Let us endeavor, all of us, of all color to hold forth freedom."[59]

The formal end of slavery did not led abolitionists to retire from active social involvement. Although some such as Edmund Quincy and Maria Weston Chapman dropped from active public life after the Civil War, and others such as Parker Pillsbury came to endorse a notion of black inferiority, most continued to fight for racial equality. Following the war Higginson moved to Newport, Rhode Island, and worked to end segregated schools in that state. For that activity he was dropped from the state School Committee.[60] Even into old age these veterans continued to hold to the principles of complete racial equality. Late in the century Henry Ingersoll Bowditch attended the Douglass Dinner, sponsored by the "Colored Young Men's" Wendell Phillips Club, to honor the old veterans of the struggle. Although impatient with the "old guard" going on and on about past accomplishments, Bowditch did find hope in the sight of "a hundred or more black men sitting at tables and waited upon by certainly white waiters. What changes in my day. . . . Thank God that I early became an abolitionist."[61]

Higginson's opposition to the "greed of monopolists" and "corporate wealth" and to imperialism led him into alliance with William Jennings Bryan and his campaign for a people's nation against the power of gold.[62] But Higginson split with Bryan over racial equality. In a series of correspondences over race, Bryan admitted that he did not believe in absolute equality between blacks and whites. As Elizabeth Buffum Chace warned, Bryan was afraid of intermarriage: "I do not see where the line can be drawn between social equality and intermarriage, and I am not in favor of intermarriage. . . . There is a line that can be drawn between equality of rights and social equality."[63] Higginson, anticipating W. E. B. Du Bois, responded to Bryan that, although monopoly and imperialism were important issues, racial equality, socially as well as civilly and politically, was the paramount issue before the nation.

As a founding member of the Rhode Island Woman's Club, Elizabeth Buffum Chace created a scandal when the Club refused admission to a black woman. Elizabeth and her daughter resigned.[64] In 1909, when William Bowditch died, the Colored Men's Republican League "acknowledge our regret that his death removed from our midst almost the last of that cycle of great men whose irrepressible devotion to the cause of liberty and whose firm adherence to the divine principle of justice and right imposed upon them a sacrifice which we as a race truly appreciate and for which the nation as the greater beneficiary will, we trust, some time fittingly recognize."[65]

For seekers after the challenge of the high goals of the Declaration of

Independence, the abolitionist vision of an egalitarian society encompassed more than just an end to racial discrimination. Embracing a natural rights argument, the radical abolitionists argued that the role of the state was to guarantee basic rights and freedoms, and they had an expansive vision of those rights and freedoms.[66] In the South they saw the possibility of new state governments, embracing both white and black citizens, enacting a broad program of land distribution, education, and social reform. The role of the federal government was to guarantee that all the South's citizens, black and white, rich and poor, had equal representation and voice in the new governments. To perform that protective function, federal troops and federal freedmen's activity were necessary. But beyond the tasks of Reconstruction, these abolitionists were not champions of a new activist government. The federal role, they believed, was to allow state governments to enact programs of social justice. In New England, where the state governments were at least in the early years after the war in the hands of the radicals, abolitionists saw the opportunity to have the state step forward to guarantee all its citizens the human rights implied by the Declaration of Independence.

But even as abolitionists wanted to move forward on their reform agenda, conflict emerged over the expansion of natural rights to women. In 1866 Wendell Phillips, a long-time supporter of women's rights, argued that women's right to vote should wait until black male suffrage had been achieved. "This hour belongs to the Negro," he proclaimed to the National Women's Rights Convention.[67] Not all agreed. Nor did the conflict end once black males did receive the vote.

Chapter 6

"Blessed Are They Who When Some Great Cause . . . Calls Them . . . Come"

In the process of overthrowing one great wrong, there is always laid bare some other wrong.

—*Elizabeth Buffum Chace*

So when the cause of slave-holding was overcome they became the leaders in the Woman suffrage cause, their children, as a rule following in their footsteps in the broader more world-wide reformation than was the conflict for the overthrow of slavery. For, although we have not the chain, the lash, the auction block, in their literal sense, to complain of, there is enough that is unjust and degrading in the condition of women to convince us that the work to which this generation of reformers is called is of far wider significance to the progress of all mankind than was the anti-slavery struggle.

—*Elizabeth Buffum Chace*

In 1868, when Julia Ward Howe came to the stage and sat down among those "champions, who had fought so long and so valiantly," she looked across the stage to where Lucy Stone sat next to her husband Henry Blackwell. Although they were to become fast friends, up to that point Julia had not been friendly to Lucy Stone. It must have pained Julia to see Stone sitting next to "the husband whose devotion so ably surrounded her life-work."[1] Julia struggled her whole married life against her husband in order that she be able to do her life-work, while Lucy Stone's marriage appeared to be a model of gender equality.[2] No wonder Julia admitted that Stone "had long been the object of one of my imaginary dislikes."

Lucy Stone did live an extraordinary life. When the dynamic Abigail Kelley spoke at Oberlin College in 1849, she inspired Stone to become an anti-slavery organizer for the Massachusetts Anti-Slavery Society. Stone's speaking was mesmerizing. Thomas Wentworth Higginson begged his mother to hear her, for "she is simply one of the noblest and gentlest persons I know with her homely face and her little bloomerfied-

Quakerism person and her voice—I think the very sweetest voice I ever heard in public speaking."[3] Lucy's support of bloomers—woman's dress reform—and opposition to corsets was offputting to traditionalists like Mary Higginson. But Mary was soon won over by Lucy's personality and argument.[4]

After lecturing on abolitionism for three years, Stone wrote to Samuel May that she would lecture on slavery for another week but "after that week I think I shall lecture on Women's Rights or at least see whether it can be done."[5] After a week of lecturing on women's rights Stone told May she would work on anti-slavery on weekends but the weekdays she "want to use for Women's rights and the two need not interfere that I see. I want to hold meetings on my own account . . . for my first series of Women's Rights."[6]

While testifying in 1853 before the Massachusetts State Constitutional Convention in favor of women's suffrage, she met Henry Blackwell, an abolitionist activist. Blackwell came from an activist family;[7] his sister Elizabeth broke new ground for women in the professions as one of the first female physicians in the country. Lucy's marriage to Blackwell was an event publicized around the country. She had not only established a reputation as an anti-slavery lecturer but by the mid-1850s had become a full-time lecturer on women's rights.

Lucy's decision to marry was not made lightly. She told Higginson on the eve of her marriage, "I felt that I never could be married for I had this public work to do and that seemed incompatible with a home," but she reflected, "I am sure now that I am doing right. But I feel so weak before the great responsibility I am undertaking; and then it is so wicked to oblige a woman to surrender her legal existence in order to become a wife."[8] Once she decided to marry, she put her property in the hands of a trustee, "so that my husband shall not control it. Think what a thing that is for a woman to have to do! But I am determined that it shall be held by a trained woman in some way, so my sister is a trustee. Harry says that I ought to be very thankful that a woman has this much freedom, but that is like telling a fugitive slave to be thankful there is a Canada when he knows he ought to be free without going there."[9]

Lucy also announced that her marriage would be totally egalitarian. The announcement vastly limited the number of ministers who would perform the ceremony, but Thomas Wentworth Higginson did so gladly. The "great occasion" at the Stone family farm began with Stone and Blackwell issuing a joint protest over the unequal and oppressive nature of traditional marriage obligations.

While we acknowledge our mutual affection by publicly assuming the sacred relationship of husband and wife yet in justice to ourselves and the great principle we deem it a duty to declare that this act on our part implies no sanction of nor promise of voluntary obedience to such of the present laws of marriage as refuse to recognize the wife as an independent rational being, while they confer upon the husband an injurious and unnatural superiority investing him with legal powers which no honorable man would exercise and which no man should possess. We protest especially against the laws which give to the husband 1 the custody of the wife's person, 2 the exclusive control and guardianship of their children, 3 the sole ownership of her personal and use of her real estate . . . 4 the absolute right to the product of her industry . . . finally against the whole system by which the legal existence of the wife is suspended during marriage. . . . We believe that personal independence and equal human rights can never be forfeited except for crime; that marriage should be an equal and permanent partnership and so recognized in law; that until it is so recognized married partners should protest against the radical injustice of the present laws by every means in their power.[10]

When Higginson came to the part of the ceremony where the wife pledged to honor and obey, Lucy pledged to "love and honor."

Knowledge of Lucy's unorthodox wedding spread throughout the region as Higginson published it as one of his stories to the *Atlantic Monthly*, noting especially that Lucy pledged to "love and honor" and not obey.[11] Lucy also did not assume her husband's name.[12] When James Buffum, who agreed to be trustee of Lucy's estate, mistakenly addressed a letter to her as Lucy Stone Blackwell, he received a quick and sharp reply. "When you write do not add Blackwell to my name! I do not take it at all! A wife should no more take her husband's name than he should hers."[13] As her trustee, Buffum was also on the receiving end of many a tirade against the injustice of having to have a trustee at all. "It is a shame that a married woman can't hold her property anywhere without any trustee."[14]

When in 1851 Stone announced she would work at both anti-slavery and women's rights, she noted, "you know that all reforms are fractions of a unit, and what helps one aids all."[15] Her movement from abolitionism to woman's rights seemed a natural progression for many of those involved in the struggle. As Elizabeth Buffum Chace reminded readers in 1891, women's inequality

requires for its removal, the same self-sacrificing spirit, the same consecration to duty as accomplished the preceding reform. So it has ever been. In the progress of the anti-slavery movement, experience revealed the great injustice, the detriment to human welfare of the subordinated, disfranchised, condition of women. Every step in that great reform was impeded by the inequality that depressed and degraded her. And these experiences were to the abolitionists in this as in other directions a liberal education.[16]

Stone remembered the importance of all the friends involved in abolitionism and their continued struggle for social justice.

The noble men and women [who] met in the anti-slavery office . . . seeing the object of their many years of labor accomplished, . . . kept on with their hearts open and hands ready to labor in behalf of equal rights of woman; and those familiar faces, so genial and cordial we always saw in the anti-slavery meetings and *Liberator* office and we now greet with renewed affection in the office of the *Woman's Journal*. . . . Surely the mantle of the antislavery office has fallen upon the *Woman's Journal* office, a blessing indeed.[17]

Thomas Wentworth Higginson remembered that "most of the early advocates of the woman suffrage reform had served previously as abolitionists for they had been thereby trained in courage and self-sacrifice."[18] That training began at the very formation of the American Anti-Slavery Society. Meeting in Philadelphia in 1833, the delegates discussed Garrison's draft of the organization's pledge. Lucretia Mott rose and suggested that the pledge would be stronger if it were based first on the principles of the Declaration of Independence and then upon Divine Revelation.[19] Many in the crowd were surprised that Mott, a woman, had spoken and that Beriah Green, the chair, had recognized her.[20] It was just the beginning of women's involvement in the organization. Lydia Maria Child left Boston for New York to take over the *National Anti-Slavery Standard*, dragging along her rather useless husband.[21] The fiery Abby Kelley began speaking out against slavery in Lynn, Massachusetts, and soon attracted enough attention that the Massachusetts Anti-Slavery Society hired her as a speaker along with the dynamic Grimke sisters. Boston female abolitionists organized a petition drive in 1839 to reform Massachusetts laws on marriage and divorce that were unfair to women and "repugnant to rights and freedom." They got the endorsement of the Massachusetts Anti-Slavery Society. When the women went before the state legislature with their petition, the legislature "found the Abolitionists made common cause" with the women.[22] This support was both ideological and social. Anne Weston rewarded the male abolitionists who came and testified with the woman by having "a hang out," social event.

The 1840 attempt to keep Abby Kelley off the executive board inflamed female abolitionists.[23] Maria Weston Chapman wrote that to deny "women's rights, they trample on human rights."[24] Although women may have been, as Chapman noted, "accustomed to suffering under the many indignities which men unconsciously inflict," these abolitionists began to fight those indignities.[25] When the traditionalists resigned from the American Anti-Slavery Society, women's rights supporters replaced them with Chapman, Lucretia Mott, and Lydia Maria Child.[26] When American abolitionists attended the World Anti-Slavery Convention in 1840, several delegates were women. When the international body refused to recognize the American female delegates, the American male delegates fought for equal recognition. Ann Phillips told her husband Wendell, "don't shilly-shally Wendell" but to demand women's equal rights. Phillips unsuccessfully proposed the motion for women's equal participation.[27]

Abby Kelley continued her speaking and agitating. In 1846 she married radical abolitionist Stephan Foster, whom she met while both were AASS organizers in Ohio. After the birth of her first child she turned the baby over to Stephan, who had returned to a farm in Worcester, Massachusetts, and went back out on the lecture tour.[28]

When the World Temperance Convention was held in 1853, Lucy Stone, Abby Kelley Foster, and Susan B. Anthony came in bloomers and demanded to be treated with equality. Traditionalists hooted down the women and their male supporters, Higginson, Garrison, and Phillips. Higginson proposed Anthony to membership on one of the executive committees. When women attempted to speak for the motion, the chair ruled against those supporting women's rights. Stone, Foster, Anthony, Garrison, Phillips, and Higginson, along with Lucretia Mott, and Elizabeth Cady Stanton, walked out of the meeting and withdrew their membership from the organization.[29]

Just two years after the famous Seneca Falls Gathering of 1848 that rewrote the Declaration of Independence as a document for women, a call went out for a national women's rights convention in Worcester, Massachusetts. The eighty-nine signatories for the call included most of New England's leading abolitionists, and the convention resolved not to forget "the trampled womanhood of the plantation, and omit no effort to raise it to a share in the rights we claim ourselves."[30] The Worcester meeting was followed up by meetings throughout New England with leading abolitionists behind them all.[31]

Lucy Stone's commitment to abolition was absolute, but so was her commitment to women's rights. When Garrison asked her to go to Cincinnati to talk on anti-slavery, she complained to her friend Samuel May that she was overworked. "I wish there were more agents at such a time more are needed. Where are they?"[32] She was afraid that if she took on the Cincinnati assignment it would detract from her women's rights work. "I must have a large part of my time for Women's Rights."[33]

These activists grounded their demand for women's rights on the assumption that women should have equal opportunity in all areas of society, not just the "woman's sphere" where they "attended their own special duties." The Cleveland Woman's Rights Convention, dominated by New England abolitionists, created a committee on women's opportunity in society and sent out a call for information about the possibilities and limitations on women. The call "to friends of the cause of woman" was signed by Wendell Phillips, Lucy Stone, Lucretia Mott, Thomas Wentworth Higginson, and Ernestine Rose.[34]

Lucy Stone's claim "that all reforms are fractions of a unit" made sense to these abolitionists because they based their opposition to slavery not only on moral grounds but also on the principle of natural rights.[35] And natural rights encompassed not just males but all the human race. Wendell Phillips noted, women's rights "involved the freedom of one half the human race."[36] Thomas Wentworth Higginson wrote in *Common Sense About Women* that it "was impossible to deny the natural right of women . . . except on grounds which exclude all natural right."[37] Lucretia Mott reminded the delegates at the first meeting of the American Anti-Slavery Society that the Declaration of Independence established the principle of natural rights, and anti-slavery needed to rest first upon that principle. Higginson argued that the Declaration of Independence established not just the principle of natural rights but the concept that governments exist to protect those rights and must rest on the consent of the governed. Since women were governed, they deserved the vote as a natural right.

For these abolitionists the argument against slavery and the argument for women's rights rested on the same foundation. Action for one led easily to action for the other. In the midst of the crisis over the Anthony Burns rendition, when Boston was in an uproar and several of its leading abolitionists were under threat of jail, Theodore Parker, one of those threatened with prison, spoke out against the "new assault upon freedom." To explain the crisis he called up the basic principles of New England: opposition to tyranny and slavery,

to affirm as a principle and establish as a measure the natural equality of men and women in all that pertained to human rights. It is only to affirm that woman is human and has the same quality of human substance with man. If difference in condition, as rich and poor, or as ability as strong or weak, does not affect the substance of manhood and the rights thence accruing, no more does difference of sex, masculine or feminine make one master and the other slave. Not only the proletary, the servant, the slave, but exploited woman also must rise as despotocracy goes down.[38]

Parker's sermons on women's rights and Elizabeth Cady Stanton's writings were considered at the time the most powerful arguments in behalf of women.[39] Higginson pushed to have them published around the world. Parker disputed the idea of a separate sphere for woman, although he did accept gendered divisions of labor. "The domestic function of woman as a housekeeper, wife, mother does not exhaust her powers. . . . To make one half of the human race consume all their energies in the functions of housekeeper, wife and mother, is a monstrous waste of the most precious material that God ever made."[40]

Parker argued that women had different personalities just as men did. For some women, "domestic function is little or is nothing. . . . Womankind is advancing from that period when every woman was a slave . . . I say woman is advancing . . . to a state of independence, where woman shall not be subordinated to man, but the two coordinated together."[41] The role of housekeeper in Parker's world is not enough for the woman as "human-being, more than it would be function enough . . . for the man."

In a truly just world Parker believed some women would be mothers and do domestic work and other things in the world, some women would be mothers but not do domestic work, some woman would not do either but would pursue science and the arts and link up with men who appreciated learned and accomplished woman, or stay single. But whatever women chose to do, "those who believe in justice and natural rights would support them and demand they be paid equal to a man doing the same activity."

The justice of this position, Parker claimed, was based upon the principle that a woman has "the same natural human rights . . . to life, liberty and pursuit of happiness—the same human duties; and they are as unalienable in a woman as in a man."[42] But Parker also understood that declaring these as rights was not enough. "For these rights to be meaningful they must be exercised in a larger community and through social institutions." This of course was the challenge that faced the community of reformers. In nineteenth-century common practice an oceanic distance separated Parker's goals for the future from everyday behavior.

It was a separation Julia Ward Howe understood. Both she and her husband were close friends with the Parkers. In many ways Julia exemplified Parker's woman who "had no taste and no talent for the domestic function," one who kept house but put her energy and intelligence to other functions.

Julia's reputation as an essayist, poet, and finally author of the "Battle Hymn of the Republic" grew throughout the late 1850s and early 1860s. In 1863 she announced to her husband her plans to give a series of public lectures on ethical subjects. She had been studying Kant, Hegel, and Fichte in their original German, and she read Comte and Rousseau in French. She wanted to work up a series of lectures criticizing their thought and developing her own. She hoped to charge for these lectures.

Samuel Gridley Howe's opposition to her assuming such a public role did not stop her.[43] That year she accepted an offer to speak, along with Emerson, at the Emancipation Day Celebration before a huge mixed audience in Boston. James Freeman Clarke asked her to deliver a lecture before a group gathered to discuss ethics, theology, and philosophy.

Her husband refused to attend.[44] Conflict over her public lectures continued through the 1860s. Whenever she asked for his approval to give a public lecture, he refused and she had to lecture in the face of his opposition. When she gave a successful series of lectures on philosophy and ethics in Washington, D.C., her long-time friend Charles Sumner refused to come and pronounced that she was incompetent to lecture on the topic, because Samuel Gridley Howe had asked him to oppose her lectures. Her husband enlisted the children on his behalf, claiming that her public lectures and published work were humiliating him, making him sick, and leading her to neglect the family. Julia would not give in to this family opposition.[45] Using the examples of the Quakers, Julia argued that "natural logic . . . allows women to speak. . . . I feel that a woman's whole moral responsibility is lowered by the fact that she must never obey a transcendent command of conscience. Man can give her nothing to take the place of this. It is the divine right of the human soul."[46]

Her fight with her family for the right to speak publicly, her commitment to equal rights for blacks, her opposition to slavery, and her reading of Kant moved Julia more and more to the position of equal rights for women. She found Kant's emphasis on freedom exciting. Her own intense religious beliefs rested on the principle of a common morality. Although she had not yet embraced suffrage for women, by 1866 she was comparing the oppression of slaves with that of women, saying "our slaves had no rights. Women have few."[47]

At the turn of the new year 1868, Julia, amid the conflict with her family over her public lectures, was asked by some old abolitionist friends to come to a meeting to discuss forming a club where women could come together away from men to share ideas and talk about serious issues concerning women and the nation. This was a novel idea for Julia, whose intellectual world had been mostly made up of men— Parker, Higginson, Clarke, Emerson, Field, and others. She remembered that until then she had tended to measure herself against men. She had assumed that her intellectual interests were the interests of men and that she would have to push herself into that masculine world.[48] And indeed, with the exception of her husband and some of his close friends, many of the men she associated with accepted her as an equal. At the same time her involvement with women abolitionists like Maria Weston Chapman led her to respect the capacities of women as thinkers and organizers. Her activities in the war effort threw her into fellowship with dozens of ordinary women who had energy, interest, and active minds that longed for some intellectual and social outlet.

Julia went with "languid assent" to the organizing meeting of the New

England Women's Club. What she found at that meeting were that "women no longer [wanted] an ancillary relation . . . to man" but wanted to be "as a free agent, fully sharing with man every human right and every human responsibility."[49] Julia realized that the Women's Club could become a forum for women to come together and discuss their ideas and to talk about philosophy, public affairs, and the interests of women. It would be a serious center for advancing women intellectually. Originally she thought that the club could be a place to find company for her studies, but it soon did much more. It "taught me much more about my own sex than I had ever known."[50] The organizing meeting decided to hold the first formal meeting of the New England Woman's Club the following May. At that meeting Julia presided and gave a short speech arguing that women's organizations have been ridiculed, but "half the horizon of the world, social, moral, and political," belonged to women, "by simple human right."[51] In 1870 Julia was elected president, a position she held for the rest of her life.

The Women's Club idea quickly caught on, and soon clubs spread up across the country. Shortly after Julia helped organize the New England Women's Club, Thomas Wentworth Higginson asked her to lend her name to the call for a Women's Rights Convention at Boston's Horticultural Hall. The call also included Higginson, Bronson Alcott, Samuel May, Francis Bird, Samuel Sewall, Stephan Foster, Lilian Emerson, Angelina Grimke Weld, Caroline Severance, Elizabeth Peabody, Mary Mann, Louisa May Alcott, and Lydia Maria Child.

Although what Julia saw as she approached the platform in Horticultural Hall was unity and community, the movement for women's rights was splitting apart. The motivation behind the meeting itself was linked to the growing conflict within the movement.[52] Women were divided in 1868 over the question of suffrage for blacks and the inclusion of the word "male" in the Fourteenth Amendment. The American Equal Rights Association, created in 1866, hoped to harness the reform energy Wendell Phillips claimed was on the ascendance to secure the franchise for both women and blacks. As the vote for black male suffrage approached, women split over whether to insist on male and female suffrage together or accept the idea of the "negro hour," as Phillips called it, and push for female suffrage afterward.[53] At the May meeting of the New England Anti-Slavery Society, Stephan Foster and Parker Pillsbury argued that the organization should endorse a resolution recognizing equal natural rights of women and blacks and demand a franchise bill guaranteeing the vote to women as well as black males. Phillips, a long-time advocate of women's rights and franchise, argued that now was not the time to commit an anti-slavery organization to women's franchise if it in any way threatened winning the franchise for black males.[54] Phillips won the argument, but many female abolitionists felt betrayed.[55] After Congress ratified the Fifteenth Amendment, which talked about the "right to vote" of "any male inhabitant," Susan B. Anthony and Elizabeth Cady Stanton argued that women should not support the Amendment or any others that did not guarantee women's suffrage.

This conflict played itself out over the next year in Kansas, confirming the worst sentiments and fears of both groups. In 1868 the voters of Kansas had the opportunity to vote on both black male and female franchise. The American Equal Rights Association and the New England Anti-Slavery Society sent organizers to Kansas. Lucy Stone and Henry Blackwell and Susan B. Anthony and Elizabeth Cady Stanton went west to organize for the expanded franchise. In Kansas they found a Republican Party willing to work for the black male franchise but uninterested in women's right to vote. Worse yet, some Kansas state Republicans openly attacked women's franchise. Stone and Blackwell tried to dissuade Republicans from attacking women's rights while at the same time they worked to get the black male franchise bill passed. Anthony and Stanton were furious at the betrayal of women's rights by the Republicans. In angry response, they allied with Democrats opposed to the black franchise, in hopes of winning Democratic support and votes for the women's franchise bill. Desperate for support, Anthony and Stanton turned to George Francis Train, a wealthy openly racist Democrat who supported white women's rights. Anthony and Stanton not only accepted Train in his praise of white woman and his tirades against blacks as inferior, ignorant rapists who if given the vote and equal rights would endanger white womanhood, but organized a lecture tour of Kansas with him.[56]

The Train episode doomed the American Equal Rights Association. Abolitionists accused Stanton and Anthony of selling out to the racists.[57] Samuel May proclaimed, "I should rejoice to be in a society today with such as Lucy Stone, for the securing of women's every rights, civil and political, and social; but I must take the very best care not to be identified with Mrs. Stanton or G. F. Train or their like." Stone claimed that Train's association with women's suffrage drove supporters away and doomed it. Anthony and Stanton accused the abolitionists of abandoning women for black males and dooming both by failing to push both equally. More accusations flew when Anthony and Stanton accepted Train's money to fund their suffrage newspaper, *Revolution*, with Parker Pillsbury as one of the editors.[58]

The conflict between Anthony and Stone soon became personal and enmeshed in a dispute over money. As discussed earlier, Francis Jackson's will stipulated that money should be set aside for anti-slavery work and work for women's rights. The heirs contested the will, and the courts ruled that the Jackson fund could not be used for women's rights. One of the heirs, Eliza Eddy, upset that the money would not go to women's rights, created a new fund with Phillips, Susan B. Anthony, and Lucy Stone as trustees. Later Phillips left, and William Bowditch was added in his place.[59] Another heir, James Jackson, left a third of his estate, with Bowditch as trustee, to help with a women's journal.

Anthony asked for money from the Eddy fund for her work in Kansas, and initially both Phillips and Stone seemed in support. But by 1868 the conflict between Stone and Anthony over Anthony's increasing hostility to black male suffrage and strident attacks on Radical Republicans and blacks flowed back to the management of the Eddy funds.[60] In 1869, to keep the money out of Anthony's hands, Stone argued that Jackson would have wanted the money to be used in New England, not Kansas. Anthony argued that, since the trustees could not agree on how the money should be spent, it should be divided, with each trustee deciding how to use a third. She claimed she worked hard in Kansas lecturing and putting out tracts and should be paid for that work from the Eddy fund, and accused Stone and Phillips of "injustice . . . if [they] persist in not giving to me at least one third of what remains."[61] Stone and Phillips voted to keep the money in New England; Stone proposed using some to fund lectures by Mrs. Campbell and Mrs. Churchill in New England. Anthony, no longer on speaking terms with either, withdrew an invitation to Phillips to talk to the American Equal Rights Association.[62] Stanton attempted to mediate by asking Stone "to lay aside [her] personal feud with Susan." Stone was not receptive to the offer, especially given that Stanton called Stone's position "petty." The conflict festered for the rest of their lives.[63]

The conflict between Anthony and Stone and Phillips became personal, but the issues were political and tactical. Anthony, Stanton, and Pillsbury led the campaign in the Equal Rights Association in opposing the Fifteenth Amendment because it did not endorse suffrage for women. They accused abolitionist supporters of the Amendment of willingness to sell out women to curry favor with Radical Republicans for the advancement of black males.[64] They were particularly furious with Phillips, who argued that white women were able to exercise influence in society, so their need for the political protection of the ballot was not as acute as that of freed slaves. Phillips, Stone, Blackwell, Bowditch, and Julia Ward Howe supported the amendment, believing it was vital to protect ex-slaves and would at a later date open the door for women's suffrage.

Concerned that women's suffrage not be lost in the larger battle for rights, while at the same time not wanting to sacrifice black rights, New

England abolitionists issued the call for the 1868 Horticultural Hall Convention. Out of that convention came the New England Woman Suffrage Association with Julia Ward Howe as president. Julia had made it clear she supported woman suffrage, but only with the securing of black suffrage. She also believed they could move forward together: "Let us endeavor, all of us, of all colors to hold forth freedom," she noted in an address to African Americans. "Any class that wishes to be free must endeavor to free others as well as itself. Men can not be free while women are enslaved."[65] By working at the state level for woman suffrage, the Association would not conflict with the struggle for the Fifteenth Amendment.[66]

Differences among suffrage supporters broke out at the 1869 Equal Rights Association Convention, which not only failed to heal the conflict but furthered it. At the convention Stephan Foster, Abby's husband, with Frederick Douglass accused Stanton and Anthony of racism. Lucy Stone attempted to chart a course for women's rights and black equality on equal footings while also asking for support of the Fifteenth Amendment. In the end the Association collapsed in discord. In its wake Anthony and Stanton organized the National Woman Suffrage Association, for women only.[67]

As the arguments heated up, both camps claimed that issues of principle were involved. Pillsbury, Stanton, and Anthony began to argue that newly freed slaves were not ready for the franchise. Pillsbury claimed that "blacks [were] more irresponsible than women," and should face "educational tests" before being allowed to vote.[68] For Phillips, Stone, Higginson, Howe, and Bowditch, even with their misgivings about the appropriateness of uneducated ex-slaves voting, the right to the franchise was bundled with natural rights, not a matter of privilege that one had to prove by responsible behavior or educational attainment. The vote was a basic human right that would allow citizens to participate in the process of giving consent to the government and provide a means of protection from denial of those natural rights. Their position on women's suffrage rested on the same foundation. When Phillips argued for female suffrage before the Massachusetts State Legislature in 1869, he stressed that "the power of the state backed by universal suffrage would end discrimination and abuse of power."[69] When detractors claimed that women would lose respect if they mixed in the messy world of politics, Julia Ward Howe countered with a vision of the vote as an instrument of authority that should be granted to all. "Blackmen and Irishmen," she noted, "use the franchise to gain power that commands respect. Women likewise will be respected for themselves in an egalitarian world where they have the power of the vote and not treated as an undifferentiated group."[70]

Julia continued her leadership in the women's suffrage movement despite her husband's increasingly shrill complaints (ironically, he supported women's suffrage).[71] By the end of 1868 Stone, Howe, Higginson, and other New England abolitionists became convinced that Anthony, Stanton, Pillsbury, and Train were driving old abolitionist friends from women's suffrage and that there needed to be another women's suffrage organization that championed women's rights on a natural rights basis that embraced black as well as women's franchise.[72] To that end Howe, Stone, Higginson, and Mary Livermore sent out a call for a convention in Cleveland to form a new organization, the American Woman Suffrage Association. Anthony, Stanton, and Pillsbury countered by reorganizing their earlier association into the National Woman Suffrage Association.[73] In a letter to Garrison, Stone justified the need for a new organization, separate from the Anthony-Stanton one.

If in the heat of the anti-slavery battle there had been only such a national association and again as the woman's cause now have, would you not have felt that in justice to the Negro no matter what difficulties were in the way he was entitled to be the benefit of a national association that would end slavery. . . . Woman needs the united help of all those who sympathize with her cause—who can have faith in each other and who know that no influence is so great as that which comes from the simple honest straight forward advocacy of principle as its own merits. . . . We shall not quarrel with the other organization. I wish we could work with them. I should rejoice more than any man can do if we had the basis of cooperation, but it does not exist.[74]

Julia Ward Howe's speech before the 1869 Cleveland Convention captured the delegates' feelings that cooperation with the National Woman Suffrage Association was impossible. She began on grounds that few women's rights advocates would not support. The issues before the nation, she argued, were "the partial laws, the unequal judgments, the inferiority of education, and the greater inequality of the distribution of wages. Half the human race has hitherto been negated by the other half." But she also warned that there would be no progress for women at the expense of others. "Treason to humanity can not be fidelity to woman. We can not put back the age to put forward our measure. . . . Let not over our haste go around those who go in with or before us."[75]

In lectures and letters, Julia pushed hard for the vision of an egalitarian society where all members would move forward. In a talk at Concord in 1870, she noted that within the space of a year women's rights "have brought to all the vexations of society an unexpected question," the failure to grant women their rights. "The more thoughtful men now found that women were a good plan, and more would be the better, the more they were allowed to be women, and not simply no man. . . . Justice to ourselves is no longer injustice to others."[76] In another speech Julia pointed out that women were perceived to be the property of men to pick and choose from and then afterward to be for women. She attacked the system by which men assumed control over "the sexual aspect of women. . . . Men ask that women shall intoxicate him, that the physical attraction of her beauty shall be heightened by dress." Women were to submit totally to "blind confidence in the man—acquiesce in his judgments." Julia argued that this was a form of idolatry and that the false idol, man, would fail her.

Despite the reality of her own marriage, Julia called for equality in marriage, where there would be "the joys of sympathy or mutual help, steadfast goods of love. . . . This will give us the equal marriage, the egalitarian train." She refuted the argument that independent women were "unwomanly women." "Are the women who are moved by men like puppets with a string womanly? No, they do what men have them do. They can not dare not act about the womanly inspirations of their heart." To women who submit to men, she warned, "you know not our own business. Men cannot track it to you because they do not know it. And you will follow their foreign suggestions instead of driving to the heart of the nature which it so much imparts to you to understand and what you alone can understand."[77]

Unlike the NWSA, which excluded males from any leadership position (though Pillsbury did edit the *Revolution*), Julia Ward Howe and the AWSA supported male involvement. Yet they also understood that women had to speak for themselves. The idea that men could speak for women had been the logic behind the denial of female suffrage, and it was something Julia absolutely rejected. Progressive men may ask women how to undo "injustice which the common law perpetuates against women," but men cannot "tell us how we feel. We know it better than they do. So why are we to persuade men to make laws for us when we are able to make them ourselves."[78] Women, Julia reminded a Concord audience in 1870, wanted simply "justice."[79]

The AWSA and its New England affiliate swept old abolitionists into the cause. Garrison and Phillips had not been speaking to each other since the conflict over the Jackson Trust, nor had Garrison been talking to Abby Kelley Foster. Garrison and Douglass had been at odds since the publication of the *North Star*. But when Howe, Stone, and Foster organized an AWSA protest rally at Faneuil Hall on December 20, 1873, under the banner "Taxation Without Representation Is Tyranny," Garrison gladly shared the stage with Douglass, Phillips, Stone, Howe, and Foster. Reunited with Phillips, Douglass, and Foster, Garrison attended an emotionally laden AWSA Fourth of July picnic in

Framingham as he formerly used to attend the MASS Framingham picnics.

The 1873 rally at Fanueil Hall grew out of the work of William Bowditch. Bowditch, who traded the presidency of the New England Woman Suffrage Association with Julia Ward Howe, had the year before (1872) published what became one of the most important women's rights tracts of the nineteenth century, *Woman Suffrage: A Right Not a Privilege*. He argued that "women without the right to vote can't give consent to govern." Bowditch claimed that the right of suffrage existed prior to legislative enactment, that such enactments only codified a pre-existing right. "Suffrage is neither a manly act nor yet a womanly act, but the act of a human being who as part of the people has an inherent right to express or refuse consent to the form of government under which he or she lives, because it is and ever must continue to be a self-evident truth, that Government derives its just power from the consent of the governed, men and woman and from no other source under heaven." Men had the right of franchise, Bowditch claimed, because they are men; it is not a privilege bestowed on them by government since the government is the agent of the people. "Since the right in-heres for men simply and solely because they are part of the people, the same rights also inhere in women simply and solely because they are part of the people."[80]

Furthermore, Bowditch argued, women paid taxes but as taxpayers were unable to vote on the use of the money raised. They were denied a fundamental liberty that lay at the heart of the American Revolution. In a 71-page pamphlet, *Taxation of Women in Massachusetts*, which like *Suffrage: A Right Not a Privilege* became a widely circulated propaganda piece for the movement, Bowditch presented massive statistical evidence concerning women's tax contribution and the significance of their lack of the right to vote.[81] After he read the piece, Garrison, who also had not been on speaking terms with Bowditch since the Jackson Trust conflict, wrote to Bowditch in the old language of natural rights and equality that the pamphlet made a powerful argument for women's suffrage:

The injustice is glaring and monstrous. It is a cruel blow at womanhood, crush-ing it into absolute subjection to the will of man and treating it as unworthy to stand upon the plain of human equality. It is the old proscription of the Negro on the alleged ground of his complexion and natural inferiority, but applied not to a particular race but to one half of mankind. Surely a proscription so senseless and a usurpation of power so indefensible must ere long give way by the dissemination of light and truth, and then, for the first time, shall the world behold the advent of a people's government, wherein all shall be put in posses-sion of equal rights and immunities.[82]

The campaign for women's rights worked at the local, state, and national level. William Bowditch and his wife Sarah Higginson Bowditch organized petition drives in Brookline to give women the vote in local elections as well as sponsoring petitions for universal suffrage.[83] Abby May, Samuel May's sister, who had joined Julia in the New England Woman's Club, worked for suffrage and ran and was elected to the Boston School Committee in 1873. In 1879 she was appointed to the State Board of Education, where she championed the rights of female teachers and education for girls.[84] At the state level Henry Ingersoll Bowditch, Julia Ward Howe, Lucy Stone and her husband Henry Blackwell, William Bowditch, Thomas Wentworth Higginson, Abby Foster and her husband Stephan, and dozens of other old abolitionists pushed the legislature year after year to consider suffrage for women and came before them to argue the point.

Julia Ward Howe reminded legislators of the constancy of suffrage supporters during the 1880s when she began her testimony: "We who belong to Massachusetts have every year to come to the state house in Boston to make our request for suffrage." She noted that the legislature had plenty of time to hear from the railroad interests and the manufacturers, but little time to hear the pleading from the women of Massachusetts.[85] At one point when opponents to suffrage argued that women were physiologically unfit to vote, Henry Ingersoll Bowditch, an octogenarian and deathly ill, roused himself once again to go before the state legislature and refute the idea as utter nonsense and bad science.[86] The New England Woman's Suffrage Association also organized a women's nonpayment of taxes campaign until they received the vote.[87]

The women's movement involved more than just suffrage, although most activists saw it as the key to addressing many other issues. William Bowditch also attacked the wage disparity between male and female workers. Noting that women "almost never receive the same wages" as men for the same or equivalent work, Bowditch argued that this disparity only proved that men were incapable of exercising power over women fairly, and how urgently women needed the power of the vote to protect themselves against the arbitrary power of males.[88]

As in the days of the anti-slavery campaigns, women's suffrage campaigners held political leaders to a standard of justice above the norm of contemporary party politics. In 1871 Higginson went to Washington to demand of Representative George Hoar, the old abolitionist, that he support women's rights. Hoar agreed and claimed that he would support legislation requiring half the juries as well as half the judges be women. Needless to say, the legislation never came forward.[89] But these old campaigners did not accept rhetoric as a substitution for action.

They met regularly to decide which candidates to support and oppose. Suffrage supporters sent representatives to party conventions and demanded women's issues be addressed.[90]

Despite their efforts they more often than not found the candidates and parties wanting. William Bowditch noted in 1885, "When the great parties in their platforms talk about a free ballot and that all citizens shall have an equal voice and all such like twaddle, they both forget the women, and are united in treating half the people of the country as if they were neither citizens nor persons."[91] A year later Bowditch told Lucy Stone that the movement should support neither the Democratic nor the Republican candidates, given their position on women's rights. Even old friends like George Hoar were not let off the hook. In a series of exchanges with Hoar, now senator, Bowditch wrote that he agreed with Higginson that not only had the Republican Party "failed the Negro in the South, [it had] done nothing to secure the vote for women." Hoar claimed the party was doing everything it could to secure the vote for women. Bowditch responded that he voted for neither Cleveland, because of his party's duplicity in the oppression of blacks in the South, nor Harrison, who showed no commitment to women's suffrage.[92]

But these reformers looked beyond suffrage. Suffrage was for them part of the larger campaign for human rights and equal rights for women. Julia Ward Howe organized industrial circles in each state and a Woman's Industrial Convention to encourage and provide support for women in industrial occupations.[93] Howe also supported dress reform and more equitable marriage and divorce laws. She considered that traditional women's dress "undermined the strength of our young women and are the invention of men." Rather than look to males, women should avail themselves of the inventions and fashions of "women who understand the regulation of their own sex."[94] "The inequality of the marital yoke," Julia believed, "made it unjust, uneven, and difficult to bear. The marriage condition involves so many essentials of slavery that a woman . . . can not . . . accept it as just."[95] Despite her vigorous language, Julia's vision of equality was not consistent. At times she argued strongly that women deserved the franchise because of their essential equality with men. Yet she also played the difference card, claiming that women's heightened morality and experience of motherhood gave them a unique perspective and claim upon civil and political society.[96] For these women the call to struggle "till every yoke is broken" included the yoke of sexual inequality.

Despite the strong support of the AWSA in New England, especially among old abolitionists and their children, by the late 1880s it was losing its national reach while the NWSA retained a national membership.[97]

Many of the old AWSA members were dead, Abby Foster in 1887, for example, and others were infirm. Lucy Stone was in her seventies and not in good health. In 1887 Alice Stone Blackwell, Lucy's daughter, decided that it was time to merge the two organizations. Negotiations for merger required more than three years. Skepticism was high on both sides. Julia Ward Howe was concerned that the Stanton- Anthony wing of the NWSA would dominate and that the new organization would abandon black rights.[98]

She had reason. Elizabeth Cady Stanton, first president of the newly merged organization, did not support universal franchise, only educated franchise, and increasingly focused on difference, not equality.[99] In a letter to William Lloyd Garrison II, she defended the war in the Philippines, arguing that the people of the Philippines were better off under American domination. "What would this continent have been if left to the Indians?" she asked rhetorically. Although she supported the war, Stanton did allow that there were other issues of importance besides uplifting the people of other isles, such as "the repression of the feminine element."[100] Julia fought vigorously, although unsuccessfully, to keep equal rights for all as part of the new organization. In 1890, the year of the merger, Julia told an audience in Toronto that it was vital that women put their rights within the framework of the wider struggle for rights, or else women's rights would be a "dead weight on the victorious march." Women, she argued, had to "move forward without prejudice"; otherwise they would abandon principle. "The way of humanity is onward, women must maintain a commitment to larger justice."[101]

To placate the concerns of the activists from the AWSA, Julia Ward Howe was made vice president of the new organization. But despite her insistence on the importance of universal justice, she was constrained in her ability to affect the direction of the merged organization.

Julia was seventy-one years old, and her attentions were divided. She was in a battle to keep the New England Women's Club, of which she was still a leader, from joining the federation movement of women's clubs. In 1890 Julia argued that general federation of clubs would encourage them to become increasingly conservative. She noted that by 1880 many if not a majority of the clubs opposed suffrage. Julia successfully argued that the New England Woman's Club should not send delegates to the first General Federation of Women's Clubs, although the following year the club outvoted her and sent delegates.[102] She helped organize the Association for the Advancement of Woman in 1874 and was its president for most of its twenty-five years.[103] She continued her lectures on ethics and philosophy and was the force behind the intellectual Town and Country Club and the Radical Club.[104] She was involved in prison reform with William Bowditch, and human rights for Cretans and Russians as well as rights of immigrants in America. Julia's ability to influence the direction of the National American Women's Suffrage Association was limited, however. In 1893 the movement split again, with Sarah Pugh, Carrie Burnham, and Ellen Davis bolting because they felt the NAWSA was too "exclusive and so terrible afraid of its reputation."[105]

Chapter 7

Bringing Together the Professional and the Political

A Life Long Earnest Worker in Every Good Cause.
—*Henry Ingersoll Bowditch*

I prefer to be remembered only as a woman who was willing to work for the elevation of women.
—*Marie Elizabeth Zakrzewska*

The Right to Clean Air, Clean Water and Clean Soil
—*Massachusetts Board of Health*

On December 8, 1852, Henry Ingersoll Bowditch, by now one of Boston's most distinguished, although also notorious, physicians and a leading member of the Massachusetts Medical Society, presented a petition to the Society on behalf of Nancy Talbot Clark to be examined by the Society "as to [her] knowledge of medicine and [her] ability to practice it . . . [so that she would] be publicly lifted from the rank of mere pretenders of learning."[1] Clark wanted recognition by the Society to gain credibility for her practice. At the time, before there was a state board of examiners, any person could claim to be a doctor. Physicians were listed in directories under categories: members of the Massachusetts Medical Society, members of the Homeopathic Medical Society, members of the Massachusetts Eclectic Society, and others. The Massachusetts Medical Society listing carried a cachet. Members were required to have attended a recognized medical training institution and to pass a society examination. Women, however, could not be members. Nancy Clark felt her training and knowledge worthy of being examined. Bowditch agreed. But the society refused to examine Clark, let alone allow her to become a member. Thus began a decades-long battle for Bowditch to get women admitted as equals in the American medical establishment. For him it was an issue of simple justice and basic human rights.

Four years after Nancy Clark was denied the opportunity to be examined by the Massachusetts Medical Society, Marie Zakrzewska arrived in Boston to raise money for Elizabeth Blackwell's New York Infirmary for Women. Blackwell, Lucy Stone's sister-in law, like Bowditch, had trained for medicine in Europe. She met Marie Zakrzewska in New York. Marie, born in 1829, daughter of a radical German family, completed midwifery school in Germany. Chafing under the discrimination women faced in medicine, she came to America, where she found things no better. She did knitting to pay her bills and drifted into reform circles, where she met Elizabeth Blackwell. Blackwell encouraged Zakrzewska to continue her medical studies and helped her get into the Cleveland Medical College. Within two years she finished her training and returned to New York to work with Blackwell. Blackwell and Zakrzewska realized there were no adequate training places for women's medicine and opened the Infirmary to train nurses and treat women. They were soon joined by Elizabeth's sister Emily, who had completed her medical education in England.[2]

While working with Elizabeth and Emily in New York, Marie fell in with the circle of female abolitionists. When she went to Boston to raise money for the Infirmary, she stayed with New England abolitionists and looked to them for support of the Infirmary. Not surprisingly, Henry Ingersoll Bowditch was one of the first to contribute funds. Marie remembered his being "the only physician in Boston who encouraged my undertaking when I first came to this city in 1856."[3]

Boston's reform community took to Zakrzewska (Dr. Zak, as she was called by friends), and in 1859 asked her to come to Boston permanently. Once there, she attended Theodore Parker's radical church and threw herself into abolitionist and women's rights activity. She socialized within the abolitionist community, and until she was settled she stayed with abolitionist families. Soon she counted Julia Ward Howe, Francis Jackson, and the Garrisons, Phillipses, Sewalls, Clarkes, Bowditches, and Mays as close friends.[4] Her friends had in common, she remembered, "abolitionism and the advancement of women."[5] Lucy Sewall and Helen Morton, both children of abolitionist families, studied under Dr. Zak.

Marie Zakrzewska found much less acceptance in the New England medical establishment. Many of the region's leading physicians opposed female doctors, even those who found Zakrzewska a competent physician. Bowditch encouraged her to apply for admission to the Massachusetts Medical Society. He was convinced she had the capabilities to pass the examination. But as in the case of Nancy Clark, the Society refused to examine her on the grounds that it only accepted male candidates. Bowditch was furious, but the coming of the war distracted him from further action.

In the meantime, Zakrzewska came to believe there was a need in Boston for a hospital that concentrated on treating women and children and would assist women in the study of medicine. With support from old abolitionists, particularly Sewall and the May family, Dr. Zak rented a house at 60 Pleasant Street and on June 22, 1862, opened it as a hospital to treat women and teach medicine. By July 1, the New England Hospital for Woman began work, training nurses, providing care to women by competent physicians of their own sex, and assisting women in the study of medicine.[6] A year later Lucy Sewell returned from her study of medicine in Europe to assist Zakrzewska, and in 1867 Helen Morton joined the hospital on her return from studying medicine in Paris.

The hospital not only offered female patients care by a female staff, but also provided hospital training for female doctors. No other hospital in Boston would admit females to their wards for clinical instruction.[7] The Boston medical establishment's hostility to females practicing medicine was directed at the new enterprise. Dr. Zak needed allies, and she found them in the abolitionist community. Bowditch and his abolitionist friend Samuel Cabot, both strong supporters of medical education for women and their admission into the medical establishment, came forward to be consulting physicians for the new hospital and remained supporters throughout their lives.[8] Bowditch as a consulting physician provided instruction and training to the female interns at the hospital.[9] For him, support of the hospital was a simple matter of "right and justice." He explained to Zakrzewska that his advocacy of the examination of women and his support to the hospital came from his commitment to "justice to every human being. My old anti-slavery warfare and its principles, with the experience gained in that fight against prejudice . . . support me."[10]

At the end of the war Bowditch again took up the battle for women in medicine. In 1867, as an officer in the AMA, he advocated women's equal membership. Despite the fact that the AMA was disgusted by his "views on women doctors," Bowditch joined the "battle for [this] unpopular idea, I cannot sit by and see an honest cause abused."[11] When one delegate at the AMA conference rose to argue that studying anatomy would "unsex" a woman, Bowditch called that reasoning "twaddle . . . and self complacency." In 1877 Bowditch was elected president of the American Medical Association. He used his presidency to push for both preventive medicine and women's equal membership in the AMA.[12]

Bowditch proudly called himself as "a decided woman's rights man." He renewed his battle for women's rights with the Massachusetts Medical Society.[13] To achieve his ends he became an officer of the Society

and appointed a committee on the admission of women. He put himself on the committee and made sure he had a majority of members
who would report favorably. Bowditch authored the report the committee issued in 1875, noting that admission to the Society was a significant
privilege because it implied competence as a physician. It was a privilege that was conferred as a right to any man who proved his ability, but
women were refused the right to prove themselves, even women
"equally well educated."[14] He argued that this refusal could not be defended "on principles of abstract justice." The women were not asking
for special privileges, only the right to be examined and to prove their
ability. The committee argued that claims about the suitability of
women to study medicine were irrelevant. Women who presented themselves to be examined should be given the opportunity to prove themselves, not be prejudged unfit to be judged. Moreover, Bowditch argued
that the physiological arguments were identical to the arguments used
by supporters of slavery, "who quoted the physiological inferiority of the
Negro race as a reason for excluding that race from the rights of freedmen." He also noted that persisting in denying women was only putting
off the inevitable.

Despite Bowditch's attempt to guarantee the report would lead to a
successful motion, two members of the committee, W. W. Wellington
and Samuel Fisk, objected in a minority report. Wellington repeated
the old arguments that "physically and mentally [women] are not fitted
for such work. Medicine is essentially based on science. The female
mind is emotional and not adapted to scientific pursuits." Using the
language of the "Cult of Domesticity," he argued "the sphere of women
is distinct from that of man. . . . Every true home has two sides and inside and an outside. It is the sphere and mission of women to reside in
the former, of man in the latter." Taking a page from Stephan Douglas,
he argued that the MMS was formed by men and for men and women
had no claim to a right to membership. Moreover he felt that since the
Society was formed to advance science, and admitting women would
not lead to the advance of science, it was "not only our right but our
duty to exclude" them.[15]

Wellington and Fisk also believed that letting in women would lower
standards in the society. The society was bound by codes of ethics and
rules; once in, women could be expected to "commit irregularities mer-
iting expulsion. Should this happen and should one of them be tried
and expelled aside from the trouble and excitement [this] . . . would
cause," the minority report authors felt the "public press would be sure
to pour out upon us for our alleged bigotry and intolerance," and the
MMS would probably capitulate in face of such charge and that would
lead to a "laxity of discipline."[16] Contrary to Bowditch's claim that denying

women equality in medicine was only prolonging the inevitable, Fisk and Wellington argued that "the woman movement, so called may not amount to much after all." They felt that the movement was "a whim of this period and will be short lived."

Wellington was concerned that admission to the MSS "would be only an entering wedge. Very soon the demand will be made that Hospitals and Medical Schools be alike open to both sexes." Such an event was almost more than Fisk and Wellington could bear, "the thought of mixed classes of young men and young women pursuing their studies together in the same medical school and the same hospitals is simply disgusting. It is difficult to conceive of any decent woman wishing to join such classes and one would suppose a professor would resign his professorship rather than to take charge of them."[17] The MSS voted 36 to 27 against Bowditch's majority report and indefinitely postponed action on admitting women. The setback did not stop Bowditch and Cabot. Bowditch came back in 1878 with another report in support of admission of women. Again the successful opposition was led by Samuel Fisk.[18]

Although the separate spheres and women's brains are different arguments, and Fisk and Wellington were old and increasingly outmoded, they were right that demands would be made to open medical schools to women. And they probably suspected that Bowditch would be the one pushing the issue. If they did, they were right. Bowditch had been arguing for women's admission to established medical schools since the 1860s. He supported Emma Call and C. Augusta Pope when they argued before the American Social Science Association for women's admission into major medical schools along with men.[19] In 1881 he wrote an article for the *Boston Medical and Surgical Society Journal* attacking not only the Massachusetts Medical Society but also Harvard Medical School for not admitting women.[20] Although the University of Michigan had accepted women to its medical school since the 1870s, and the homeopathic and eclectic schools also did, no traditional school of medicine in New England accepted women. Eclectics and homeopaths were the two major challenges to the medical establishment in the second half of the nineteenth century. Both relied heavily on herbal medicines and both set up their own schools. Most eclectic and homeopathic schools accepted women. But graduation from a homeopathic or eclectic medical school did not gain one admission into the medical establishment. Indeed, medical societies discouraged members from even consulting with those educated at homeopathic or eclectic medical schools. When Boston University formed its medical school in 1873, it asked homeopathic doctors to staff its faculty. For those who wanted acceptance in the medical establishment and access to the list of the Massachusetts Medical Society, it was not the homeopathic school at Boston University from which they needed to graduate but rather one of the mainstream medical schools such as Harvard. And it was Harvard that Bowditch fought to get women accepted.

Bowditch's was not the only campaign to get women into Harvard. In the 1870s a group led by old abolitionist-alumni, including James Freeman Clarke, Hoar, Bowditch and Higginson, met with Harvard president Eliot about accepting women in the college and letting them sit for examinations. Eliot patiently listened to the group but failed to act. Despite his failure to admit women, Higginson saw Eliot as "honest and manly."[21] Julia Ward Howe was not impressed. She publicly attacked the university and President Eliot for failing accept women.[22] Eventually the university offered women what Bowditch critically termed "a small center connected with [the] University; an annex."[23] Bowditch rejected Harvard's compromise and claimed that the "annex . . . shows [Harvard's] low estimation of women. I never can think of it save with a certain contempt. . . . The corporation virtually says 'you women shall not join in the academic race because you are inferior to us.'"

Bowditch led the unsuccessful campaign to support Harriet Hunt's attempt to be admitted to Harvard Medical School. Using Edith Varney's offer of financial support, Bowditch finally forced the university to create a committee to look into accepting women. The committee, headed by Theodore Lyman, a conservative Boston Brahmin, made no recommendation. It reported that the medical school faculty, although having no objection to the medical education of women, were opposed to their admission to Harvard. Moreover, the medical school had struggled to increase its standards, and the "addition of a mass of women to the students would probably result either in seriously deranging the machinery of the school or the standards of the school and of medical education."[24] The Board of Overseers, which also included Lyman, voted against accepting women. Bowditch was furious. He called the medical school faculty's reasoning and the Board's position "absurd." Convinced that Harvard would one day be "thoroughly ashamed, Bowditch joined Julia Ward Howe in accusing President Eliot of cowardice. "Thank Heaven!" he wrote Edith Varney, "Other Universities in this country and in Europe have higher ideals in regards to women."[25]

Bowditch was defeated at Harvard, but he finally was successful with the Massachusetts Medical Society. After thirty-two years of struggle, he persuaded the MMS to examine a female for membership. In 1884 Emma Louisa Call, a University of Michigan School of Medicine graduate of 1873, was examined and admitted into the MMS. Bowditch had the privilege of sending her the certificate of membership. In the letter enclosing the certificate, he congratulated Call and also the MMS for finally abandoning its "refusal to do justice even to the most accomplished female physicians who have practiced in Boston."[26]

Women were not the only group in New England facing antagonism, including that from the medical establishment. Boston's hostility to Catholics went deep and touched on many sectors of the community, from wealthy Beacon Hill to the poorer sections of the North End. Fearing that their coreligionists would face discrimination, prejudice, and proselytizing in the city's main hospitals, nuns attempted to found a charity hospital for Catholics, but they could not find doctors to act as consultants. Bowditch, believing that all citizens had a right to medical care regardless of background or religion, and having an intense dislike of religious intolerance, stepped forward and became a consulting physician for the Carney Hospital and the Catholic Orphans Asylum. Sister Superior of the Hospital Anne Alexis commented that, if it were not for Bowditch's fight against the prejudice of Protestant Boston, the hospital would never have happened. Championing the rights of Catholics to medical care fit Bowditch's vision of fighting a "good cause."[27]

Bowditch was a dedicated physician, and being a physician was also very much part of his sense of himself. Throughout the struggle against slavery he juggled to maintain his medical practice. Although he was accused by the hostile press of neglecting medicine for agitating, he claimed his patients never suffered because of his political involvement. Yet he felt the tension of balancing the separate spheres of medicine and political activism. When the war against slavery ended, Bowditch continued working for equal rights for blacks and women, but, as in his work for women's rights in medicine, he thought about how to bring the two parts of his public world together. He did so in the campaign for preventive medicine, or as he called it, state medicine.

Bowditch held to the idea that governments were created to protect basic natural rights. Among those rights were life, liberty, and the pursuit of happiness. This was the basis for Bowditch's claim that the government needed to protect the basic rights of the newly freed slaves and to provide schools, hospitals, libraries, and other services to citizens of both races. He also claimed that life and the pursuit of happiness required health, and it was the responsibility of the state to protect the health of the citizens so they could exercise their basic rights. To this end Bowditch argued for the creation of a state board of health.[28]

His was not the only voice, nor the first, to call for a state board of health. Josiah Curtis's report on health conditions in Lowell in 1848 and Lemuel Shattuck's on Boston in 1850 both pointed to the need for a general board of health to keep records and recommend new action.[29]

Edward Jarvis, a physician in Dorchester, president of the American Statistical Society and a friend of Howes and English sanitary reformer Edwin Chadwick, also argued for a board to gather the state's health statistics.[30] Chadwick, a follower of radical reformer Jeremy Bentham, influenced a whole generation of American reformers.[31] Although he would not endorse the notion that poverty caused crime, he did argue that poor living and working conditions contributed to disease and the impoverishment of the working classes.[32] Jarvis, who saw Chadwick as the father of sanitary reform, was in regular correspondence with him about issues of poverty, education, and tenement reform as well as sanitation.[33] But despite Chadwick's support and calls for a state board of health, neither Shattuck nor Jarvis was able to mount a politically viable campaign.[34]

Bowditch, on the other hand, cut his political teeth on issues of power and politics. In 1862 he delivered a speech before the Massachusetts Medical Society in which he argued for a state board of health, "by whose agencies all these great questions, now so utterly ignored may be investigated."[35] Pittsfield Democrat Representative Thomas Plunkett's wife read Bowditch's appeal, and when an epidemic hit a girls' finishing school on whose board she served, she pushed Plunkett to get a board of health bill through the state legislature.[36] It met little opposition, and on June 21, 1869, Governor John Andrew signed the bill and promptly appointed a Board of Health consisting of Richard Frothingham, William Chapin, William Sawyer, Emory Aldrich, Dr. Robert Davis, Dr. George Derby, and Bowditch.[37]

Davis, Derby, and Bowditch were the only doctors on the board, and they were friends. Bowditch knew Davis, an Irish-born Quaker from Fall River, from involvement in radical anti-slavery activity.[38] Davis briefly sat on the State Board of Charities with Franklin Sanborn, another radical abolitionist and co-conspirator in the anti-slavery activity of John Brown.[39] (John Hoadley, an engineer who replaced Sawyer on the board, was also involved in radical abolitionist activity.) Derby, a classmate of William Bowditch at Harvard College, was one of the original members of Henry Ingersoll Bowditch's Boston Society for Medical Education, which brought Louis's clinical approach to America. Derby's abolitionist activity was limited until the Civil War, when he jumped at the opportunity to fight slavery. Graduating from Harvard Medical School in 1843, Derby retrained as a surgeon and served the Union Army till the end of the war, rising to the rank of lieutenant colonel. After the war he became a surgeon at Boston City Hospital and threw himself into reform activity.[40] The war convinced Derby of the need for sanitary action.

In the minds of these nineteenth-century reformers, any efforts to clean up what they believed to be environmental hazards to health, particularly foul air such as that emitted from unventilated water-closets or stagnant air, dirty, visibly unclean surfaces, or polluted water, were considered sanitary reform, and Derby soon became an expert on it. Eventually he was appointed lecturer on "Sanitary Science and Hygiene" at Harvard Medical School. In 1868, in a Boston address before the American Social Science Association, Derby added his name to those calling for a state board to work to prevent disease.[41]

The experience of the war also created a context for sanitary reform. Sanitary commissions at the state level publicized the actions of doctors to improve sanitary conditions for the soldiers. Doctors used their claims of expertise to demand changes in the organization of hospitals, medical care, and sanitation in the field. Working with volunteer nurses, these "men of science and medicine" convinced the public of the importance of sanitary reform backed by scientific knowledge. When the war ended, doctors such as Derby and Josiah Curtis, who worked as a brigadier surgeon, returned to New England committed to bringing their sanitary reforms home as well.[42] With the support of Derby and Davis, Bowditch was appointed chairman; Derby was chosen secretary.

Bowditch had strong medical credentials. He was a renowned expert on pulmonary issues, and author of dozens of medical papers read throughout the world. By 1869 he was one of Boston's leading physicians and, despite his agitation for women in the Massachusetts Medical Society, he was a major force in the society, a professor at Harvard, a volunteer medical examiner for the state, a volunteer doctor for the Union Army in Virginia in the last months of war, a strong supporter of the Republican Party, the force behind the Army Medical Ambulance Service, and a man whose son had fallen at Ford's Crossing in 1863.[43] By the 1860s, with old radical abolitionist John Albion Andrew governor and abolitionists controlling most of the Massachusetts legislative delegation, Bowditch's positions no longer seemed as threatening as in the two previous decades.

What Bowditch brought to the board was a sense of politics. He understood power. His experience in the abolitionist struggle led him to see the board as an agency not just to educate about sanitation and gather statistics but also to advance social justice by being a voice for those suffering from the injustice of an unhealthy environment. Other members, particularly Davis and Derby, shared his sense that the board's mission should be broad and embrace justice, but Bowditch's position in the inner circle of New England abolitionists had taught him important political lessons. He knew how to use the language of rights to advance a political agenda. He also had a deep network of ties to call on in the radical reform community.

Bowditch wanted the board to move to advocacy for the "right" of a healthy environment. He saw state power as something to be contested for and used to rectify wrongs and believed the board could take its limited charge from the state to expand its authority.

In his first address to the board, Bowditch argued that it could "increase the state authority."[44] He did not want the board to "simply sit and gravely hear complaints . . . and after sifting evidence," make recommendations, but argued that it should go out "officially as an organ of state power" and take "vigorous action."[45] Bowditch believed that the state legislature created "openings" for "state medicine," where the board, if it acted "in light of the broadest philanthropy," could prevent disease and improve the quality of life for the citizens of the state.[46]

Bowditch, of course, was also a scientist and believed in the power of scientific observations. He noted that, although statistics and scientific observations could be "tedious" they were "the foundation of preventative medicine. Without them the Board of Health would be left in wordy talk . . . with no basis for fact."[47] He believed that the power of the board would be used for public good because it was informed by both science and an understanding of human rights. "The last legislature, unconsciously, perhaps on the part of many members there . . . has proposed a system that may be made by us capable of good to the citizens in all future time."[48] The board, Bowditch argued at its first meeting, "was a special function of a state authority which until these latter days of scientific investigations has been left almost unperformed or exercised only under the greatest incitements . . . such as the coming of the plague, cholera, small pox, or other especially malignant disease. By this function the authorities of the state are bound to take care of the public health, to investigate the cause of epidemics and other diseases in order that each citizen may not only have as long a life as nature would give him, but liberalize as healthy a life as possible."[49]

Bowditch was not alone in this broad vision of the board. In a letter to Bowditch at its creation, Dr. Edward Jarvis argued that one of the first things it should do was tackle the high city mortality rates, that it was the responsibility of the state to do it. Jarvis noted that crowded tenements accounted for the difference and the state had a role in that "factories are created . . . encouraged by favoring legislation which gives them control of ponds and water courses. With, however, the financial provision that whatever lands may be enclosed, grass submerged, or travel terminated, the mill owners shall pay the costs. But whoever is endangered in his vitality, he has no claim for remuneration, no grounds to demand a removal of the malicious provider of disease or unhealthy." Jarvis claimed that the legislature made "long efforts" for the mills but little for health. He urged the board to take action against crowded tenements and "particularly unhealthy working conditions," including "excessive labor." He believed the board should get the legislature to act as forcefully as if "someone were robbing their house."[50] Bowditch and Jarvis wanted a board that used the power of the state actively to prevent disease and the conditions of disease, not just gather statistics and report on disease prevalence.[51] In a letter to his daughter Bowditch stated he wanted "nuisance makers in . . . the state [to] feel the power the legislature granted us."[52]

At the 1878 American Medical Association Conference, Bowditch noted that advocates of preventive medicine needed to "draw to our aid all the influence of the people and all the power of the state." He also noted it was important to follow the example of England where "the private citizen, however humble, is as justly entitled to protection by the state against the public enemies of his health and life as against highway robbery and murder."[53]

Bowditch argued that, although historically man served the state, in the new Lockean age, as demonstrated in the Declaration of Independence, the reverse could be true: "the state claims to have the tenderest interest in the welfare of each and every one, the humblest or richest of its citizens." Bowditch claimed that since man had demonstrated the power to prevent disease, natural law dictated the state's role in using "its moral power and material resources in the aid of State or Preventative Medicine."[54] "The state will annually," he believed, "become more alive to its best interests and to its duties toward the people."

Bowditch also understood there would be resistance to this new active state working for the general good, particularly from manufacturers and landlords. For Bowditch the "Hunkers" were now replaced with "self-seeking capitalists" and landlords interested only in making money at the expense of the people.[55]

Although more cautious that Bowditch, Derby shared his activist vision of the board. Derby also had an acute sense of how to move the other board members to embrace this vision.[56] At his urging the first two board projects involved tackling the problem of the Brighton slaughterhouses and diseases associated with poor housing.

Brighton's slaughterhouses were a good opening salvo. Notoriously noxious, they had been targets of nuisance cases in the courts for years. And unlike other corporations, slaughterhouses seldom got positive rulings from the courts. Derby's, Davis's, and Bowditch's strategy was to initiate the other board members in an area where few could fail to see the necessity of strong action for the public good. Derby and Bowditch took the other board members to Brighton to investigate the filthy and foul-smelling conditions there. Once confronted with the filth, they got the other members to support "vigorous action."[57] The board reported to the state on the conditions in Brighton and asked for greater power to shut down the slaughterhouses.[58]

In 1870 Bowditch traveled to London on behalf of the board to investigate reform activities in England.[59] Bowditch had other reasons for visiting England, including many friends in Europe from his activities in the anti-slavery campaigns and his studies in France.[60] He used these connections when he arrived in London. He visited Octavia Hill's managed tenements, visited with John Ruskin, and looked at the Peabody Trust's model housing. In this connection he met with model tenement house philanthropist Angela Burdett-Coutts and the Rev. Samuel Barnett, soon to be the founder of the first university settlement house. He looked into sewage disposal, and toured London's worst slums. He also met with Harriet Martineau and other old abolitionist friends.

Bowditch's trip to England did not convince him of the need for a broad systemic attack against the conditions of poverty; he went already dedicated to that perspective. What his trip provided was evidence and data to prove to others the necessity for such an attack. In a letter back to the Massachusetts board, Bowditch noted all that was being done in England in cleaning up tenements. He commented that public authorities in London were committed to providing shelter and cleaning facilities in the casual wards, (homeless shelters), and wondered how long it would be before public authorities would provide decent housing for the poor for the good of society and public health.[61]

What Bowditch did not report back was the intense paternalism and Christian moralizing, especially of Barnett and Hill, who referred to "my dear poor."[62] The difference between Bowditch's view and the paternalistic vision was also reflected in Bowditch's attitude toward alcohol. When the state legislature created the Board of Health it charged the board, among other things, to deal with the problem of alcohol consumption. Temperance had long been an issue among New England reformers. But Bowditch's handling of the issue did not win him many friends in the temperance movement. Following the state legislature's interest in intemperance, the board did investigate the issue in 1870. Reporting back to the legislature, Bowditch argued that, although drunkenness was a problem, the quality of alcohol the poor drank was of greater concern. Bowditch felt that the state should not outlaw liquor, but curb abuse by encouraging substituting beer and wine for "the wretched stuff offered to the poor." His position led to the prohibitionists accusing him of favoring "free rum."[63] He responded by claiming total abstinence an absurd position like saying that "all men and women avoid sexual intercourse because many are aroused by improper use of that instinct . . . that [is] almost necessity for the well being of many of both sexes."[64]

For Bowditch health was related to general physical and environmental conditions. His work on tuberculosis emphasized that certain physical environments exacerbated the diseases. He also believed that an inadequate physical environment that bred disease and deadened the spirit was an evil correctable by human action. In his address to the Harvard graduating class of 1863, he argued that all humans desire "enjoyment of the outward world experience and a perfectly healthful physical existence, friendship and love, and free enjoyment of his intellect." Denial of these things harmed the soul, was detrimental to human society, and was a violation of basic natural rights. When the poor lived in miserable conditions and "terrible life-long toil," the consequence was a plague spot on society. He believed that it was "public authorities'" responsibility, for "surely the [conditions] in which the poor live and love and have their being ought . . . like the schools . . . be cared for by the public; if not for humanity's sake, then for the sake of public health."[65]

To do nothing in the face of evil was for Bowditch unmanly and immoral, just as doing nothing in face of slavery was immoral and unmanly.[66] To do anything short of direct action to correct a wrong was to be part of the system that sustained and maintained an evil. He viewed evil as a product of evildoers, and evil was sustained by the failure of people of conscience to confront those evildoers.[67]

The ill health and immiseration of poverty were evils similar to slavery for Bowditch. They were evils that could be corrected by human agency, but only if people of good will stepped forward and used the instruments available to them to eradicate the evils. For Bowditch the state was an instrument of power that could be directed toward public good, as it ultimately had in ending slavery.[68] But Bowditch also understood that one had to contest for state power. Evil forces could also use the state to thwart the public good, as they had with the Fugitive Slave Law. Bowditch, early on, believed in contesting for state power to do public good. He broke with Garrison over the issue of electoral politics when he ran for office as a Liberty Party candidate. He continued through the 1850s to advocate that abolitionists should contend for state power by engaging in the political arena. The state was not an enemy for Bowditch but an instrument of power for which to contest.

Bowditch brought to his position as chair of the Massachusetts Board of Health his vision of social justice and his understanding of the potential power and enlarging sphere of state activism. He also brought his understanding that society was constituted around interests and that justice required people of conscience to stand up against interests arrayed against those with little power or authority. In that spirit Bowditch, in an attack against child labor, claimed that the health of children required that they should be allowed to play outside.[69]

The campaign against the slaughterhouses succeeded in expanding the scope and power of the board. The campaign for tenement house reform proved more difficult. In 1870 the Massachusetts Bureau of Labor Statistics reported that "there are no places within the settled portions of the city of Boston, where the low paid toilers can find a house of decency and comfort."[70] The Bureau suggested the Board of Health investigate the health implications of the inadequate and overpriced housing for the poor. Bowditch did not need to be convinced. He had been pushing for tenement house reform since the 1840s.[71] Following the war, Bowditch became part of a tenement reform project, the Crystal Palace, which attempted to provide remodeled housing for the poor.[72] During his trip to London, Bowditch focused much of his investigation on tenement house reform. In 1874 he reported that the "large tenements for the poor [where] all the amenities of human life are set at naught, in which it is impossible to educate a family in decency [should be declared by the state] public nuisances and pesthouses."[73] The campaign for tenement reform continued to occupy Bowditch, and the board. Massachusetts had passed a Tenement House Act of 1868, but landlord resistance made real results elusive.[74] By contrast, the campaign against industrial pollution ignited a firestorm of protest from leading industrialists around the state.

For the first three quarters of the nineteenth century epidemiologically oriented physicians believed that many diseases were caused by bad air. One could actually smell disease-causing air because disease arose from filth. As air passed over sewage, decaying vegetable matter, wet smelly soil, stagnant water, and rotting carcasses it picked up disease that then spread through the air, searing the lungs and weakening the body. Given this widespread belief, the courts often found against both people and companies that were responsible for creating bad air. For most of the nineteenth century these cases were directed against slaughterhouses, or individuals dumping wastes into ponds or maintaining stagnant waste pits. Since it was assumed that running water cleaned itself, few cases were brought against companies and cities dumping wastes into running rivers and streams.

Industries were located on running water for power, but also to dispose of wastes. As the Massachusetts State Board of Health noted in 1872, "manufacturers are located on river banks . . . particularly because running water affords the opportunity of readily disposing of waste liquors and other refuse."[75] Massachusetts Superior Judge Gray noted in 1871 that "one great natural office of the sea and of all running water is to carry off and dissipate . . . impurities."[76]

By the second half of the nineteenth century, dumping industrial and sewage wastes into running streams had become so widespread as to turn fresh water into frothing mixtures of toxic wastes, killing fish and sending forth foul stinks.[77] Given the believed link between disease and smelly water, public health advocates began studying water pollution and disease. Before the widespread acceptance of the germ theory of disease causation, the correlation between disease and unclean water provided the causal link, so that the Massachusetts Board of Health began agitating for broad power to enforce the clean up of the state's waters.

For Bowditch and Derby it was a matter of rights. The Massachusetts Board of Health claimed that every citizen had a right to "clean water, clean air, and clean soil." Bowditch and the abolitionists had fought slavery with the rhetoric of rights. Now Bowditch attempted to extend the concept of natural rights to include health and "clean air, clean water, and clean soil."[78] Since, as Locke taught, the legitimate role of government was to protect basic rights, then the government had to protect the rights of citizens to "clean air, water, and soil." Bowditch saw public health as a means for the state to extend the ideal of rights and to protect the rights of those unable to protect themselves.[79] The citizens could not protect themselves, as fugitive slaves could not protect themselves, because of the unequal distribution of power in society. Polluters and landlords had more power and control than the poor over resources. The Board of Health, by championing the rights of the citizens to clean air, water, and soil, would correct that wrong of inequality by using state power to counter private power.

Bowditch's understanding of the struggle over clean air and water as a struggle over rights and power captured much of the nineteenth-century world. Although Bowditch was constructing a world where the state acted proactively to protect rights, America was to a great extent a place where individuals defended their rights through court action. It was to the courts that the citizens of Northampton went to demand redress to the foul, stagnant waters created by a navigational canal's dam. Yet when owners of the mills dumping toxic wastes into the region's waters defended their actions as in the general good and in harmony with God's design, such defenses usually found support in the courts.[80] Bowditch and the early public health advocates articulated a different understanding of how rights should be defended. They looked to the state to defend the rights of the poor and weak against the powerful. The Connecticut Board of Health argued, "it is certainly the duty of the government to protect the weak from the oppression of the strong . . . and especially to protect that class called the poor."[81]

Since corporations were dumping wastes into the region's waters and threatening the natural rights of the poor to clean air, water, and soil and a healthy environment, Bowditch and the early board looked to the legislature to outlaw the practice. The board used its forum to publicize industrial pollution and the corruption of the environment. Its annual reports contained extensive investigations of water pollution and its threat to the public health. It lobbied the legislature for increased power and laws prohibiting pollution of streams and rivers.

Corporations fought back. They threatened to leave the state and leave behind unemployed workers. One corporate leader argued that pollution laws would compel the manufacturing interests to move out of the state and leave behind unemployed "villagers which depend upon the mills for their prosperity."[82] Industrialists asked the governor to limit the power of the board. When, in a close contest between the Democrats and Republicans, the Board of Health was merged with the Board of Lunacy and Charity, the manufacturers managed to get Charles Donnelly appointed chair of the new merged board. Failure of the new board under Donnelly to move against industrial polluters led to Bowditch's resignation. When even the moderate public health advocate Henry Walcott continued to push the issue of industrial pollution, manufacturers successfully pressured the governor to remove Walcott from the board. This act stirred major public controversy and eventually got the Board of Health reestablished with Walcott as chair.[83]

The corporations' opposition to the board's attempt to push legislation restricting the dumping of industrial pollution into the state's waterways reconfirmed Bowditch's worldview. Once again the avaricious and "greed" of the powerful were working to push down and exploit the weak. The construction of the battle as a fight by "greedy capitalists" polluting the public health against the will of the people and the public recalled the earlier political vision of these ex-abolitionists.[84] Just as the abolitionists constructed their battle against slavery as a battle of justice of the common people against the "hunkers," and "lords of the loom," these public health reformers constructed their battle as a battle of the people against selfish industrialists.[85]

This construction reflected reality. The corporations did attack the Massachusetts Board of Health broad reform agenda. When the political conflict and concerns to save money led to the merger of the Massachusetts Board of Health with the Board of Charity and Lunacy, the beneficiaries were industries under pressure to reduce pollution, large municipalities dumping sewage, and slumlords. The immediate political issue behind the merger was irrelevant to Bowditch, coming from a worldview centered on the idea of the struggle of interests. The powerful self-seeking interests of the corporations were behind the merger, and the merger was designed to cripple the larger reform agenda of the board. By attacking the anti-pollution campaign, the chair of the new board, Charles Donnelly, reinforced that perspective. Donnelly also claimed that medicine should be about curing the sick, not preventing disease.[86]

Following the battle over the reestablishment of the Board of Health, Walcott did not turn away from the expanded power Bowditch, Davis, Derby, and the former board had sought. But changes in science and technology coupled with resistance on the part of the state's manufacturing interests redirected the board away from confrontation with the industrialists.[87] The new germ theory and the success of the board's Lawrence Experimental Station increasingly led it to projects centered on germs: reporting on water quality to prove the need for water filtration, cleaning up and monitoring milk supplies, and tracking disease incidents.

The very success of these enterprises diverted the new board from its earlier focus on tenement house reform, its concern over child labor, and its more general rights and justice agenda. The most radical visionaries on the early board no longer served. Derby died, Bowditch resigned, and Davis was running for Congress and increasingly lost his reform zeal as he adapted himself to the mainstream of the Republican Party with its advocacy of the protective the tariff. Walcott's focus on filtering municipal water and tracking down germs paid off in terms of public health. Deaths from cholera and typhoid fell. Not unreasonably the Board came to believe that educating the public on the dangers of germs was of utmost importance.[88] As the public health movement began to rack up successes, it won converts to its side, but the side was considerably altered from what Bowditch had envisioned in 1869–75. Bowditch called for "state medicine." He envisioned an active state directed by knowledgeable, informed medical professionals moving against the larger social causes of ill-health whether they were over crowded tenements, exploited children, or polluted air or water. It was his expanded understanding of social justice that informed him and his vision.[89] Bowditch believed in the power of science, but he was also a deeply committed fighter for social justice. As he saw it the public health movement brought science and social justice together.

The success of the public health movement in the late nineteenth century more and more grew from the work of trained specialists, not scientist-doctors like Bowditch but bacteriologists, chemists, biologists, and engineers. These people believed that by separating issues of value and justice from facts they could achieve "objective science." Even Walcott, trained as a physician and influenced by Jarvis, came to rely on specialists to provide the detailed reports, analysis of water, and plans for water treatment facilities. The professionals justified themselves to the state not by claims to be advancing social justice and "rights," but by their ability to achieve specific results and to understand things others could not. The idea that the state had a responsibility to advance the "right" of good health was replaced with the idea that the state should provide the opportunity for health education and encourage individuals to pursue good health.

The shift of public health from the struggle for rights and justice to the struggle against ignorance, although particular to public health, was also part of a larger story of political struggle. Bowditch and his old abolitionist friends were slowly being pushed aside by a new generation of social movers and that new generation had a different vision of reform and the reformer.

Chapter 8

"Public Society Owes Perfect Protection": The State and the People's Rights

Justice to All! Let Us Stand on That.
—*Julia Ward Howe*

Utter Truth and Labor for Right.
—*Wendell Phillips*

Fifty years after the organizing of the American Anti-Slavery Society, the old comrades came together in Philadelphia to commemorate the event. It was a moment partly to celebrate that slavery had been abolished, partly to reinforce commitment to racial equality in face of repeated attacks, and partly to remember fallen comrades: Garrison had died the year before. Wendell Phillips could not make the gathering, but he sent a letter that was read before the group. In it he proclaimed that the struggle against slavery was a struggle for social justice, and that it did not end until justice reined on earth. "Let it not be said," Phillips reminded those gathered, "that the old abolitionist stopped with the Negro, and was never able to see that the same principles he had advocated at such cost claimed his utmost effort to protect all labor, white and black, and to further the discussion of every claim of down-trodden humanity. Let it be seen that our experience made us not merely abolitionists, but philanthropists."[1]

Phillips saw philanthropy not as moral uplift or Christian charity, but as action to redress the wrongs of inequality. "Labor . . . claim[s] our aid in the name of that same humanity and justice which originally stirred us. We always proclaimed that it was not only the protection of the Negro we aim at, but that we sought to establish a principle, the right of human nature. In that view it seems to me we are narrow and wanting if we do not contribute the energy and skill which so many years have aroused and created to those questions which flow so naturally out of ours and belong to the same great brotherhood."[2] Although Octavia Hill and Samuel Barnett demonstrate that his view was not universally held, Phillips was not alone in seeing philanthropy and charity not as social control or noblesse oblige but rather as action for social justice and natural rights. Franklin Sanborn proclaimed, "Philanthropic enterprises . . . had for their object the amelioration of the woes or redress of the wrongs of humanity."[3]

This large vision of philanthropy was shared by many of those who had come through the abolitionist struggle, including Massachusetts governor John Andrew. By the time of the Civil War many of these abolitionists who for so many years had been shunned and held outside of the circles of influence were now at the center of power. The political abolitionist group known as the Bird Club had created a political machine that by the 1860s dominated Massachusetts state power.

In 1863 Governor John Andrew, active abolitionist and radical Republican, pushed the state legislature to create a "State Board of Charities" to look at the issue of poverty and need in the state. Andrew reached deep inside the abolitionist community for many of his appointments to the board, which included Robert Davis of Fall River, Franklin Sanborn of Concord, Edward Earle, a member of the Underground Railroad in Worcester, and Moses Kimball and Julius Clarke, both from abolitionist families. In late 1864 the governor added Samuel Gridley Howe.

Initially Howe did not have time for this new challenge. He was still busy with the Sanitary Commission, and his involvement in the Emancipation League kept him linked to radical Republican political activity. In 1864 Secretary of War Stanton appointed Howe to the Freedmen's Inquiry Commission to look into what to do for the freed slaves. But by 1865 Howe had more time on his hands. Julia's increased public involvement drove him to distraction, and he needed a place to direct his energy beyond his wife.

In 1865 the Massachusetts Board of Charities issued its first report. Franklin Sanborn wrote the report, which reflected the sentiments of Howe as well as most of the board. Although it was far short of what Phillips had in mind for an aggressive state working to promote equality and social justice, it did lay out an argument for seeing poverty as a product of society's as well as individuals' failings. It argued for state action to mitigate social conditions that contributed to poverty.

Sanborn began his report with the current views that too much charity could lead to vagrancy and pauperism or limit individual freedom, and that the state had to be careful not to become overburdened with it.[4] But the report quickly moved to more innovative ground. Poverty was not a crime, Sanborn noted, but failure to address poverty could lead to crime. He argued that the state had an obligation on both fronts, one to alleviate poverty, the other to prevent crime. "Society . . . owes necessary subsistence to those who cannot procure it for themselves."[5]

Sanborn used both the idea of rights and the metaphor of preventative medicine to encourage action against poverty. "As prevention, in the diseases of the body is less painful, less expensive and more efficacious than the more skillful cure; so in . . . society."[6] The report argued that the state needed to take "more active measures as our population increases and habits of society change." Particularly it needed "to secure fair wages to every laborer, to discourage monopolies, foster education and promote temperance."

In this first report Sanborn was optimistic for substantive state action to deal with the problems of poverty. The state had, after all, a tradition of strong "fine public institutions" and citizens whose kindness flowed "deep and strong from the great heart of the people." Nothing, he believed, "can prevent the progress of needed reforms."[7]

When Howe assumed the chair of the Board of Charities, he continued to argue for aggressive state action to promote greater equality. Ending slavery, Howe claimed, would not bring peace "so long as the labors and drudgery of the world is thrown actively upon one class, while another class is entirely exempt from it. There is a radical injustice in it. And injustice in society is like a rotten timber in the foundation of a house."[8] To deal with the problems of this inequality, Howe suggested that the state should institute a "sliding scale of taxation proportionate to income." He noted that the wealthy would see such a taxation proposal as an "invasion of right," but he noted that the laboring classes were often forced to submit to "invasion of natural rights."[9]

In the Second Annual Report Howe took over as the principal author. Following his plan of action when he took over the school for the blind, he noted that the board should first establish the best methods for action based on examples from at home and abroad, and that it should understand the conditions of poverty through statistical study. But at the same time it was important not to label the poor: "it is undesirable . . . to use such terms as pauper class, the criminal class or the like," for doing so undermines equality and assumes poverty is ingrained. The existence of "dependents and of destructives, is phenomenal not essential in society," Howe argued; "their numbers depend upon social conditions within human control."[10]

Howe used older notions of poverty, "poor stock," but claimed that "poor stock" was itself caused by "poor nutrition, use of stimulants, or abuse of functions." Action by the state could "correct the constitutional tendencies to disease."[11] "Foremost among the measures for social reform must be those which improve the material conditions and the daily habits" of the poor. He asked the state for "improvement of dwellings; of ownership of homesteads; increased facility for buying clothing and wholesome food; decreased facility for buying rum and unwholesome food; [and] restriction of exhausting labor."[12]

Howe, like Sanborn, believed that the history of Massachusetts indicated reform was within grasp. "The people of Massachusetts took the insane out of garrets"; so too Howe believed they would deal with poverty. But he was conflicted about how they should go about it. He argued that the state should build large "public institutions only in the last resort"; he supported private charity and small institutions. Charitable institutions or no, the state should act against abuses, to outlaw child labor, bad tenements, and abusive working conditions.[13]

Three years later, in 1869, Howe wrote his most comprehensive statement on poverty and the role of the state based upon a natural rights argument. "Work, which justly divided among men is honorable, easy, invigorating, and which brings blessing in its train, becomes by unjust partition dishonorable, hard, and exhausting and brings curses and rottenness upon the social fabric. Some of the lower classes have instinctive perceptions of this wrong." The oppressed poor then "feel their justice denied and yearn for their stolen birthright, the pursuit of happiness."[14] If it was the responsibility of the state to protect natural rights, including "pursuit of happiness," then the state needed to take action "to furnish industrial occupations with fair wages," as well as maintain "pleasant schools and interesting methods of instruction, and to facilitate access to the country and places of pleasant resort."[15]

Besides fair wages and ending child labor, Howe and the board struggled with the question of adequate housing. They thought of decent housing as a basic right. "Place-space-room is essential to physical welfare and without enough of it there can not be for the masses, at least, any moral well-being." "Men . . . require freedom in space. Without it they cannot be developed freely and normally."[16] Poor housing not only stunted social growth, it encouraged class division. "Overcrowding . . . tends to array class against class," but it was also "entirely within our control. The common weal, the common safety require that neither the landlord's greed, nor the tenant's ignorance shall be allowed to poison the air and vitiate the moral atmosphere. The legislature has clearly the power to prevent this, and . . . it should hasten to do so."[17]

Sanborn and Howe were not the only old abolitionists campaigning for tenement house reform. James Freeman Clarke and Henry Ingersoll Bowditch had been fighting for decent housing for the poor for decades. In 1846 Bowditch helped organize a campaign for "workingmen's tenements." He and George Derby lobbied the legislature for the

passage of tenement house reform that would outlaw poorly lit, venti-
lated, and constructed tenement houses. That effort partially paid off
with the passage of the Tenement House Act of 1868, which provided
that there be at least one privy for every twenty persons, waste disposal
be linked to city sewers, and health inspectors check on tenements at
regular intervals. Unfortunately resistance by landlords prevented strict
enforcement of the law, and in 1871 Derby and a number of other investigating physicians resigned from their positions.

While in England investigating health reform for the Board of Health,
Bowditch contacted Octavia Hill. Hill, who had been active in tenement
house reform since the early 1860s,[18] had persuaded philanthropist Lady
Penbroke to fund purchasing and rehabilitating housing for the poor.[19]
Hill managed the tenements she rehabilitated, keeping strict control
over the behavior of the tenants, whom she referred to as "my tenants."[20]
She and her fellow reformers William Barnett and his wife Yetta were concerned about poverty, the poor, and housing, but they never argued that
the poor had a natural right to decent housing—the position of
Bowditch, Howe, Sanborn, and other ex-abolitionists. Hill noted that the
poor "are dear to me because they are poor and needy, but [they] are not
individual living men and women to me."[21] For the Barnetts and Hill, tenement house reform and moral uplift would bring the poor closer to
Christ.[22] Poverty, they felt, was the result of the poor's "neglect of God's
laws."[23] Rather than seeing the poor as having rights that the state had a
responsibility to protect, English reformers saw private charity as the
agent to uplift the poor for social control and as a reflection of the Christian character of the leaders of private and public life.[24]

Hill believed decent housing was not a right but rather a privilege
that the poor should earn through good behavior. Unlike Bowditch
and his group of Americans, Hill, Barnett, and other leaders in English
charity did not want the government to get involved in housing reform.
Barnett argued that what was required for decent housing was "not legislation. It is individual interest which will put things useful. . . . A reconstruction of society would not make the poor rich."[25]

Bowditch was well received by the English reformers, but it was not
their philosophy but the products of their activity that interested him. "I
hoped that I might gain something that might possibly be of service to
dear New England."[26] He visited the model tenements Hill managed and
inspected public bathhouses. What he saw was a commitment to improve the conditions of life. Although Barnett and Hill were suspicious
of public involvement in charity, Bowditch saw their actions as intermin-
gled with the public projects of bathhouses. He ignored their hostility to
government and focused instead on his vision of public and private action to further the rights of the poor to a decent life. "Surely the homes

in which the poor live and love and have their being ought [like the schools] be cared for by the public," he argued in 1870.[27]

Back in Boston in 1871, Bowditch helped secure passage of legislation establishing the Boston Cooperative Building Company for building decent housing for the poor.[28] Utilizing this company, Bowditch, Derby, and Clarke began raising money to eliminate one of Boston's worst slums, the Crystal Palace on Lincoln Street in southeast Boston near South Station. The area, notorious for poor ventilation, lack of sanitation, overcrowding, and appalling filth, was home to hundreds of poor—mostly recent immigrants to the city. The group rehabilitated the Crystal Palace and offered the refurbished housing to the poor at reduced rents.[29]

At the Crystal Palace Bowditch and the other old abolitionists set up a Five Cent Savings Bank to give the poor a safe place to save. Bowditch, much as he had at the old Warren Street Chapel, organized classes and activities especially for the youth of the tenement. He set up woodworking classes, where the children made crafts that Bowditch helped sell.[30] In the depression of the 1870s the Crystal Palace project went bankrupt, but even before then Bowditch came to believe the project could not succeed because it concentrated too many poor people in crowded conditions. Housing reform should involve housing for the poor scattered across the community with easy access to open spaces.[31]

Many of these old abolitionists considered themselves "most energetically at work in every good cause," which they understood as one that opposed oppression and furthered equality.[32] Both Henry Ingersoll Bowditch and Julia Ward Howe objected to hierarchies in school for fear they would breed inequality. At a meeting of women in Newport, Julia was surprised when the idea was put forward that there should be special education for "children of genius where they be set apart and able to expand their ability." She attacked the inequality such an idea would foster and "gave the card house a tolerable shaking . . . and brought it down."[33] Bowditch went farther and objected even to "prizes and marks" as "vile influences," that set people apart.[34] He similarly spoke out against the growing popularity of Social Darwinism.

For Wendell Phillips, Abby and Stephan Foster, Henry Blackwell, and Parker Pillsbury, workers' rights became a major issue of social justice. Phillips and Julia Ward Howe embraced the eight-hour day movement.[35] Unlike most labor reformers, Phillips did not think strikes an effective weapon for labor but instead advocated state intervention. He argued that the state had a responsibility to guarantee workers a decent life, so workers should use the power of the vote to get legislation that would protect their rights.[36] Phillips, the Fosters, Blackwell, and Pillsbury argued that capitalists, "greedy capitalists," Pillsbury called them, like slave owners, enriched themselves at the expense of labor. "Capital massed, monopolized, rules the nation," Pillsbury claimed, "ruling, and grinding labor of both men and women to death."[37]

Although he died in 1860, Theodore Parker, minister to the abolitionists, laid the groundwork for thinking on issues of labor and inequality. He sermonized in 1854 that like slavery the inequality between labor and capital "threatened the rights of man in America."[38] Arguing that in America "money is power" and legislation "almost invariably favors capital and not the laboring hand," he admitted that using political power would not be easy and that the rich kept the poor from political power. But he argued for workers to "stir again" and use the ballot to check the power of capital.[39]

Believing that inequality should be addressed by vigorous state action, many of the old abolitionists supported Henry George and then Edward Bellamy's nationalist movement.[40] Higginson, Julia Ward Howe, Lucy Stone, and Bowditch helped form the Boston Nationalist Club. In a letter to Higginson, Bellamy noted that he wanted the support of "all good men and women who have hearts to feel the evils of the day and the courage to work for better things."[41] That was certainly how the abolitionists saw themselves.

When others were arguing that inequality was the consequence of one's effort, Julia Ward Howe argued that "idleness is impossible in the poorer classes, in the richer, it is promiscuous. Among the poor the necessity for industry, economy, exertion [force] labor upon them."[42] She argued for "the necessary equality on some one fundamental point without which human society can not operate." To achieve that equality the state needed to be an active force. "The state represents that unity of action without whose inauguration society could not enter, when its existence and internal wholesome maintenance [failed] its existence could not be maintained."

As the conflict between Samuel Gridley Howe's public pronouncements for women's equality and his private oppression of his wife reflects, these abolitionists were not ideal persons, nor were they totally free from the prejudices of their time. The Brahmins among them could be patronizing. Julia Ward Howe's belief when confronted with slaves in Cuba that slavery degrades the intellect and morals of blacks did not rest comfortably with her commitments to equality and earned her a severe rebuke by William Lloyd Garrison.[43] But unlike most of their contemporaries abolitionists carried from their earlier campaigns a bundle of beliefs that encouraged them to search out and confront inequality and injustice no matter how uncomfortable. The social movement for abolition created a community of activists who reinforced each other in their continuing battle for human rights.

At a time in Boston when more and more old established families considered immigrants the bane and downfall of the city, the former abolitionists fought against these ideas as contrary to the ideals of equality and justice. Julia Ward Howe claimed that everyone, immigrant as well as native born, was entitled to human rights. Arguing that the answer to the problem of "aliens in America" was more social "justice," Howe proclaimed, "justice is established in the heavens. Her rule is without exception."[44]

Rather than bemoan Irish political activity, Howe and Bowditch saw it as an example of political success that would be a model for black suffrage. Bowditch argued that Irish suffrage in Boston led to the successful election of "an excellent man" for mayor by "his Irish followers." Because the Irish were able to elect a person who understood their concerns, the new administration governed "with an eye to the public good."[45]

Justice was also for those abroad. Abolitionism was an international struggle. American abolitionists had regularly traveled to England and Europe to raise money and build international links. While there, they had taken an interest not just in reform activity in England and Europe but also in the international struggle for rights. As exemplified by their support for Irish nationalists and Howe's efforts for the Greeks and Poles, abolitionists saw social justice as transcending national boundaries. As Samuel May noted at an earlier time, "because we have calls at home it is no reason we should be deaf to those abroad."[46] Samuel Howe's internationalism was rooted in his earliest adult experiences, so it should be no surprise that in 1866, when the people of Crete rose in rebellion against the Turks, Howe organized a committee to support the uprising. To raise the committee Howe turned to his old abolitionist comrades Wendell Phillips, John Albion Andrew, and Bowditch's friend Edward Jarvis for help.[47] For Julia Ward Howe, who joined her husband in the campaign for Crete, the issue was one of universal rights. All humanity, she reminded an audience, must be seen as "neighbors." People do not choose their misfortune, but the "justice" of their cause called upon Americans to act.[48]

Returning from Crete, where she and Samuel Gridley distributed clothing from New England, Julia Ward Howe decided to organize a fair modeled on the old abolitionists' bazaars to raise money for relief in the island of Crete. Julia looked to the abolitionist community for help and found Abby May, daughter of an old abolitionist family and a prewar summer companion to Julia, who did much to make sure the week-long affair of sales and entertainments realized more than thirty thousand dollars.[49]

It was not just romantic Greece that pulled these old abolitionists into action. In 1891 Julia Ward Howe called together a veritable Who's

Who of living abolitionists, including Thomas Wentworth Higginson, Franklin Sanborn, James Russell Lowell, John Whittier, F. W. Bird, and Henry Ingersoll Bowditch (a year before his death at age eighty-four), as well as children of prominent abolitionists such as William Lloyd Garrison II (Garrison's son), Lillie Buffum Chace, and Alice Freeman Palmer, to form a Society of American Friends of Russian Freedom.[50] While in England in 1892, Julia Ward Howe lectured at Toynbee Hall not only on women's suffrage, public ownership of utilities, and the eight-hour day, but also on the rights of the Irish to home rule, an issue Phillips also campaigned for till the end of his life.[51] Howe's 1892 lectures on Home Rule for Ireland were not her first involvement with this issue. In 1872, when she was in England to organize an International Women's Peace Association, she met with several Irish home rule activists and pledged her support.[52]

With her involvement in the Boston Woman's Club and her activity in the campaign for woman's rights, Julia Ward Howe began to see a unique role for women in the campaign for justice. The campaign for women's rights had been haunted by attacks that it was a movement of independent women who rejected motherhood. Although some women saw in Abby Kelley Foster's action of giving birth and leaving her child in her husband's care as she went on the road to lecture an act of independence and mutuality in marriage, others used it to attack independent women as unmotherly. Ironically for a woman attacked by her husband and children for neglecting her family and children for scholarship and public lectures, Julia Ward Howe countered that attack by cultivating an image of an elderly matron. She used the ideal of motherhood as a means to diffuse criticism while at the same time calling mothers to action for justice.

Injustice, Howe noted, was rooted in more locations than the actions of evildoers. Women, particularly mothers, often suffered the consequences of this injustice in fallen sons and failed promises. Howe came to believe that "mothers of mankind [needed to] interfere in these matters."[53] To mobilize women to address these issues, Howe planned a Congress of Women for Peace. She began by turning to her old female abolitionist friends and organized meetings in Boston and New York to drum up support for the Congress. From these meetings Howe sent out an appeal to women around the world to come to a London Congress of Peace.[54]

In 1872 Howe left for London in order to advance her idea of a Women's International Peace Association.[55] In London she was asked to speak before the National Prison Reform Congress on women's public education, but she was unsuccessful in her attempt to organize a World's Congress of Women for Peace.[56] Frustrated in England, Howe returned to the United States and, using her old abolitionist contacts, she adopted Maria Weston Chapman's idea of a "Festival" to organize an Annual Peace Festival to be held June 2 of each year.[57] Howe called her Festival "Mother's Day dedicated to Peace." At the first festival, June 2, 1873, Howe asked eighty-year-old Lucretia Mott to speak as well as William Lloyd Garrison. She felt that the speakers "both did nobly for me."[58] Thomas Wentworth Higginson commented that Mott spoke "an hour clearly and forcibly."[59]

Although she spent the first half of her adult life privately studying philosophy, publicly publishing books and plays on travel, poetry, and romance, and fighting her husband for a more public persona, by the 1870s Julia Ward Howe had established her public voice, and it was no longer the voice of romance, but the voice for justice. She was not only an officer in the American Woman Suffrage Association and vice president of the National American Woman Suffrage Association, but a regularly invited speaker to any number of national and international organizations, including the Daughters of the American Revolution, where she argued for suffrage and justice for women. In 1903 at age eighty-four Howe wrote an editorial letter to the *Chicago Tribune* denouncing lynching. She noted that lynching was murder and states were pledged to enforce laws against murder; "those who lynch are criminals and should be treated as such." Since the laws against murder were not being enforced she called for the formation of organizations of people "for the protection of legal rights."[60]

Where a person stood in the campaigns for justice and human rights became for Julia Ward Howe the defining element of a person's character. Given her tendency to cover up her personal misery with her husband, one would expect Julia Ward Howe's remembrance of her husband to gloss over his faults. Even so, how she remembered him tells much about her sense of what made a life honorable and what she herself valued. Julia Ward Howe said of her husband, "in a world as he would have had it, there should have been neither paupers nor outcasts." "The zeal for the rights of others," she felt motivated her husband, "a champion of human freedom."[61] But mostly she noted "he stood with the heroic few who dared to advocate the abolition of slavery."

In 1908, only two years before her death, Julia had a dream that she related to her daughter. She called the dream her "vision of the world"; in it she saw

men and women of every clime, working like bees to unwrap the evils of society and to discover the whole web of vice and misery and to apply the remedies and also to find the influences that should best counter act the evil and its attendant suffering. There seemed to be a new, a wondrous, ever permeating light, the glory of which I can not attempt to put into human words—the light of the newborn hope and sympathy—blazing. The source of this light was born of human endeavor. The men and the women were standing side by side, shoulder to shoulder a common lofty and indomitable purpose lighting every face with a glow not of this earth. All were advancing with one end in view, one foe to trample, one everlasting goal to gain . . . and then I saw the victory. All of evil was gone from the earth. Misery was blotted out. Mankind was emancipated and ready to march forward in a new era of human understanding, all encompassing sympathy and ever-present help, the Era of perfect love, of peace passing understanding.[62]

Julia Ward Howe believed in God. Yet although this dream is packed with religious images, of "ever penetrating light" that had about it a "glory" and a blaze of "newborn" hope, it was very much centered in human endeavor in the material world. It reflected the earlier "perfectionism" of Garrison and Charles Finney, the idea that humans could become perfectly sanctified by a second blessing and create a more perfect society fit for the second coming. Yet Howe's vision encompassed a call to a particularly universal human agency. Evil could be eliminated from the land if people, men and women, of all races joined together to work "like bees" to discover the root causes of misery and want and to eradicate them. Julia's dream reflected her understanding of what was important in the world and the highest calling of human endeavor. For Julia, one gained nobility and sanctity in the struggle to right wrongs. Julia's dream of the world was an interracial, co-sexual perfectionist vision. The world's rebirth came when people's hearts were filled with sympathy, love, and help and they acted to eliminate misery and emancipate all humankind.

If the world was still short of this new millennium, Julia and even her difficult husband had achieved personal salvation through their struggle to realize this new world. In looking over her life she found her place as among those working like bees to discover the sources of misery and marching shoulder to shoulder to eradicate that want.

Julia Ward Howe was not the only old reformer looking back and finding comfort in the lifelong struggle for social justice. Henry Ingersoll Bowditch wrote at the end of his life to Marie that he thanked God for the "opportunity to fight for simple right and justice."[63] Zakrzewska echoed that point when in her last message she noted that she was fortunate to "work for the benefit of womankind in general, irrespective of country or race."[64] Julia Ward Howe's eulogy to Marie at her funeral emphasized that Marie was privileged to have lived to serve for the betterment of humankind.[65]

Marie Zakrzewska came to America to escape the restrictions she felt on her life in Europe. In America she quickly moved into the circle of abolitionist reformers. Zakrzewska concentrated her work with the New

England Hospital, but that did not keep her from active involvement in abolitionism. Following the war she continued her reform work in actively pushing for women's rights. She joined and was a central participant in the American Woman Suffrage Association. Her hospital work involved not only the training of women nurses and doctors but also offering female-centered medical care to women patients, particularly poor women. Dr. Zak and the other women involved in the hospital, including Bowditch's daughter Liz, considered poor women one of the primary purposes of the hospital and treated them without charge. But, as Dr. Zak said many times, it was "not Charity which we must cultivate and practice, it is justice to one another."[66]

Despite its title, the early members of the State Board of Charities wanted justice among Massachusetts residents to be based upon the notion of rights and not charity. To be sure they also shared notions of paternalism and the idea that if poverty were not dealt with the poor would turn to crime, but in its early years, under the leadership of Howe and Sanborn, the board also argued that poverty was as much a product of the lack of "favoring circumstances" as personal failings.[67] In his report to the state legislators Howe reminded them "What [the poor and criminals] are we might have been; what we are (and even higher) they or their children may be." Howe suggested to the legislators "to respect and to economize property, a man must own something. To improve he must have some free agency."[68] By linking self-improvement with free agency Howe was harkening back to those basic rights promised in the Declaration of Independence, "liberty and pursuit of happiness." The state had a responsibility to protect life, liberty, and the pursuit of happiness, as well as property. Although not fully embracing the idea of cooperative ownership, as his wife and friends did at the end of the century when they formed the Boston Nationalist Club, Howe did suggest the basis for vigorous state action for the general welfare.

But Howe faced resistance on the board to his broad vision of general welfare. In 1873 Howe contemplated resigning from the board. He even wrote a resignation letter and sent it to Sanborn to give to the governor at the appropriate time. The resignation of one of the conservative members, however, encouraged Howe to remain chair for another year before Sanborn took over from him.[69]

Although Howe was optimistic that the replacement of the conservative member might "open the door of hope to having one with whom I could work more sympathetically," the board slowly retreated from Howe's broad vision. During the summer of Howe's last year as chair, the board sent Secretary Pierce to visit Europe to investigate charity, welfare, and charitable institutions. Pierce returned with a weighty report that unfortunately focused on philanthropy and the organization of charity.

Bowditch came back from Europe claiming that the experience argued for greater state action and an expanded vision; ignoring all the evidence to the contrary, Pierce emphasized private charity. Although he admitted that "the general assumption is that poor relief can not be left to private charity," it was privately administered charity that most excited him. "In no other country probably are the thoughts of the best minds so much given to the subject of poor relief as in England." So Pierce looked to the English for his model of how to approach the issue of charity and general welfare. He visited the London Charity Organization Society with whom Octavia Hill had been so involved. He was impressed that "local committees of the Charity Organization Society organized a corps of visitors, generally ladies to each of whom is assigned a small sub-district. Any application for relief made to the local poor-law authorities is referred to the local committee."[70] The committee-volunteer, usually an upper-middle- or upper-class woman, investigated the case and made a recommendation to the authorities. The authorities usually followed the recommendation. It was these volunteers that Octavia Hill beseeched not to be too generous to the poor. Believing that discipline and the pain of poverty should not be too easily relieved, Hill argued for limited or no relief in most cases.[71] Pierce praised the Charity Organization Society for its role not in eliminating want but in urging the "repression of vagrancy."[72]

Pierce, like Bowditch, reported on Hill's work "to provide a better class of homes for working people." But unlike Bowditch, who came away arguing for state construction of decent housing, Pierce was most interested in the idea of housing "that realizes a fair income on the capital invested." Pierce also argued that the English system of widely providing free medical services had led to abuse, and he noted that the English were abandoning such services.

As Howe declined in health, so too did his influence on the State Board of Charities. Although Sanborn took over as chair in 1874 the institution that both he and Howe had hoped would help launch a new era of state activism was increasingly looking toward private organizations and limited state involvement. In 1875 the governor replaced Howe with Charles Donnelly. Donnelly was a wealthy conservative Catholic, born in Ireland but raised in New England. He graduated from Harvard in 1859 and was a successful Boston lawyer, the legal representative of several textile manufacturers, and an advisor to Bishop Williams of Boston. Concerned that Catholic orphans might be put in non-Catholic homes, Williams asked Donnelly to become involved with the state Board of Charities. Donnelly concerned himself with protecting Catholic orphans but also opposed the expansive vision of Howe and Sanborn. The president of the Charitable Irish Society, Donnelly felt that private charity should handle the problems of the poor and that the state should not interfere in the affairs of the individual or of industry. Believing that manufacturers brought prosperity to the region and employment to the poor, he was not at all sympathetic to an active Board of Charities involving itself in wages, hours, or conditions of work or housing.[73] Donnelly also believed that Massachusetts was providing too much support for the poor and needed to tighten restrictions on gaining relief. Although Ben Butler refused to reappoint Donnelly to the merged Board of Health, Lunacy and Charity, Governor Robinson, who defeated the radical Butler in 1883, put Donnelly back on the board and made him chair, a position he held until 1907. Donnelly used his position to redirect the board away from its former activist position. His appointment as chair and his success in refocusing the board reflected not so much his powers of persuasion as a general shift in political and ideological currents. The older generation of abolitionist reformers were fewer and fewer, and the new generation of reformers were more interested in government corruption than government action. The board and the general public made a fundamental shift away from the insights of the abolitionists' human rights campaigns. They viewed poverty not as a product of circumstances or the responsibility of the state, but as a product of individual failure. Pauperism, the term Howe believed should be banned from use, became increasingly part of the lexicon of the board as it moved through the final decades of the nineteenth century.

Chapter 9

"A Relative Right"

In 1884 Wendell Phillips died. At the memorial service in Faneuil Hall, Julia Ward Howe spoke of the place's appropriateness: "the people's meeting hall, the place of all others where the *people* should commemorate Wendell Phillips." Julia recalled to the gathering Phillips's "splendid service to humanity" in connection to Labor Reform, anti-slavery, Ireland, and suffrage. Thomas Wentworth Higginson, also a speaker, took it upon himself to criticize Phillips. The service was symbolic in many ways. Old friends gathered to celebrate a lost comrade, but old friends were also increasingly divided about how to go into the future.[1]

Although Julia Ward Howe thought Faneuil Hall an appropriate venue, it was also an ironic location for the event. It was there in 1837 that Wendell Phillips dramatically declared himself an abolitionist when he leaped onto the stage, called abolitionism the heir to Boston's revolutionary past, and denounced those who justified the mob action and murder of Elijah Lovejoy. His oratory won the crowd. Thirty-eight years later in that same hall Phillips heard calls for support of those in Louisiana using lynching and gun violence to drive black voters from the polls. Again Phillips came to the stage and denounced those who supported mob rule. "I should deem myself wanted in my duty as an old abolitionist, if I did not do everything in my power to prevent a word going out from this hall that will make a Negro or a white Republican more exposed to danger." Phillips then called on the "men of Boston" not to support mob rule in Louisiana.[2] This time his oratory failed to carry the day. He managed to sway a large number of the audience, but an even larger number booed and hissed his calls for support of black voters in Louisiana.

Although Phillips failed to sway the crowd in 1875 as he had in 1837, the ideals of the abolitionists were not totally swept from the stage. The optimism of the early postwar years had been tempered by the conflicts of Reconstruction. The failure of various Republican administrations in Washington to fulfill the promise of equality and justice to the freed slaves weighed heavily on the abolitionist community. With lynching and racial violence increasingly driving down black political influence in the South, Reconstruction seemed to more and more Americans a failure. This failure played into a larger national stage and also back into the reform movement. Yet the abolitionists continued to push forward with their vision of a new Common Weal despite setbacks and disagreements among themselves.

For Wendell Phillips, Julia Ward Howe, and the Bowditch brothers, the fight for justice involved fighting the assault against black equality as well as advancing the larger ideal of an egalitarian society. On the other hand, Thomas Wentworth Higginson's confused and contradictory approach to the postwar era captured the shifting currents within the reform community.

When Lincoln called for volunteers to put down the Southern rebellion, Higginson, like many abolitionists, questioned where Lincoln's actions would lead. Abolition of slavery and black equality were their concerns, and until Lincoln demonstrated a movement in those directions Higginson kept a distance, although he privately believed that the war would either end or weaken slavery.[3] When the Union Army experienced a series of defeats, Higginson called for volunteers, and in the fall of 1862 General Rufus Saxton, the military governor of the Southern Department, wrote to Higginson asking if he were interested in a colonelcy of the First South Carolina Volunteers, a regiment of freed slaves.

Higginson took the offer and was soon in the heat of battle leading the first authorized regiment of black troops.[4] Seth Wright, a fellow Worcester abolitionist, joined him as regimental surgeon. In the early years after the war Higginson's position on black equality and political rights followed those of the other abolitionists. He denounced Parker Pillsbury when Pillsbury joined with Elizabeth Cady Stanton and Susan B. Anthony in their claim that black males should not be given the franchise ahead of white women and attacked black male voters as ignorant and unworthy of the vote. Higginson supported Lucy Stone in her argument that black rights and women's rights needed to be coupled not separated but that black male suffrage must be achieved even if it meant putting off women's rights and accepting language in the Fourteenth and Fifteenth amendments contrary to those rights. He approved of the radical Reconstruction in the South and stationing federal troops to guarantee black suffrage. When his old companion in the Town and Country Club, James Lowell, seemed to be moving away from his earlier positions on black equality, Higginson accused him of taking a "reactionary position compared to his former self."[5]

Through the 1870s Higginson continued to be politically active and to visit with his old crowd of radical abolitionists. Withdrawing from the ministry to write full time, Higginson and his wife Mary, whose arthritis was debilitating, moved to Newport, Rhode Island. Newport was also the summer home of the Howes and other leading reformers. Higginson and his neighbor, sanitary reformer Colonel George Waring, regularly dropped in to visit the Howes. Old abolitionists came as guests to the Howes' or Higginsons.'[6] Julia Ward Howe remembers these summers as a time when a band of old reformers combined to "improve the beautiful summer season by picnics, sailing parties, and household soirees."[7]

But although Higginson was a courageous fighter and insightful writer, consistency was not one of his characteristics. In the 1880s he became an active supporter of Civil Service reform. When he joined the campaign he began to make arguments that differed little from those coming out of the South in attacks against black voters and Reconstruction. He ran for Congress in 1888 on the Civil Service reform ticket, claiming that voters' ignorance helped explain the corrupt spoils system and urging voters to put all other issues aside until Civil Service reform was achieved.[8]

When challenged by his old abolitionist friends Higginson backed himself into the corner of privilege, responding that "suffrage is a relative right belonging to a certain stage of human progress." It was a position not even his closest friends found acceptable. Frederick Douglass denounced him, as did women in the American Woman Suffrage Association.[9] Higginson responded by breaking his connection with the *Woman's Journal.*[10] His 1885 review of the biography of William Lloyd Garrison by Garrison's sons was so hostile that Anne Weston wrote to Samuel May that the review "had the genuine old pro-slavery ring of 40 years ago." "Why a man should try to make himself solidaire with unsuccessful sin and inequity is a curious psychological study."[11]

Higginson's break with his old friends and comrades came over the issue of Civil Service reform, but it had its origins in his ambivalent attitude toward Reconstruction. Frustrated by the failure of Reconstruction to usher in a new world of racial equality in the South, Higginson argued that blacks would be no worse off under a Democratic administration than a Republican one. He was joined in this position by William Lloyd Garrison, II, son of the old abolitionist fighter.[12] Abandoning the core idea of natural rights, during the 1880s Higginson argued that Reconstruction "failed' because southern blacks were not ready for the franchise. Rather than see the impact of violence and intimidation, Higginson saw low black voter turnout as "lack of interest" in politics.[13]

Higginson did not persist in these positions for long. By 1890, with continued and increasing racial violence in the South, he claimed that Democratic rule was proving disastrous for blacks.[14] Blacks, he stated at the end of the century, had a "right to the freedom of civilization, the freedom of political rights, the freedom not merely to escape being held as slaves, but to have a position as free men that is worth having. The trouble is that the freedom of these people in the South is nominal not real freedom."[15] Yet Higginson's approach to the nation's race problems continued to be more cautious and conservative than that of most of his fellow abolitionists. In 1905, when the last surviving abolitionists turned to the Niagara Movement and the forming of the NAACP, Higginson stayed loyal to the gradualist approach of Booker T. Washington.[16] But by the end of his life Higginson once again attacked lynching, claiming that violence against blacks was "about defense of caste," not about defense of white womanhood. At the same time he optimistically believed that "colorphobia will cease to control our society; and marriage may come to be founded not on the color of the skin, but . . . upon genuine sympathies of heart and mind."[17]

Although Higginson returned to a natural rights argument for black rights, many Americans attributed the failure of Reconstruction to the behavior of blacks not yet ready for the franchise. It was a popular attitude that continued to plague abolitionist attempts to push forward a progressive agenda based upon natural rights. Typical of the feelings of many post-Civil War reformers, too young or not active in the abolitionist campaign, were those of Charles Folsom, a young colleague of Henry Ingersoll Bowditch in the public health movement. While Bowditch was arguing for broadened democracy, Folsom wrote to Edwin Chadwick in England in 1878 that conditions in the South were deplorable because "ignorant, impoverished, immoral and jittery [blacks]" and "abominable carpet bag government" had driven the states into debt.[18] Oliver Wendell Holmes, whose father had shown little sympathy for the abolitionists, carried on the family tradition by renouncing Reconstruction and the whole idea of transforming society.[19]

With few exceptions abolitionists refused to abandon their original call for total equality.[20] Yet the nation wanted to forget the cause of the war, and to celebrate valor for its own sake. Americans were uneasy, if not openly hostile, to the very possibility of black equality. Over the years the abolitionists' call for state action to defend basic natural rights found fewer and fewer supporters.[21] The violence against blacks in the South, rather than lending support for more state action in defense of rights, became an argument against defense of rights.

Confronted with a powerful opponent in the Republican Party, the Democrats embraced the strategy that Stephen Douglas had used against Lincoln in their now famous debates. They embraced white supremacy and attacked the Republican Party as the party of racial equality. Picturing Reconstruction as a total failure and a product of

Republican Party repression of innocent southern whites, the Democrats claimed that the "failure of Reconstruction" proved the failure of racial equality. The South, the Democrats repeated over and over again, was being oppressed by "ignorant" black rule. Everywhere, they claimed, whites in the South were being abused and subjected to indignity; Reconstruction governments were dominated by corrupt and ignorant black politicians, and their policies were laying the South waste. This failure proved the folly of extending the franchise to blacks and the evils of aggressive state action that went against local customs.

Conservatives in the Republican Party had always been uneasy over the influence of the egalitarian ideals of the abolitionists within the Party, and northern conservative Democrats loathed the very idea of racial equality. Neither group felt an urge to step forward to defend the Reconstruction governments in the South. Conservative Republicans, fearing a racial backlash if they came to the defense of Reconstruction, distanced themselves from the idea of black rule in the South even before the Compromise of 1877. Without strong support among non-abolitionists in the North, the idea of the failure of Reconstruction took hold in the nation. Reconstruction's failure was not laid at the feet of white violence, but blamed on the failure of "black voters" to use the franchise wisely. It became part of the national lore that Reconstruction failed because blacks were either "not ready" for the vote (the more benign view) or incapable of self-rule (the more conservative view). For conservatives Reconstruction itself proved the need for elites to assume authority in society: in the South where order was threatened by "ignorant" black rule, and in the North where it was threatened by unruly immigrants.

The "failure of Reconstruction" also played against the abolitionists' larger reform agenda. It undermined claims for extending the franchise to women, and, in positing that the franchise was something for which one had to prove one's readiness, it subverted the natural rights-based argument for reform.

When William Bowditch pushed Amos Lawrence in 1874 to support women's rights, Lawrence responded negatively that "universal manhood suffrage has proved to be a failure in the cities and thickly settled communities and all though the South chiefly because it is not based on intelligence, nor on character, nor on property. To give the right to vote to all the women would only be to increase the evil."[22]

Although Julia Ward Howe argued that women could not move through the door of progress if it were closed to others, other strategists within the suffrage campaign came to believe that women had no chance of gaining suffrage if they tied their interests to those of the least favored in American society. At a time when black male voters were being driven from the polls with claims that they were unfit to vote, it would have been unrealistic and self-defeating, these activists argued, to champion both women's rights and black rights. The activists in the National Woman Suffrage Association argued that women needed to narrow their focus on women's right to vote, even if that meant accepting black disenfranchisement in the South.

Although most of the old reformers continued to hold to their core belief in natural rights, the political winds of the nation were shifting rightward. The claim of rights put forth by the old abolitionists was based on the assumption of a birthright that all people were born equal with certain unalienable rights. Their conviction was rooted in a natural rights philosophy that was the language of the seventeenth and eighteenth centuries. For conservatives, the natural rights philosophy supported the defense of property. They saw the role of the state as limited to protecting the rights of property, not as a vehicle for human rights reform.[23]

The abolitionists took that same philosophy and attached it to the car of progress, using its universalism to attack slavery and inequality. In the postwar period they used Locke's conception of the role of the state as a means to defend not just property but the basic human rights of life, liberty, and pursuit of happiness. Their vision involved an activist state that would promote reforms to protect individuals from the forces and interests allied against a person's ability to fully experience a liberated life. That vision meant that the state should aggressively step in to protect the freed slaves from intimidation, guarantee their full rights as citizens, including the right to vote, and provide the resources necessary for them to pursue happiness on equal terms with their white neighbors.[24] It also meant that the state should work to protect the ability of workers to enjoy a free and decent life, protect women from discrimination, and protect the poor from indecent housing and an unhealthy environment.

With the natural rights position used to advance a reform agenda, conservatives turned elsewhere to defend their laissez-faire society, where those at the top of the social hierarchy would be free from the power of the state to interfere with their world or their position in the hierarchy. For a philosophy that would defend their position against the attack by the postwar reformers, conservatives turned to the new science of biology and Darwinism. Although conservatives, particularly in Europe, had traditionally been skeptical of the democratic potential of the new scientific revolution, American conservatives were more practical in their approach to science. When Herbert Spencer simplified Darwin's ideas about evolution through natural selection to propose a regime of "survival of the fittest" for human society, American conservatives found a scientific interpretation they could enthusiastically embrace.[25] If the dominant discourse of the eighteenth and early nineteenth centuries was natural rights, the metaphors of biological science shaped the language of the late nineteenth century in the form of Social Darwinism.[26]

Social Darwinism was a comforting science for the American middle class. It relieved them from any responsibility for the growing inequality within industrial America. Herbert Spencer railed against state intervention in the economy as unscientific and counterproductive. In his *Social Statistics*, Spencer attacked Jeremy Bentham's claim that science showed that the greatest happiness could be attained by social legislation to reform society. Spencer argued that evolution and progress depended on allowing his imagined laws of nature to work without interference. He claimed that the fault for poverty lay with the poor rather than with the failure of the state to fulfill its promise to protect life, liberty, and the pursuit of happiness. He argued against not only aid to the poor but also state support for schools and even sanitary reform.[27]

For Americans horrified at the terrible costs of the war and impatient at the calls for ever greater action and sacrifice for those at the bottom of society, Spencer provided a reason for inaction.[28] William Graham Sumner, a professor of theology at Yale, led the way in popularizing Spencer's views in America. Sumner argued that it was irrelevant what one wanted; society could "not go outside of this alternative: liberty, inequality, survival of the fittest: not-liberty, equality, survival of the unfittest. The former carries society forward and favors all its best members: The latter carries society downwards and favors all its worst members."[29] For many Americans those "worst members" were the newly freed slaves and newly arriving immigrants.

Social Darwinism fit nicely with the racism that found deep roots in American soil. Social Darwinists argued that Reconstruction failed not because of a lack of will on the part of society and the state, but because black Americans were not yet evolved to take the responsibility of full citizenship. Abolitionists attacked Social Darwinism as providing intellectual respectability to the failure of society to deliver on its promise of equality and racial justice.[30] But abolitionists were increasingly shunted aside in the national debates as anachronisms. The Social Darwinists argued that the claim of the old abolitionists for an activist state promoting equality was based on bad science. The scientific metaphors of Social Darwinism supported a laissez-faire state that allowed the individual to express his or her own ability without aid or support. Social Darwinism also merged with the scientific racism that had been haunting the back corners of the American psyche for several decades. Linked with Darwinism, the new scientific racism gained legitimacy at the very time that Americans were anxiously trying to understand their new industrial world.

When Samuel Gridley Howe claimed that logic and science declared that the state needed to step in and guarantee fair wages, safe working conditions, and decent housing, Americans were confronting a world where a smaller proportion of its population could expect decent housing or working conditions.[31] American cities, like their European counterparts, had always suffered from overcrowding and inadequate housing and sanitation. But until the late nineteenth century few Americans lived in cities. In 1860 urban dwellers made up only 20 percent of the nation, while 35 percent of New England lived in towns and cities. But the last four decades of the nineteenth century saw a burgeoning urban population, especially in the Northeast. The century ended with more than 40 percent of the nation and 60 percent of New England living in urban areas. Who these people were changed as well. Until 1850 most of New England's urban population came from the surrounding countryside and shared religion and often kinship with those already residing in the cities. But the Irish potato famine radically changed the makeup of the region's urban population, and New England did not respond well to the new immigrants. The rise and power of the anti-immigrant, anti-Catholic Know Nothing Party in New England, although fleeting, nonetheless reflected deep hostility to the mostly Catholic newcomers. Yet Boston's immigrant Irish population was only 23 percent in 1870, with all foreign-born making up 35 percent. By the end of the century New England added Italians, Poles, Slavs, and Jews to the Irish, Canadian, German, Scotch, Scotch-Irish, English, and Welsh. The percentage of foreign-born and children of foreign-born grew dramatically, making up almost half the populations of the region's cities. These immigrants, unlike the migrants to the cities of the first half of the century, came with few resources and huddled into overcrowded slums and tenements.

The overcrowding that caused Bowditch so much concern was now magnified a thousand-fold. For Bowditch the answer was a thousand-fold greater effort to alleviate the conditions that thwarted human potential. Julia Ward Howe believed that, since "justice is established in the heavens," the answer to the problem of "aliens in America" was more social justice.[32] Other Americans, like Amos Lawrence, saw the new immigrants as menacing. Social Darwinists assured those like Lawrence that responsibility for the immigrants' poverty and disease rested with the immigrants themselves. Not state action but at best benign neglect was called for. The Social Darwinists argued that it was an injustice to those who had prospered to expect them to give to those at the bottom of society.[33]

Civil Service reform became the cause of those who championed conservative reform. The Republican Party had failed black Americans in the South, and increasingly in the North it ceased to be the party of Lincoln or of reform; rather it became the party of business.[34] Scandals and corruption plagued the GOP. For many the party of equal rights had become the party of the railroads. In the campaign for clean politics, like the campaign for women's suffrage, there was a temptation to tap into the rich political seam of ethnic and racial hostility. Social Darwinism sweetened that temptation.

Not all who came to champion Civil Service reform followed this line into ethnic and racial stereotyping. Bowditch carefully contexualized his support for Civil Service reform as anti-monopoly, not anti-immigrant. Bowditch broke with the Republican Party in 1884 and voted for Cleveland because he felt the Republican Party had been taken over by "thieving scoundrels," especially the western raiload interests.[35] But Bowditch's position was not the dominant one in Civil Service reform circles.

Civil Service reform was partly a reaction to the failure of the Republican Party to carry forward the ideals of Lincoln, but it challenged government corruption, not inequality and deprivation. It muted the political edge of the reform movement. It found support from people like Amos Lawrence, who saw it as a vehicle to keep immigrants off the public payroll. Others, like Theodore Lyman, made wealthy by investments in the region's textiles and railroads and whose father's mayoral action during the anti-Garrison riot Maria Weston Chapman found so duplicitous, ran for Congress on the Civil Service reform ticket. Lyman ran to fulfill what he believed was his paternalistic obligation to serve the region and bring clean government to the nation. He believed corruption involved people of poor character winning political office and using that office for personal advantage by payment from those favored by government action or some other direct financial benefit. Not only did he believe his "moral character" would prevent such corruption, but being independently wealthy he did not feel he would be subject to such temptation. In office Lyman's championing of good government meant not only support of science and the Smithsonian Institution, but also economy in government and strong support of the tariffs, particularly those on textiles. He did not feel there was a contradiction between support of clean government and voting high tariffs that provided special benefits for his class and family.[36]

Civil Service reformers, or mugwumps, saw themselves as the supporters of progress. But Civil Service reform also fit nicely within the framework of Social Darwinism. For society to move forward it needed to be led by those who had proved their fitness by the positions they already held. The leading families had succeeded first as merchants in the rough and tumble competitive world of commerce; they had gone on to success as bankers and industrialists. These leaders believed their wealth reflected their value to society. Civil servants chosen according to ability rather than party attachment would lead to social improvement, just as New England had improved because it was led (and should be led if it wanted to continue to progress) by those who had emerged at the top of the highly competitive world of commerce and industry.

As New England entered the last decade of the nineteenth century, most of the dwindling number of old abolitionists continued to champion social justice. Their names and voices were heard at meetings in support of liberty of those abroad as well as for social justice for the least fortunate within the nation. They protested lynching, poverty, racism, and sexual discrimination. But more often they gathered not to protest but to mourn as they laid more and more of their number in the ground. Their names appeared in the local papers under memorials, not calls for conventions and conferences. In these tributes and at these funerals the heroics of the old abolitionists' struggles were recounted, but less and less was said about their continued struggle for social justice.[37] In 1889 Harriet Winslow Sewall found it ironic that now so many people felt free to talk about the evils of slavery while ignoring the evils about them. "It does not require much moral courage to decry the injustice of fifty years ago," she noted to William Lloyd Garrison's son Francis.[38]

By the end of the century a new generation of reformers began to influence the affairs of the nation. These progressives were not of the abolitionist generation. They did not grow up with a world divided between free and slave and a politics constantly circling back to the issue of slavery and natural rights. The world of the progressives was the world of Social Darwinism, the ascendancy of racism, and the crisis of the immigrant poor and urban slums. It was also the world of Marxism and socialism. The radical wing of the progressives attacked the beliefs of Social Darwinism from the vantage point of the environmentalism of scientific socialism. The religion of the progressives was not the millennialism of the perfectionists but the gradualism of the Social Gospel movement.

As Richard Hofstadter noted fifty years ago, the progressives responded to a world of immigration and bureaucratic industrialization by calling for more individual accountability, responsibility, and opportunity. They attacked monopoly, corruption, and spoils and advocated advancement, appointment, and policy itself on the basis of merit, not interest. For Hofstadter, at their roots progressives reacted against the massive change in the American socioeconomic world with reforms that attempted to recapture a homogeneous Yankee world of individual responsibility and competition.[39]

This vision certainly captures much about the progressive reformers, but it loses much in simplifying their understanding of history and their intellectual age. The progressives were aware of the increasingly restructuring bureaucratic world of large corporations, impersonal urban centers, and political machines. But the progressives were also cognizant of the earlier reform campaigns of the postwar era. They were acutely aware of the power of Social Darwinism and racism to structure the form and content of political discourse.

The American world they confronted at the turn of the century was not just the lost world of homogeneous Yankeedom. It was also a world of immense misery and poverty: teeming slums with astounding death rates, especially of tuberculosis, dysentery, and typhoid, unparalleled inequalities of wealth and privilege, surpassed in our national past only by the disparity between slave and free. It was a world of rapacious destruction of public resources for private gain, where workers attempting to unionize were shot and their families shot down and burned out by public armed forces acting on private behalf.

Such a world surely called for radical root and branch reform. It was the kind of change the old abolitionists understood. It was a world where state action to protect the natural rights of liberty and pursuit of happiness was needed. Yet as Hofstadter noted the reforms of the progressive response were limited. The progressives worked on a more constrained stage. That stage was to a great extent the consequence of the failure of the radical postwar reform era. In a world where racism and Social Darwinism had routed natural rights ideals of equality and social justice, the progressives proceeded more cautiously. They called for protection for competition and recognition of "legitimate" privilege rather than a rejection of privilege itself. Henry Ingersoll Bowditch's belief that schools should not award honors because they create feelings of superiority and inferiority gave way to calls for rigorous tests to ensure that titles and claims to privilege were "fair and legitimate." The argument shifted from the legitimacy of privilege itself to making sure that the deserving received their full due of privilege. When a Rhode Island Woman's Club member argued for special schools for bright and talented children, Julia Ward Howe attacked the idea of special schools for gifted children. The progressives were more concerned that deserving would have fair access to such schools. To be sure, they tended to envision the deserving as Yankee Protestants, but they nonetheless clung to the idea that they wanted a society where privilege and hierarchy were based upon merit, not connections. Social Darwinism had legitimized privilege and hierarchy; the progressives wanted reforms that would ensure fair access to that hierarchy.

The progressives were a new generation; their language and their battles were different from those of the old abolitionists. Yet something did pass down from the abolitionists to the new generation of reformers. Many, like Jane Addams and Florence Kelley, came out of abolitionist families, and they grew up hearing the stories of the old battles and the old beliefs. And in some ways they recreated the community of struggle of the older abolitionists in the settlement houses that symbolized the progressive spirit of the turn-of-the-century reformers. The abolitionists would never let the idea of a racially just society die, and their ideas nourished the formation of the NAACP. The old abolitionists also gave to the new reformers the idea that through government action society could improve conditions particularly for those at the bottom of economic ladder.

The new reformers may have armed themselves with new ideological weapons—socialist or liberal economics, the social gospel, pragmatism-but they carried from the abolitionists the basic beliefs in a just society and the value of the struggle for social justice. Abolitionists also provided models of action and moral courage to which future generations continued to refer: a model of commitment to struggle "till every yoke is broken."

Abbreviations

BPL	Boston Public Library, Anti-Slavery Collection
BFP, Peabody	Bowditch Family Papers, Peabody Essex Museum
BFP, MHS	Bowditch Family Papers, Massachusetts Historical Society
Bowditch, *Life*	Vincent Y. Bowditch, *Life and Correspondence of Henry Ingersoll Bowditch* (Boston: Houghton, Mifflin, 1902)
GFP	Garrison Family Papers, Sophia Smith Collection, Smith College
HIB, Harvard	Henry Ingersoll Bowditch Papers, Countway Library, Harvard University
HIB, Harvard, MJ	Miscellaneous Journals 1827–1888, Archives 6a9.2, Vol. 1842–1889 MJ
HIB, Harvard, Seq.	Journal de 1884 et Sequentes Vol. 3 Archives 6a9.20 Vol. 3
HIB, B MS	Misc.2fd Letters
HIB, MHS chusetts Historical Society,	Henry Ingersoll Bowditch Papers, Massachusetts Historical Society, Miscellaneous Volumes, Box 1
HIB, MHS, Scrapbook	Miscellaneous Volumes, Box 2, Scrapbook compiled in memory of Henry I. Bowditch and Olivia Y. Bowditch, by Vincent Yardley Bowditch, 1894.
HIB, MHS, *Annual Report*	*Annual Report of the New England Hospital for Women and Children*
JWH, Houghton	Julia Ward Howe Papers, Houghton Library, Harvard University bMs Am 2214
MHS	Massachusetts Historical Society

OH, LPE	Octavia Hill Papers, British Library of Political and Economic Science, London, Collection 51
SGH, Houghton	Samuel Gridley Howe Papers, Houghton Library, Harvard University, bMS AM 2119
TWH, Houghton	Thomas Wentworth Higginson Papers, Houghton Library, Harvard University, bMs Am 784
WBP, Peabody	William Bowditch Papers, BFP, Peabody

Notes

Preface

1. See Brian Donahue, *The Great Meadow: Farmers and the Land in Colonial Concord* (New Haven, Conn.: Yale University Press, 2004) for an excellent example of a historical work, in this case about colonial agriculture, informed by the experience of working the land.

Introduction: "Till Every Yoke Is Broken"

1. *Commemoration of the Fiftieth Anniversary of the Organization of the American Anti-Slavery Society in Philadelphia* (Philadelphia: T.S. Dando, 1884), 15.

2. Richard Hofstadter presented abolitionism as a one-issue religious crusade: "when the Civil War ended most abolitionists returned to their workday pursuits, content to rest upon their formal success and to luxuriate in their new roles as respected citizens who had once been the prophets of a great moral reform." Richard Hofstadter, *American Political Tradition and the Men Who Made It* (New York: Knopf, 1948), 155. Although Hofstadter exempted Phillips from this characterization, he missed the extent to which Phillips was not alone but part of a larger social movement or community of reformers who carried on past Reconstruction. This perspective in turn affected Hofstadter's understanding of the seeds of the Age of Reform. Hofstadter, *The Age of Reform: From Bryan to F.D.R.* (New York: Knopf, 1955). Hofstadter was not alone in this view of the abolitionists as retiring veterans of a successful campaign. George Fredrickson in his seminal work on northern intellectuals saw prewar public thinkers, including abolitionists, as effectively pushed aside or withdrawn from the public scene after the war. Because of his focus on the Transcendentalists and the anti-state abolitionists such as William Lloyd Garrison, he saw a pattern of withdrawal after the war. His analysis does not work if one takes a broader view of the abolitionists. This broader view points to abolitionists aggressively taking their natural rights arguments forward and supporting a more activist state. George Fredrickson, *The Inner Civil War: Northern Intellectuals and the Crisis of the Union* (New York: Harper and Row, 1965).

Focusing on the generation of intellectuals who came to maturity during and after the war, Louis Menand and David Blight argue that the war experience itself so traumatized that generation that they rejected radical reform. David

Blight, *Beyond the Battlefield: Race, Memory, and the American Civil War* (Amherst: University of Massachusetts Press, 2002); Louis Menand, *The Metaphysical Club* (New York: Farrar, Straus and Giroux, 2001). Although this may have been true of many of the war generation, it fails to capture the experience and influence of those "bred in the old anti-slavery reform." In recent years scholars of women's history and biographies of activists have pointed to the continuation of political activism by former abolitionists, particularly feminists. Lori D. Ginzberg, *Women and the Work of Benevolence: Morality, Politics, and Class in the Nineteenth-Century United States* (New Haven, Conn.: Yale University Press, 1990), sees the continued activism of what she calls the ultra-reformers in the postwar period, but argues that in general reformers moved away from broad moral-based reform toward social control. Ellen DuBois, among other women's historians, has argued that female abolitionists carried on the battle for equal rights for women, using the abolitionist ideal of natural rights. DuBois, in her work on feminism and the emergence of the women's movement, focuses on the role of abolitionism and of natural rights in setting the stage for later suffrage activism. Ellen Carol DuBois, *Feminism and Suffrage: The Emergence of an Independent Women's Movement in America, 1848–1869* (Ithaca, N.Y.: Cornell University Press, 1978). This work argues that what DuBois and others have found about the suffrage applies to a wide range of reform activism. The push to broaden the natural rights argument beyond slavery affected far more than just suffrage supporters. For other works that look at the abolitionist influence on the women's movement, see Jean Fagan Yellin, *Women and Sisters: Antislavery Feminists in American Culture* (New Haven, Conn.: Yale University Press, 1990); Blanche G. Hersh, *The Slavery of Sex: Feminist Abolitionists in America* (Urbana: University of Illinois Press, 1978); see also Wendy Hamand Venet, *Neither Ballots Nor Bullets: Women Abolitionists and the Civil War* (Charlottesville: University of Virginia Press, 1991) for a discussion of women pushing the gender boundaries during the war. See Nancy Isenberg, *Sex and Citizenship in Antebellum America* (Chapel Hill: University of North Carolina Press, 1998) for how women's use of rights enabled them to develop a critique of traditional social roles and paved the way for a broad based feminist movement.

3. James McPherson has written on how abolitionists continued to engage the issue of rights for the freed slave. James McPherson, *The Abolitionist Legacy: From Reconstruction to the NAACP* (Princeton, N.J.: Princeton University Press, 1975). Although the works of McPherson and women's historians are a healthy counterbalance to the vision of abolitionists as retiring from active engagement following emancipation, focusing on only activism for black rights or women's rights, these histories imply that such activists were exceptions rather than part of a larger pattern of social engagement.

4. DuBois is not the only historian to suggest that ideas developed to oppose slavery were later used to push for other reforms. See David Montgomery's classic study of the attempt to expand the struggle for equality to include labor rights, *Beyond Equality: Labor and the Radical Republicans, 1862–1872* (New York: Knopf, 1967). Amy Dru Stanley argues in *From Bondage to Contract: Wage Labor, Marriage, and the Market in the Age of Slave Emancipation* (Cambridge: Cambridge University Press, 1998) that ideas about contracts and free labor developed by critics of slavery continued to influence political debate in many areas in the postwar years. Indeed, Stanley argues that abolitionist notions about contracts and free labor in conflict with the interests and aspirations of the freed people in the South undermined Reconstruction and caused considerable conflict in

the North as reformers attempted to meld notions of contract, free labor, gender roles, and marriage into a coherent worldview. See Kathryn Kish Sklar, *Florence Kelley and the Nation's Work* (New Haven, Conn.: Yale University Press, 1995) for how the earlier generation of abolitionists influenced Florence Kelley; see also Sklar, *Women's Rights Emerges Within the Anti-Slavery Movement 1830–1870: A Brief History with Documents* (Boston: Bedford/St. Martin's, 2000).

5. It wasn't just the Garrisonian abolitionists who sustained themselves around social events. The political abolitionists involved in the Liberty and then the Free Soil Party, who ultimately took over the state Republican Party and dominated Massachusetts politics for over a decade, began as an informal gathering of anti-slavery activists. What was known as the Bird Club evolved into a regular informal Saturday meal where several dozen people would gather. Francis Bird, Howe, Andrew, Sumner, Stearns, and Sanborn were central to this gathering. See Lawrence Friedman, *Gregarious Saints: Self and Community in American Abolitionism, 1830–1870* (Cambridge: Cambridge University Press, 1982) for the social interactions among abolitionists. See also biographies of individual abolitionists, such as Henry Mayer, *All on Fire: William Lloyd Garrison and the Abolition of Slavery* (New York: St. Martin's, 1998); Russell B. Nye, *William Lloyd Garrison and the Humanitarian Reformers* (Boston: Little, Brown, 1955); Stacey Robertson, *Parker Pillsbury: Radical Abolitionist, Male Feminist* (Ithaca, N.Y.: Cornell University Press, 2000); James Brewer Stewart, *Wendell Phillips: Liberty's Hero* (Baton Rouge: Louisiana State University Press, 1986). See also Aileen S. Kraditor, *Means and Ends in American Abolitionism: Garrison and His Critics on Strategy and Tactics, 1834–1850* (New York: Pantheon, 1969).

6. It was the radicals, particularly the socialists, who looked to the abolitionists as historical models. See Ginzberg, *Women and the Work of Benevolence* for the emergence of a social control vision of reform.

7. See Lawrence Goodwyn, *Democratic Promise: The Populist Movement in America* (Oxford: Oxford University Press, 1976) for how a social movement sustains itself. This work takes a similar approach to understanding the abolitionists and what happened to them following the Civil War.

8. For a work on abolitionism that looks to understand abolitionists as people from varied backgrounds who came together and forged a common worldview, see Ronald G. Walters, *The Anti-Slavery Appeal: American Abolitionism After 1830* (Baltimore: Johns Hopkins University Press, 1978).

9. For a general study of the abolitionist movement see James Brewer Stewart, *Holy Warriors: The Abolitionists and American Slavery* (New York: Hill and Wang, 1976); Louis Filler, *The Crusade Against Slavery: 1830–1860* (New York: Harper and Rowe, 1963); Ronald Walter, *The Antislavery Appeal: American Abolitionists After 1830* (Baltimore: John Hopkins University Press, 1978). For an overview and general history of New England abolitionists and their activities, see Lawrence Lader, *The Bold Brahmins: New England's War Against Slavery: 1831–1863* (New York: E.P. Dutton, 1961).

10. Abolitionists regularly signed their letters with "till every yoke is broken," See the letters of Lydia Child and the Weston sisters, BPL. Garrison signed his letters, "Yours to break every yoke."

11. HIB, Harvard, Scrapbook.

12. See Deborah Pickman Clifford, *Mine Eyes Have Seen the Glory: A Biography of Julia Ward Howe* (Boston: Little Brown, 1979); Mary Hetherington Grant, *Private Woman, Public Person: An Account of the Life of Julia Ward Howe from*

1819–1868 (Brooklyn, N.Y.: Carlson, 1994); Jean Brown Wagoner, *Julia Ward Howe: Girl of Old New York* (New York: Bobb-Merrill, 1945); Valarie H. Ziegler, *Diva Julia: The Public Romance and Private Agony of Julia Ward Howe* (Harrisburg, Pa.: Trinity Press, 2003).

13. Bowditch's early life will get only a most sketchy coverage. Those interested in Bowditch's relationship with his father and mother will have to turn elsewhere, although anyone reading through his papers cannot but be fascinated with that story. My interest in Bowditch begins in earnest as he entered his adult years.

14. Bowditch noted that his anti-slavery activity did not force him to "neglect a single patient." HIB, Harvard, Seq., Sept. 16, 1886. In a letter to his brother Vincent Bowditch about his father, William Bowditch noted that Henry "was a committed doctor despite all his activities." BFP, MHS, Box 3, Letter from William to Vincent, Jan. 8, 1903.

15. HIB, Harvard University, Seq., Index, Nov. 19, 1885.

16. Ibid., Sept. 16, 1886.

17. Ibid., letter to his wife, n.d.

18. Most work on abolitionists focuses on those such as Wendell Phillips, William Lloyd Garrison, J. G. Birney, Frederick Douglass, Lucy Stone, Stephan Foster, or Abby Kelley Foster, whose careers were as abolitionists.

19. Theodore Weld, the intensely religious student of Lyman Beecher who led the student rebels at Lane's Seminary in revolt against the school's restriction on abolitionist activity, along with his wife Angelina Grimke Weld, Lydia Maria Child, Elizur Wright, and Stephan Foster all abandoned formal denominational religions for a more radical "religious humanity." James, Brewer Stewart, *Holy Warriors: The Abolitionists and American Slavery* (New York: Hill and Wang, 1996) 115.

20. HIB, Harvard University, Seq., May 27, 1880.

21. In his 1844 autobiographical note Bowditch noted, "I have avoided the ceremonies of Christians because they seemed to me unholy. . . . In the quiet Sabbath of my own heart I have communed with God." Bowditch believed that true faith was action for justice, "the everyday actions of life," and the sooner "we endeavor to do justly and to have mercy the sooner we shall do the world and ourselves good." Ibid., Autobiographical Note, Aug. 11, 1844. In a memorial address concerning James Deane, a Springfield doctor and abolitionist, Bowditch said, "it mattered little if one were a Catholic, or Protestant, Jew or Gentile"; what mattered was if one's "life was in the right." Library of Congress, Henry Ingersoll Bowditch Manuscripts, *An Address on the Life and Character of James Deane, M.D.* (Greenfield, Mass.: H.D. Mirick, 1858), 38.

22. HIB, Harvard, MJ, Oct. 1842.

23. Garrison, born in 1805, grew up poor in Newburyport, the son of an alcoholic. He apprenticed as a printer but aspired to be an editor. He held a number of printing jobs with various National Republican newspapers until in 1828 he took a job editing Benjamin Lundy's moderate Baltimore anti-slavery paper, *The Genius of Universal Emancipation*. Paul Goodman argued in *Of One Blood: Abolitionism and the Origins of Racial Equality* (Berkeley: University of California Press, 1998), 37–39 that it was in Baltimore that Garrison first met African Americans and became convinced that only immediate emancipation and anti-racism were the appropriate response to the evils of slavery.

24. This was not only true of the elite. Elizabeth Buffum Chace noted that when her family became militant abolitionists other Quaker families of south-

eastern Massachusetts no longer accepted them as friends. Elizabeth Buffum Chace, *Anti-Slavery Reminiscences* (Central Falls, R.I.: E.L. Freeman, 1891), GFP.

25. In an undated letter to Deborah Weston, probably 1851 Caroline Weston noted that Henry Ingersoll Bowditch was coming by to socialize and talk about what to do about the fugitive slave case. BPL, Caroline Weston letter to Deborah Weston, n.d.

26. Contrary to his later claims, Higginson showed little interest in abolitionism until after mid-1842 when he began spending more time with the Channing sisters. See TWH, Houghton, Box 4, 136, letter, July 24, 1842.

27. Some historians refer to Ann Green. I am using the spelling most consistently used in the documents.

28. Charles Sumner also introduced Julia Ward Howe to Samuel Gridley Howe.

29. Julia Ward Howe, *Reminiscences, 1819–1899* (Boston: Houghton Mifflin, 1899). In the early 1840s Samuel Gridley Howe wrote to Henry Ingersoll Bowditch expressing his reluctance to join the abolitionists, although Howe did note he objected to slavery. By the end of the decade he was more involved, and by the 1850s both he and Julia Ward Howe were deeply linked to the abolitionist community. In 1847, despite his earlier reluctance to alienate slaveholders who were open to "listening to the arguments of the north," Howe had moved into the camp of the radical abolitionists. He was on the executive committee of the Vigilance Committee, and by 1859 he was linked with John Brown and the Harpers Ferry attack. SGH, Houghton (1574), letter from Executive Committee of the Committee of Vigilance, June 3, 1847. The other members of the executive committee were Henry Ingersoll Bowditch, John W. Browne, John Andrews, John King, and William Channing.

30. Julia Ward Howe was slow to come to abolitionism, but the route she took was typical of many. She first became acquainted with Garrison and Phillips at a gathering at the home of Theodore Parker. Later as she became more socially involved with the Parkers she and her husband became more linked to the abolitionists. JWH, Houghton (320), Box 12; see also *Reminiscences.*

31. GFP, Lucy Stone letter to James Buffum, July 4, 1857.

32. See the letter of Caroline Weston to Samuel May, Oct. 21, 1871 that outlines the history of the fair, BPL, Caroline Weston Letters. See also BPL, letters of Maria Weston Chapman, Henry and Abby Foster, Henry Chapman, and Wendell Phillips; James Freeman Clarke Papers, TWH, Houghton; Lee Chambers-Schiller, "A Good Work Among the People: The Political Culture of the Boston Antislavery Fair," in Jean Fagan Yellin and John C. Van Horne, eds., *The Abolitionist Sisterhood: Women's Political Culture in Antebellum America* (Ithaca, N.Y.: Cornell University Press, 1994), 249–74.

33. The term "Hunkers" for Northern pro-slavery supporters was a constant reference for the abolitionists; see, e.g., the papers in BPL; Higginson calls the pro-slavery position of northerners "Hunkerism." TWH, Houghton, Box 4, 360. Bowditch claimed that Boston's aristocracy supported slavery while the common man was more likely to oppose it. "All the great men of respectability stood aloof." Bowditch, *Life*, 178. Julia Ward Howe remembers the city divided with the "class of wealthy conservatives and their followers" supporting slavery, and the institution being "upheld by the immense money power of the North." Howe, *Reminiscences*, 218, 252. See also note 36.

34. Henry Ingersoll Bowditch, "Notes to the Class of 1828," Pusey Library, Harvard College.

35. Recent historians have pointed out how often abolitionists slipped into patterns of paternalism particularly toward African Americans and working-class activists. See DuBois, *Feminism and Suffrage*, 96–100 and particularly 119–27. See also Yellin, *Women and Sisters*, 81. See Louis Michele Newman, *White Women's Rights: The Racial Origins of Feminism in the United States* (Oxford: Oxford University Press, 1999) for the paternalism of white reformers. Recent historiography is right to emphasize how privileged many of these reformers were. Certainly most of those who occupy the central place in this narrative came from privilege. That white abolitionists at times asserted their white privilege or that elite activists asserted their social position should not be surprising. What in many ways is more historically significant is that such behavior was not more common among these reformers. In a world so highly racialized and a region notorious for its hierarchy, these New Englanders struggled to fight racism and to some extent privilege, not only in society but in themselves. This work argues that, by painting these reformers as privileged and removed from the working-class or black community, historians miss a significant part of the story. Putting them in a social movement with a moral vision, a natural rights ideology, and a social bond will help us better understand why these reformers fought against privilege while so many of their peers did not.

36. Thomas Wentworth Higginson noted that, unlike the civil service reform, the anti-slavery movement "was predominately a people's movement, based on the simplest human instincts and far stronger for a time in the factories and shoe shops than in the pulpits or colleges." He noted that it was a common saying about abolitionists that "radicalism went with the smell of leather." Thomas Wentworth Higginson, *Cheerful Yesterdays* (Boston: Houghton Mifflin, 1898), 114.

37. Franklin Sanborn remembered the "broadcloth mob" using their influence as men of "property and standing" to attack abolitionists to maintain their "trade with South Carolina." GFP. Julia Ward Howe remembers prewar Boston divided between anti-slavery people and "the class of wealthy conservatives and their followers," and that Webster, who she felt had sold out freedom, was "the political idol of the Massachusetts aristocracy." Howe, *Reminiscences*, 218.

38. BPL, Theodore Parker, Sermons, Sermon 12, "The New Crime Against Humanity," June 4, 1854.

39. TWH, Houghton (365), TWH letter to Sam, June 29, 1851.

40. Parker made this point again and again in his sermons. In Sermon 14, he argued that in America "money is power. . . . In politics money has more influence than in most despotic countries. National legislation almost invariably favors capital and not the laboring hand. . . . There is nothing but the voter's naked ballot holds money in check." BPL, Theodore Parker, Sermons.

41. Howe, *Reminiscences*, 252.

42. BPL, Theodore Parker, Sermons.

43. Bowditch, *Life*, 2: 334–35.

44. See Gilbert Barnes, *The Anti-Slavery Impulse, 1830–1844* (Gloucester, Mass.: P. Smith, 1957). Barnes's thesis has been refined and attacked since it was first published, but the central idea that intense religious belief explains much of the abolitionist involvement has continued to be a central focus of work on abolitionism. See, e.g., Donald M. Scott, "Abolition as a Sacred Vocation," in Lewis Perry and Michael Fellman, eds., *Antislavery Reconsidered: New Perspectives on the Abolitionists* (Baton Rouge: Louisiana State University Press, 1979), 51–74; Douglas M. Strong, *Perfectionist Politics: Abolitionism and the Religious Tensions of*

American Democracy (Syracuse, N.Y.: Syracuse University Press, 1999); Lewis Perry, *Radical Abolitionism: Anarchy and the Government of God in Antislavery Thought* (Ithaca, N.Y.: Cornell University Press, 1973); Donald G. Matthews, *Slavery and Methodism: A Chapter in the American Morality, 1780–1845* (Princeton, N.J.: Princeton University Press, 1965); Friedman, *Gregarious Saints*; Stewart, *Holy Warriors.*

45. Walter, *The Antislavery Appeal* does a good job of pointing out the varied religious experiences of those involved in abolitionism and the problem of finding a common religious impetus to abolitionists' commitment. Paul Goodman made a similar point in *Of One Blood.* Once on the search for motivation, one must also ask the motivation behind those who became caught up in the revivals. See Louis Filler, *The Crusade Against Slavery, 1830–1860* (New York: Harper, 1963) for examples of abolitionists who were not identified with strong religious beliefs.

46. Other historians have looked to psychological explanations for abolitionists' commitment, such as strong mothers or harsh, judgmental fathers. Again this explanation explains less than at first appears. Many Americans with strong mothers and harsh fathers did not join the abolitionists; others with such parents supported slavery; others with weak mothers and warm fathers became abolitionists.

47. Although it is not possible to know what was in the minds of those activists, if we are to give credence to their professions of religious faith we should also give credence to their claims about natural rights.

48. Locke did accept slavery, but within very limited contexts very different from the American South. Thus it was not Locke's statement on slavery but his defense of property to which the South was attracted.

49. To be sure, there is potential for losing sight of underlying causal explanations when one accepts what historical actors say about themselves on face value. On the other hand, the tendency to find original motivations in sociopsychological factors often leads to explanations that account for only a small number of those investigated or could explain many different behaviors.

50. Some historians might find the desire for social justice a not particularly sophisticated explanation for the thinking of these abolitionists, but historians should not easily dismiss the understanding historical characters had of their own actions and motives.

51. HIB, Harvard, MJ, Oct. 18, 1842.

52. The founding document of the American Anti-Slavery Society contained the phrase "to break every yoke and let the oppressed go free."

53. Aileen Kraditor has shown that the radical anti-slavery political activists were wrong in assuming that the immediatists who rejected linking themselves to one particular party were anti-political. The immediatists were political, but afraid that linking themselves to one party would limit their ability to create pressure to end slavery and involve compromise that would undermine that objective. I am arguing here that this difference in strategy, although important to all the players at the time, did not divide them socially or even that much politically. Henry Bowditch was both a Liberty Party Candidate and supporter of the Free Soil Party and an officer in the Garrisonian Massachusetts Anti-Slavery Society. *Annual Reports, Massachusetts Anti-Slavery Society*, vols. 11– 22. See also Kraditor, Means and Ends.

54. Thomas Wentworth Higginson, *Part of a Man's Life* (Boston: Houghton Mifflin, 1903), 128.

55. Higginson also noted the conflict among abolitionists: "consider the sub-divisions of the Garrisonian abolitionists themselves, after slavery itself was abolished at a period when I remember to have seen Edmund Quincy walk halfway up a stairway and turn suddenly round to descend, merely to avoid Wendell Phillips who was coming downstairs! Having worked side by side together . . . the two men had yet separated in bitterness on the interpretation of a will made by a fellow laborer, Francis Jackson." Higginson, *Part of a Man's Life*, 128.

56. Bonnie S. Anderson, *Joyous Greetings: The First International Women's Movement, 1830–1880* (Oxford: Oxford University Press, 2000), 126.

57. In recent years much good work has been done on black abolitionism. See, e.g., the essays in Donald M. Jacobs, ed., *Courage and Conscience: Black and White Abolitionists in Boston* (Bloomington: Indiana University Press, 1993).

58. See Friedman, *Gregarious Saints*.

59. One of the "sisters of reform" in which activists such as Lucy Stone, Thomas Wentworth Higginson, and Lucretia Mott were involved was temperance. Because following the Civil War most of the reformers followed here were less involved in temperance reform, it will not play a significant role in this work, although it had a major early influence on reform activity, especially for the role of women.

60. See Montgomery, *Beyond Equality* for a discussion of labor and radical republicans.

61. Bowditch, *Life*, 1: 114, 146.

62. Beginning in the 1850s Howe worked for reforming treatment of juvenile delinquents, advocating a combination of schooling and family placement. He continued pushing this effort into his years as head of the Massachusetts Board of Charities.

63. See James McPherson, *The Struggle for Equality: Abolitionists and the Negro in the Civil War and Reconstruction* (Princeton, N.J.: Princeton University Press, 1964) and *The Abolitionist Legacy* and Fredrickson, *The Inner Civil War* for the abolitionists' view of the post-Civil War struggle for equality.

64. To be sure, Sanborn and Howe were inconsistent in their approach to charity and the infirm. They called for state intervention in wages and working conditions, but were skeptical of state charity and thought private ventures might be preferable. They also opposed large institutional settings and looked to put troubled youths in private homes of morally upright families.

65. The issue of race as well as personalities divided the National Woman Suffrage Association from the New England-based American Woman Suffrage Association. Although historians have noted that the conflict between the two organizations originated with AWSA activists arguing that the NWSA was abandoning African Americans, and many works on this split have tended to see the issue as one of personality, political expediency, and the role of males in the AWSA, the leaders of the AWSA themselves focused on the approach to race and African American rights as the crucial difference. See Newman, *White Women's Rights*. The AWSA took a strong position in favor of racial equality and women's rights. Julia Ward Howe, one of the leaders, was concerned when the two organizations merged that the Stanton-Anthony wing of the NWSA would dominate and the new organization would abandon black rights. She fought vigorously though unsuccessfully to keep equal rights for all as part of the new organization. See JWH, Houghton (320), Box 13, "Draft of address to Association for the Advancement of Women, 1890." See also TWH, Houghton, letter, Aug. 15, 1869, calling for a convention for Women's Rights, to form the AWSA.

66. *Boston Globe,* Jan. 20, 1892.

67. HIB, MHS, Miscellaneous Volumes, Box 2, Journal compiled by Vincent Yardley Bowditch. At a Wendell Phillips Club meeting honoring Frederick Douglass, Douglass noted that Henry Ingersoll Bowditch was the first to open his house to Douglass. Douglass also acknowledged Oliver Johnson and the black abolitionist Lewis Hayden, and talked of Maria Weston Chapman, Francis Jackson, Joseph Southwick, Samuel Philbrick, Ellis Gaylord, Samuel Sewell, and Edmund Quincy as important leaders of the early abolitionist struggle. HIB, Harvard, Seq. At another point Douglass said of Bowditch, "he was the first in Boston to treat me as a man."

68. GFP, Harriet Winslow Sewall letter to Francis J. Garrison, March 2, 1889.

Chapter 1. The People and the Times

Epigraph: HIB, Harvard, MS, July 30, 1880.

1. See JWH, Houghton (340), Box 10, manuscripts, where Howe reflects that she was uninterested in suffrage. She also notes that she became involved with the Women's Club to find company for her studies.

2. Julia Ward Howe, *Reminiscences, 1819–1899* (Boston: Houghton Mifflin, 1899), 374.

3. Ibid., 375.

4. Laura Howe Richards and Maud Howe Elliot, *Julia Ward Howe, 1819–1910* (Boston: Houghton Mifflin, 1925) 198.

5. Howe, *Reminiscences,* 375.

6. JWH, Houghton (322). By the 1860s Julia was speaking out in public forums on philosophy and social justice, although not yet for equal rights for women, even though her husband Samuel Gridley Howe vigorously objected to women and especially Julia speaking in public. See *Reminiscences,* 305. She wrote in her diary in 1860, "I feel that a woman's whole moral responsibility is lowered by the fact that she must never obey a transcendent command of conscience. Man can give her nothing to take the place of this. It is the divine right of the human soul." Quoted in Richards and Elliot, *Julia Ward Howe,* 115, 134. Samuel Gridley Howe's objection to Julia's independence was a constant source of conflict in their marriage. Julia demanded intellectual and moral equality with her husband even as she shunned woman's rights organizations. In an early article, "Woman's Rights Question," Julia allowed that a woman's status and rights depend upon her husband, "To him belong the functions of the outer world," yet she argued that women were morally independent and must be given moral equality. A woman "must study like a man to know what to do." JWH, Houghton (320). Theodore Parker and his wife were Julia's closest friends. She attended Parker's church until her husband insisted that for the children's sake they join another church. Besides being a radical abolitionist, Parker insisted on "the claims of the sex to equality and education" and referred to God as "Father and Mother of us all." Julia heard Lucretia Mott preach in Parker's pulpit and attended a sermon by the feminist Rev. Antoinette Brown Blackwell, Lucy Stone's sister-in-law. When, after a long fight with Samuel Gridley Howe, Julia left Parker's church, she joined James Freeman Clarke's church. Clarke like Parker was a committed radical abolitionist and woman's rights supporter. Howe, *Reminiscences,* 166, 245.

7. Quoted in Richards and Elliot, *Julia Ward Howe,* 115, 134.

8. Julia Ward Howe to her daughter, ibid., 196.

9. Ibid., 22, 23.

10. See ibid. for Julia's early life in New York as she described it to her daughters.

11. Howe, *Reminiscences*, 82.

12. Before their marriage Howe wrote to Julia's brother Sam, worried that Julia's intellectual interests would make her unfit to be a good homemaker and companion. Instead of warning Julia off the wedding, Sam assured Howe that her intellectual pursuits would in no way decrease her ability as a helpmate. See Valarie H. Ziegler, *Diva Julia: The Public Romance and Private Agony of Julia Ward Howe* (Harrisburg, Pa.: Trinity Press, 2003) for the difficulties of her marriage.

13. JWH, Houghton (320), Box 15, speeches. Speaking from her own experience in a critique of traditional marriage, Julia pictures Samuel Gridley Howe's expectation of her that she should "intoxicate him." He expected her to submit "to blind confidence" and "acquiesce in his judgment." She longed for an equal marriage "where the joys of sympathy or mutual help . . . [create the] equilateral train."

14. Ibid. Julia noted that husbands assume control over "the sexual aspect of a woman."

15. Howe, *Reminiscences*, 153.

16. JWH, Houghton (320), Box 15, speeches. In an 1870 talk in Concord, Julia noted that when first meeting Phillips at Parker's house she thought him quixotic. In another speech, Box 10, manuscripts, she noted "my husband had not been one of the early abolitionists."

17. Ibid.

18. Howe, *Reminiscences*, 218. Despite an earlier claim that her abolitionism cast her out of Boston society, Julia claimed that she could be friends with people "diverse in political persuasion."

19. Howe, *Reminiscences*, 150.

20. Howe, *Reminiscences*, 305. When Julia pointed out that his admiration of Florence Nightingale involved her public activity, Howe told her that, much as he admired Nightingale, if he had loved or been engaged to her he would have given her up if she had commenced her career as a public woman.

21. For a good description of the Howes' troubled private life, see Mary Hetherington Grant, *Private Woman, Public Person: An Account of the Life of Julia Ward Howe from 1819 to 1868* (Brooklyn, N.Y.: Carlson, 1994), 58–94. See also Deborah Pickman Clifford, *Mine Eyes Have Seen the Glory: A Biography of Julia Ward Howe* (Boston: Little Brown, 1979). Julia gave birth to three children; see Clifford for Julia's anxiety about childbirth and accompanying depressions. In 1850 the Howes went to Europe. Julia stayed on in Rome with her two younger children for her health and to continue her study of Hebrew. There she met and fell in love with a poet from Philadelphia, Horace Wallace. When word of the affair reached Samuel Gridley Howe in Boston, he was furious. He wrote her several nasty letters and demanded she return to Boston or he would divorce her. See Clifford, 105–6 and Grant 96–99 for Julia's stay in Rome; Clifford believes the relationship between Julia and Wallace was only a close friendship.

22. JWH, Houghton (320), Box 15, speeches.

23. JWH, Houghton (322), n.d., probably early 1860s.

24. Faced with Julia's growing national prominence, her husband attempted to win the adult children over to his position that she was neglecting him and her family duties. Julia tried to mediate between the demands of her family and

her intellectual and political pursuits by articulating a position that historians called "maternalism," the idea that women and mothers played a special moral role in society; see *Reminiscences*, 328. Yet she also held to the idea of universal rights and called for equal rights for women, claiming that the struggle for women's rights was part of the larger struggle for human rights. Historians have called this wing of the women's movement "equal rights" feminism. See Ellen Carol DuBois, *Woman Suffrage and Women's Rights* (New York: New York University Press, 1998). In an 1870 talk in Concord Howe argued that, although progressive men might be sympathetic to women's injustices, men "can not tell me how I feel. I know it better than [they] do. So why are we to persuade men to make laws for us when we [should be] able to make them ourselves." She also notes that "the more thoughtful men now found that women were a good plan and more would be the better, the more they were allowed to be women and not simply no men." JWH, Houghton (320), Box 15, speeches. Howe's life indicates that the divisions between difference feminism—feminists who argued that women had a unique role to play in society because of their difference—and equal rights feminism break down in the case of Julia Ward Howe.

25. TWH, Houghton, letter to his sister, Aug. 30, 1870.

26. The abolitionists referred to the mob as the "broadcloth mob" (see below), or as made up of persons or men of "property and standing." Parker called the crowds that supported the shipping of the fugitive Sims back into slavery "Gentlemen of Property and Standing." See Leonard L. Richards, *Gentlemen of Property and Standing: Anti-Abolition Mobs in Jacksonian Democracy* (London: Oxford University Press, 1970).

27. Bowditch, *Life*, 1: 99–100.

28. Ibid., 1: 100. Bowditch referred to the mob as the "broadcloth mob, and claimed that after confronting established citizens for failing to aid Garrison, he was disgusted and vowed in his heart, "I am an Abolitionist from this very moment." It should be noted that at other times in his life Bowditch would claim other moments as being the pivotal one. Bowditch, *Life*, 1: 100. The issue that incensed Bowditch in 1835 was the denial of free speech. 99, 100.

29. HIB, MHS, Miscellaneous Volumes, Box 1, "Memoir of visit to Salem, 1889."

30. Bowditch's reputation as a navigator was enhanced by the story of his sailing into Salem Harbor through a blinding snowstorm. Whether or not it was true, the story had wide currency. See Samuel Eliot Morison, *The Maritime History of Massachusetts, 1783–1860* (Boston: Houghton Mifflin, 1921).

31. The *New American Practical Navigator* was a total revision of an earlier work by John Moore. Bowditch had published two revisions of Moore in the late 1790s; with this work he completely reworked Moore's book and calculations.

32. HIB, MHS, Miscellaneous Volumes, Box 1, "Memoir of visit to Salem, 1889." Morison, *Maritime History*; see also HIB, MHS, Miscellaneous Volumes, Box 2, "Notes from Memorial Meeting of the Mass Medical Society," talk by Frederick Knight, and C. F. Folsom, "Henry Ingersoll Bowditch," *Proceedings of the American Academy of Arts and Sciences* 28.

33. The MHLIC offered depositors trusts under their own names or in someone else's. One could draw regular interest or have the interest added to the principal. Some accounts terminated in a set number of years, others lasted the life of the depositor, still others could be passed down to heirs. And in an age where husbands controlled a woman's assets, a trust could be established for female beneficiaries where the income was "for her separate use, free from

the debts, control or interference by any husband she now has or may hereafter have." Quoted in Robert F. Dalzell, Jr., *Enterprising Elite: The Boston Associ-
ates and the World They Made* (Cambridge, Mass.: Harvard University Press,
1987), 104.

34. By 1830 MHLIC had $5 million in trust deposits but only $67,000 in insurance policies and annuities. Ibid., 103.

35. Henry was privately tutored in reading and mathematics till he was old
enough to be enrolled in John Walsh's Grammar School on Green Street. The
boys at Walsh's school learned their lessons, although Henry did not stand out
as one of the school's top scholars.

36. Enjoying himself in the neighborhood involved general mischief as well
as fights with boys of other sections of town. Most of this activity, fortunately for
Bowditch, occurred below his father's radar, for Nathaniel Bowditch had little
tolerance of misbehavior and Henry very much wanted his father's approval,
which his father was niggardly in giving out. HIB, MHS, Miscellaneous Volumes, Box 1, "Memoir of visit to Salem, 1889."

37. HIB, Harvard, MJ, Vol. 1, June 23, Nov. 15, 1827.

38. Ibid., May 12, 1827.

39. Ibid., Sept. 1, 1827.

40. Bowditch chose medicine rather than surgery because he didn't want to
cut and he liked the science of problem solving in medicine. HIB, MHS, Scrapbook; Folsom, "Henry Ingersoll Bowditch," 3.

41. George Bancroft studied history and philosophy in Germany, as did J. G.
Cogswell. When Bowditch arrived in Paris, he soon fell in with several New Englanders also studying there, including Mason Warren and Copley Green, as well
as Oliver Wendell Homes and James Jackson. Theodore Lyman, the famous bi-
ologist and philanthropist, completed his studies at Harvard under Agassiz and
then sailed for Europe to complete his education.

42. Bowditch noted the generosity of his father "in giving me the means to
visit Europe. His father's translation of Pierre-Simon Laplace had put a financial burden on the family, but gave him a "high reputation" in Europe and
made for "a warm reception [for Bowditch] as his son from all the mathemati-
cians" and scientists. Even when Bowditch went to London, his father's reputation preceded him. Charles Babbidge, inventor of the calculating machine,
took Bowditch under his wing. Likewise the professors of Cambridge warmly
welcomed him. HIB, Harvard, Seq.

43. See William Coleman, *Death Is a Social Disease: Public Health and Political
Economy in Early Industrial France* (Madison: University of Wisconsin Press,
1982), for a discussion of France's development of medical education.

44. In a letter to Bowditch, Pierre Charles Alexander Louis, leader of the new
clinicians, noted that he only observed patients, he did not treat them. HIB,
Harvard, B MS Misc 2fd Letters, Louis letter to Bowditch, Oct. 1, 1840. HIB,
Harvard, MJ, Vol. 1842–1849, Sept. 15, 1872; Henry Ingersoll Bowditch, *Brief
Memories of Louis and Some of His Contemporaries in the Parisian School of Medicine
of Forty Years Ago* (Boston: John Wilson, 1872).

45. Bowditch very much missed his close friend Jackson when he returned to
Boston. Jackson's death a year after returning to Boston was a great blow to
Bowditch. See HIB, Harvard, HMSC 8.2, Bowditch letters to James Jackson Sr.,
May 16, July 3, 1834. Louis's Société Médicale d'Observation laid out its princi-
ples as to make members good students of pathology through group review of
observations; to influence medicine by bringing forward the idea of the impor-

tance of observation and recording the phenomena of disease; and to publish material based on "strict deduction from these facts the laws which regulate disease" so that the science of medicine could advance. Bowditch, *Life*, 1: 37, letter to his mother. See also Bowditch, *Brief Memories*, 11.

Louis also founded the numerical method of medicine that focused on looking at groups of patients with similar symptoms and comparing different treatments to determine what was effective. The numerical method also called for large numbers of observations. Louis noted in one letter to Bowditch that he observed 138 cases of typhoid in order to understand it and compared it to 700 other cases of acute diseases. HIB, Harvard, B MS Misc 2fd Letters, Louis letter to Bowditch, June 3, 1841.

46. Ibid. See also HIB, Harvard, MJ, Vol. 1842–1849, Sept. 15, 1875. After leaving Paris, he was in constant communication with Louis and stayed with him whenever visiting Europe. On learning of the death of Louis, August 13, 1872, Bowditch wrote in his journal about his "dear friend and most honored master in medicine," "I fear I can not review with any skill the sweet and all powerful influences exerted by Louis as a leader in Medicine and as a dear friend upon my whole life." Ibid.

47. HIB, Harvard, MJ, Vol. 1842–1849, Sept. 15, 1875.

48. Letter to his mother, Jan. 27, 1833, Bowditch, *Life*, 1: 37.

49. Bowditch, *Brief Memories*, 10.

50. HIB, Harvard, MJ, Vol. 1, Dec. 14, 1827.

51. Bowditch, *Brief Memories*, 19.

52. HIB, Harvard, MJ, Vol. 1842–1849, Sept. 15, 1872. Once back in Boston, Bowditch sent Louis Shattuck's statistical work on disease and death in Boston. Shattuck, like Louis, approached the problem of disease inductively, drawing conclusions from large aggregates of data. Bowditch connected Shattuck to Louis, and Louis and Shattuck began exchanging letters. Louis advised Shattuck on his statistical methods. HIB, Harvard, B MS Misc.2fd Letters, Louis letter to Bowditch, May 30, 1836.

53. Through his father's connections Bowditch met Adrien-Marie Legendre, Madame Laplace, and the Marquis de Lafayette. In London his father's name led him to William Herschel and Charles Babbage. HIB, MHS, Box 3.

54. For example, Victor Hugo was Louis's brother-in-law. Bowditch, *Brief Memories*.

55. HIB, Harvard, MJ, Vol. 1842–1889.

56. Bowditch wrote to his parents that troops are being used to "keep the people in as much subjection as under the old regime." See Bowditch, *Life*, 1: 42.

57. HIB, Harvard, Seq. Following his year in Paris, Bowditch was to move to London for a second year of study, but after a brief visit to the city he decided that British medical education was far behind the French, and British intellectual life was stifling. In defense of his decision to return to Paris, he wrote his father that British doctors were not serious observers of patients, nor did they seem to care for them. Subsequently, the doctor and social justice advocate in training returned to Paris for his second year. Letter to his father, Aug. 8, 1833, Bowditch, *Life*, 1: 55; Oct. 29, 1833. 1: 62, 63.

58. Bowditch argued that by his second year he had become "more American," by denouncing the troops used "to keep the people in as much subjection as under the old regime. Bowditch, *Life*, 1: 42.

59. Ibid., 1: 72.

60. Ibid., 1: 50.

61. Ibid., 1: 73.

62. Letter to his father, July 31, 1834, ibid., 1: 86; letter to his father, undated, 1: 89.

63. The bleeding lancet was such a standard medical instrument that it came to symbolize the profession. To this day the leading medical journal in Britain is the *Lancet*.

64. Bowditch, *Life*, 1: 99.

65. Henry's parents gave their approval well before Olivia came to America, but both died shortly before Olivia arrived. Letter of Nathaniel Bowditch to Olivia Yardley, March 10, 1838, Bowditch, *Life*, 1: 95, 96. See also BFP, MHS, Family Genealogy.

66. In 1852 Bowditch helped found a private medical school, Boylston Medical School, but it fell apart three years later. HIB, MHS, Scrapbook; Knight talk.

67. The home also became a meeting place of abolitionists. BFP, Peabody, Box 13, folder 11, Documents of the Vigilance Committee of the Massachusetts Anti-Slavery Society.

68. Bowditch is credited with being the first physician to use and popularize Wyman's method of relieving fluid around the lungs with thoracentesis. HIB, MHS, Miscellaneous Volumes, Box 2, Journal by Vincent Yardley Bowditch.

69. HIB, MHS, Miscellaneous, Scrapbook; Knight speech.

70. HIB, Harvard, MJ, Vol. 1842–1889, June 26, 1842.

71. Bowditch was not at all disconcerted by French anti-clericalism. At one point he argued that the "majority of churches were a hindrance to humanity; the true leaders of philanthropy were outside the church," and that the church "was faithless to humanity." Bowditch, *Life*, 1: 117.

72. Ibid., 1: 105. In college Bowditch skipped required chapel and attended a Universalist service and a Catholic mass. HIB, Harvard, MJ, Vol. 1, Sept. 7, Dec. 9, Dec. 25, 1827. In Paris the skepticism of the French anti-clerics fit well with Bowditch's belief in keeping an open mind and investigating all assumptions, including religious.

73. HIB, MHS, Miscellaneous Volumes, Box 1, Memoir of visit to Salem, 1889.

74. HIB, Harvard, MJ, Vol. 1842–1889, Aug. 9, 1845.

75. Ibid., Aug. 11, 1844.

76. Ibid.

77. HIB, MHS, Miscellaneous Volumes, Box 3, William Bowditch letter to Vincent Y. Bowditch. See Scrapbook; 3; Folsom, "Henry Ingersoll Bowditch," 3, 28

78. He also wanted his children to form their own religious faiths and respect that others who differed from their views might see the Almighty as clearly but from a different point of view. "The sun shines on one part of the earth differently from what it does on another, yet God governs all parts a little and fits each with its appropriate surroundings of his spirit." MJ, Vol. 4, letter to his wife from the Isles of Shoals, Sept. 16, 1863.

79. HIB, MHS, Miscellaneous Volumes Scrapbook, 3; Folsom, "Henry Ingersoll Bowditch."

80. HIB, Harvard, MJ, March 20, 1849.

81. Ibid., May 1880.

82. Ibid., Oct. 18, 1842.

83. See Eric C. Schneider, *In the Web of Class: Delinquents and Reformers in Boston, 1810s–1930s* (New York: New York University Press, 1992), 29 for the Warren Street Chapel and child reform.

84. HIB, Harvard, MJ, Aug. 12, 1844.

85. Bowditch, *Life*, 105.

86. HIB, Harvard, MJ, Vol. 1842–1889, Oct. 18, 1842. Ironically Bowditch broke with the Warren Street Chapel over slavery and equal rights. When the Chapel refused to let Bowditch organize a program against slavery for the community and would not accept black children in 1842, Bowditch resigned. Bowditch, *Life*, 112.

87. HIB, Harvard, MJ, Aug. 31, 1846.

88. Ibid., Oct. 18, 1842.

89. Ibid.

90. Ibid.

91. In a letter to Maria Weston Chapman, Aug. 6, 1843, explaining why he did not initially join the Massachusetts Anti-Slavery Society, Bowditch wrote, "the reasons that influenced me were a fear of losing my individuality in a society which in early times at least presented such a perfectly united band that all seemed to be of one mind. I came earnestly from Europe where the individual is much more of an individual that with us- and I determined to keep free from all shackles spiritual or temporal-religious or political." BPL, H. I. Bowditch letter to Chapman, Aug. 6, 1843.

92. HIB, Harvard, Seq., Sept. 16, 1886.

93. BPL, HIB letter to Chapman, Aug. 6, 1843.

94. HIB, Harvard, MJ, July 30, 1880.

95. Ibid., Autobiographical note, Aug. 11, 1844.

96. Ibid., Oct. 18, 1842.

97. Ibid., MJ, Vol. 3, 154.

98. Elizabeth Buffum Chace, *Anti-Slavery Reminiscences* (Central Falls, R.I.: E.L. Freeman, 1891), GFP.

Chapter 2. "With Other Good Souls"

Epigraph: HIB, MHS, Box 2, Scrapbook.

1. HIB, Harvard, Seq. See also HIB, MHS, Box 3, manuscript, 99.

2. HIB, MHS, 100.

3. Ibid., 99–100.

4. For a description of the riot and the events leading up to it, see Henry Mayer, *All on Fire: William Lloyd Garrison and the Abolition of Slavery* (New York: St. Martin's, 1998).

5. BPL, Bowditch letter to Chapman, Aug. 6, 1843.

6. Bowditch, *Life*, 100.

7. BPL, Bowditch letter to Chapman.

8. Ibid.

9. HIB, MHS, Box 2, Scrapbook; C. F. Folsom, "Henry Ingersoll Bowditch," *Proceedings of the American Association of Arts and Sciences* 28.

10. BPL, Bowditch letter to Chapman.

11. Quoted in Mayer, *All on Fire*, 176.

12. See Paul Goodman, *Of One Blood: Abolitionism and the Origins of Racial Equality* (Berkeley: University of California Press, 1998) for the abolitionists' commitment to racial equality. Although I did not find Goodman's explanation for abolitionists' egalitarianism convincing, his analysis of their commitment to the ideal of racial equality is sound.

13. Richard Hofstadter has Phillips rushing out and asking what was happening to Garrison. This event did occur, but it was Bowditch not Phillips who rushed out to confront the crowd. Phillips observed the crowd from his office window. Hofstadter, *The American Political Tradition* (New York: Knopf, 1973).

14. Ibid., 138.

15. See James Brewer Stewart, *Wendell Phillips: Liberty's Hero* (Baton Rouge: Louisiana State University Press, 1986), 24–35, for a description of Phillips's early conservatism. After law school, where he studied under Justice Joseph Story, Phillips went into practice in Lowell with Thomas Hopkins, who later led a mob against abolitionists, and was an avid supporter of Daniel Webster; he later opened a law office on Court Street. Stewart believes that beneath Phillips's youthful conservatism was a commitment to equality that would eventually dominate his views. I am more inclined to accept Phillips's early positions at face value and see his radicalism as a product of his involvement in abolitionism.

16. Ibid., 35.

17. Ibid., 139.

18. Quoted in ibid., 43.

19. Ibid., 139. Hofstadter spells Greene's first name "Anne." In this work I follow the pattern in the letters to and from her and use "Ann."

20. Stewart, *Wendell Phillips*, 42.

21. Ibid., 44.

22. Quoted in Lawrence Friedman, *Gregarious Saints: Self and Community in American Abolitionism, 1830–1870* (Cambridge: Cambridge University Press, 1982), 159.

23. Hofstadter, *American Political Tradition*, 139; see also Stewart, *Wendell Phillips*, 56–58; Mayer, *All on Fire*, 238. At the Faneuil Hall meeting Phillips began in support of free speech but ended embracing abolitionism.

24. Lewis Perry argues in *Radical Abolitionism: Anarchy and the Government of God in Antislavery Thought* (Ithaca, N.Y.: Cornell University Press, 1973) that those who came to abolitionism through religious conversion believed slavery was a sin because it came between man and God.

25. BPL, Bowditch letter to Chapman.

26. See Friedman, *Gregarious Saints* and Perry, *Radical Abolitionism* for a description of the religious motivation of those associated with the immediacy wing of anti-slavery. See also John Thomas, *The Liberator: William Lloyd Garrison, a Biography* (Boston: Little, Brown, 1963); James Brewer Stewart, *William Lloyd Garrison and the Challenge of Emancipation* (Arlington Heights, Ill.: H. Davidson, 1992); Mayer, *All on Fire*; Donald Scott, "Abolition as a Sacred Vocation," in Lewis Perry and Michael Fellman, eds., *Antislavery Reconsidered: New Perspectives on the Abolitonists* (Baton Rouge: Louisiana State University Press, 1979), for a discussion of the religious dimension of the early abolitionists. For a view of abolitionism that sees more diversity within the community see Aileen Kraditor, *Means and Ends in American Abolitionism: Garrison and His Critics on Strategy and Tactics, 1834–1850* (New York: Pantheon, 1968).

27. In other cases personal reasons reinforced religious or political reasons for joining the movement. Parker Pillsbury, a poor farm boy from New Hampshire, was influenced by the religious enthusiasm of Charles Finney to commit himself to the ministry. At Andover Theological Seminary, Pillsbury heard about Garrison and George Thompson and joined the abolitionist camp. There he met and married the fiercely abolitionist Sarah Sargent. See Stacey M.

Robertson, *Parker Pillsbury: Radical Abolitionist, Male Feminist* (Ithaca, N.Y.: Cornell University Press, 2000) for a description of Pillsbury's movement into abolitionism.

28. TWH. Houghton, Box 4 (149), TWH letter to his mother, Feb. 1843.

29. TWH, Houghton, Box 4 (91), TWH letter to Frank, Feb. 17, 1841.

30. Thomas Wentworth Higginson, *Cheerful Yesterdays* (Boston: Houghton Mifflin, 1898) 98.

31. TWH, Houghton, Box 4 (136), TWH letter to his mother, July 24, 1842. See also Higginson, *Cheerful Yesterdays*, 97, 98, 126.

32. TWH, Houghton, Box 4 (145), TWH "engagement announcement," 1842; Higginson, *Cheerful Yesterdays*, 126.

33. Higginson claims the radical abolitionists wore beards, not the custom in the 1840s. A derogatory term for them was "men with beards." Lowell's initiation into abolitionism was marked by growing a beard. Higginson, *Cheerful Yesterdays*, 118.

34. Higginson also claims he was influenced by two tracts Mary insisted he read, Lydia Maria Child, *Appeal in Favor of That Class of Americans Called Africans* (Boston: Allen and Ticknor, 1833), and Harriet Martineau, *The Martyr Age of the United States* (Boston: Weeks, Jordan, 1839). See *A Part of a Man's Life* and *Cheerful Yesterdays*, 126.

35. TWH, Houghton, Box 4 (350), TWH letter to his mother, Aug. 7, 1850.

36. TWH, Houghton, Box 4 (400). TWH letter probably to his mother, undated. Before he accepted the Worcester position, Higginson wrote his mother that he might turn it down and spend his time "in congenial pursuits" such as literature. TWH, Houghton, Box 4 (395), TWH letter to his mother, April 22, 1852. She strongly urged him to take the job and settle down. TWH, Houghton, Box 4 (395), mother's letter to TWH, April 16, 1852.

37. TWH, Houghton, Box 4 (393), TWH letter to Mary, April 16, 1852.

38. Higginson, *Cheerful Yesterdays*, 128, 132.

39. Quoted in James Tuttleton, *Thomas Wentworth Higginson* (Boston: Twayne, 1978), 29. Higginson and Phillips were not the only abolitionists influenced by the women they fell in love with. Elizabeth Buffum Chace, raised in a Quaker abolitionist family in Fall River (her father, Arnold Buffum, was the first president of the New England Anti-Slavery Society), brought her husband into abolitionism, and their home soon became a center for radical abolitionism. "When I married," she remembered, "and my husband's attention was called to the question, he readily accepted the anti-slavery principles and remained faithful to them during his life." GFP, Elizabeth Buffum Chace, *Anti-Slavery Reminiscences* (Central Falls, R.I.: E.L. Freeman, 1891), 11. Her sister Sarah married Nathaniel Borden and brought him into anti-slavery work. Their home became a safe home for runaway slaves (27).

40. Whittier's "The Hero," based on Howe, became a popular New England poem.

41. Laura Howe Richards, *Samuel Gridley Howe* (New York: Appleton-Century, 1935), 5.

42. Quoted in ibid., 24.

43. Ibid., 57.

44. See Samuel Gridley Howe, *Letters and Journal of Samuel Gridley Howe*, ed. Laura E. Richards (Boston: Dana Estes, 1906) for a description of this period of Howe's life. See also Franklin Sanborn, *Dr. S. G. Howe: The Philanthropist* (New York: Funk and Wagnalls, 1891).

45. Quoted in Harold Schwartz, *Samuel Gridley Howe: Social Reformer, 1801–1876* (Cambridge, Mass.: Harvard University Press, 1956) 151.

46. SGH, Houghton (960), SGH letter to HIB, Feb. 3, 1843.

47. Laura E. Richards and Maud Howe Elliot, *Julia Ward Howe, 1819–1910* (Boston: Houghton Mifflin, 1925), 115. See Mary H. Grant, *Private Woman, Public Person: An Account of the Life of Julia Ward Howe from 1819 to 1868* (New York: Carlson, 1994), 99, for Julia's marriage.

48. For Maria Chapman's critique of Parker's position, see BPL, Maria Weston Chapman Papers, letter to unknown, Nov. 1842. Higginson claimed Parker said that between those who did the work and those who use the work he preferred those who worked. Higginson, *Part of a Man's Life*, 104.By 1846 Parker was calling for violent opposition to slavery. He claimed the commercial classes supported slavery for profits, caring more for money than for human rights. See Schwartz, *Samuel Gridley Howe*, 155.

49. Higginson, *Part of a Man's Life*, 104. See also Howe, *Reminiscences*, 166.

50. JWH, Houghton (320), speeches. In her *Reminiscences* Howe noted that during her early years in Boston she carried a "dislike" toward the abolitionists, particularly Garrison and Phillips, but that Parker "held them in great esteem. It was through [Parker] that "I met [Garrison] at one of Parker's Sunday evenings at home...I learned to respect and honor [Garrison] more and more though as yet little foreseeing how glad I should be one day to work with and under him." *Reminiscences*, 153; for her link to Phillips through Parker see 154.

51. Ibid.

52. JWH, Houghton (320), "Address to Negroes." Howe noted that Samuel Gridley Howe was reluctant to get involved in abolitionism at this point, but found Phillips "right in principle." At that date, Julia remembered, "no one then dreamed that he would live to see the abolition of slavery and the women's question lay far behind this one in the perspectives of events. We failed at first to see our mission until the human race had arrived and the struggle was upon us."

53. Howe, *Reminiscences*, 245, 156. When a mob threatened to attack Phillips, Chapman and other women protected him from the crowd. Afterward Julia wrote to Phillips that she "should be proud to join his body-guard" (157). Mary Grant in *Private Woman, Public Person* argues that Julia was critical of abolitionists as self-righteous and self-satisfied into the 1850s. I think her criticism did not reflect rejection of the community from without as much as criticism from within; many ardent abolitionists accused Garrison in particular of being self-righteous and self-satisfied. I also suspect Julia's criticism reflected her annoyance at her husband, who publicly championed equal rights but privately attempted whenever possible to subvert Julia's equality.

54. Mann was appointed head of the Massachusetts Board of Education and used that position to advocate school reform. When opposed by the Boston school principals, he urged Sumner and Howe to run for the board to support him. They were joined by Parker in the campaign for school reform. Mann's principles did not extend to supporting the end of Boston's segregated school system. When black parents organized protests, Massachusetts abolitionists, particularly black abolitionists Lewis Hayden, William Cooper Nell, and Lenox Remond and white supporters Garrison, Phillips, Bowditch, Chapman, the Weston sisters, Jackson, Clarke, and May, supported the protests and petitioned Mann to use his position as head of the board to endorse integrated schools. Mann refused to take a stand, earning a strong denunciation in the *Liberator*. Ultimately,

without Mann's help, the black parents and their abolitionist friends won. Sumner, who argued that segregation was unconstitutional, took the case to the courts.

55. Sumner attacked regular Whig Robert Winthrop for selling out to the South for cotton. He claimed Winthrop's support of the Mexican-American War was a doctrine of "our country right or wrong," when Winthrop should be protecting Americans from unnecessary bloodshed, and called for the defeat of the American Army in Mexico. Schwartz, *Samuel Gridley Howe*, 156–57.

56. Ibid., 155.

57. Mann did not join Sumner, Dana, and Howe in this. He remained in the Whig Party and was elected to Congress as an anti-slavery Whig.

58. Quoted in Schwartz, *Samuel Gridley Howe*, 155.

59. GFP, Box 46, MS group 69, folder 1154, William Bowditch letter to William Lloyd Garrison II, April 3, 1886. HIB, Harvard, Seq., July 1, 1886.

60. WBP, Peabody, Bound Vol. 4, 87.

61. Bowditch noted that Phillips was a significant influence on him: "Wendell Phillips I loved." WBP, Peabody, Bound Vol. 5, Autobiographical Sketch.

62. BFP, Box 13, folder 1, William Bowditch letter to Ingersoll Bowditch, n.d. BFP, MHS, Box 3, William Bowditch letter to Vincent Bowditch, n.d.

63. WBP, Peabody, Bound Vol. 5, Autobiographical Sketch.

64. GFP, Box 46, MS group 69, folder 1154, William Bowditch letter to William Lloyd Garrison II, April 3, 1886.

65. Among others Bowditch hid the Crafts, whom Henry, armed to protect himself against slave-catchers, drove out of town, and Henry Brown, known as Box Brown because he was shipped out of the South in a box.

66. WBP, Peabody, Bound Vol. 5, Autobiographical Sketch; Vol. 4, 88.

67. BFP, Peabody, Box 13, folder 5, Charles Sumner letter to William Bowditch, April 2, 1852.

68. GFP, Box 46, MS group 69, folder 1154, William Bowditch letter to William Lloyd Garrison II, April 3, 1886. BFP, MHS, Box 3, William Bowditch letter to Vincent Bowditch, n,d.

69. BFP, MHS, Box 3, William Bowditch letter to Vincent Bowditch, n.d.

70. GFP, Box 46, MS group 69, folder 1154, William Bowditch letter to William Lloyd Garrison II, April 3, 1886.

71. See Stewart, *Wendell Phillips*, 166 for this conflict.

72. GFP, Maria Weston Chapman, *Right and Wrong in Massachusetts* (Boston: Dow And Jackson, 1840), 13.

73. See Keith Melder, "Abby Kelley and the Process of Liberation," in Jean Fagan Yellin and John C. Van Horne, eds., *The Abolitionist Sisterhood: Women's Political Culture n Antebellum America* (Ithaca, N.Y.: Cornell University Press, 1994), 230–48 for Abby Kelley's movement into abolitionism.

74. In 1838 conservatives inside the Massachusetts Anti-Slavery Society attempted to deny women full membership but lost. Maria Weston Chapman claimed Phelps was one of the organizers of this anti-woman position. Chapman, *Right and Wrong in Massachusetts*, 53.

75. BPL, Edmund Quincy letter to Maria Weston Chapman, Jan. 11, 1842.

76. TWH, Houghton, Journal, 1849.

77. Maria Weston Chapman, who could be a vicious fighter for her position, as Whittier was more than willing to testify, claimed that, despite all the conflicts, abolitionists tolerated fierce internal differences for the general cause. GFP, Chapman, *Right and Wrong in Massachusetts*, 15.

78. The July 4 gathering in Framingham was organized by abolitionists after fugitive slave Anthony Burns was captured and sent south. The community was disheartened and discouraged. It had failed to rescue Burns and several members were under threat of being jailed. The celebration was designed to rally the community and renew the commitment to prevent any more fugitive slaves from being removed. Garrison and Phillips spoke along with radical black abolitionist from Salem Charles Lenox Remond and the inspiring Sojourner Truth. Austin Bearse, *Reminiscences of Fugitive-Slave Law Days in Boston* (Boston: W. Richardson, 1880), 12.

79. Quoted in Friedman, *Gregarious Saints*, 66.

80. Chace, *Anti-Slavery Remininscences*, 22.

81. Caroline Wells Healey Dall Papers 1832, Box 1, 8 Journal Jan. 28, 1853, May 26, 1853, Schlesinger Library, Harvard University. Within a year she was attending James Freeman Clarke's and Theodore Parker's services, outraged not at the abolitionist rhetoric but the "miserable set of Southerners," April 6, 1854, June 1, 1854, Feb. 24, 1856.

82. Schwartz, *Samuel Gridley Howe*, 165, 195, 196.

83. Although his main focus is on the transformation of abolitionism that occurred just prior to the focus of this work, Richard S. Newman, *The Transformation of American Abolitionism: Fighting Slavery in the Early Republic* (Chapel Hill: University of North Carolina Press, 2002) does an excellent job of describing the early organizing actions of New England abolitionists. Newman's work provides insights into how second wave abolitionists created a mass based grassroots movement, particularly focusing on new tactics and new venues of activism.

84. BPL, Caroline Weston letter to Samuel May, Oct. 21, 1871.

85. Caroline Weston claimed this 1835 fair was held in Chapman's parents' house, while others placed it in Chapman's house. See Lee Chambers-Schiller, "A Good Work Among the People: the Political Culture of the Boston Antislavery Fair," in Yellin and Van Horne, eds., *The Abolitionist Sisterhood*, for the early history of the fair. See also Julia Roy Jeffrey, *The Great Army of Abolitionism: Ordinary Women in the Anti-Slavery Movement* (Chapel Hill: University of North Carolina Press, 1998), 107–10.

86. BPL, Caroline Weston letter to Samuel May, Oct. 21, 1871.

87. Quote from Debra Gold Hansen, "The Boston Female Anti-Slavery Society," in Yellin and Van Horne, eds., *The Abolitionist Sisterhood*, 60. Hansen argues that it was predominately the wealthier women who supported a more open role for women, while the conservative supporters of the clerical position were more likely to be Congregational or Baptist middle-class women who shunned outward political activity. Hansen, "The Boston Female Anti-Slavery Society," 61, 62.

88. The supporters of Phelps then disbanded the BFASS, organized the Massachusetts Female Emancipation Society, and affiliated with Phelps's Massachusetts Abolition Society. Chapman reorganized the BFASS in 1840. Neither society flourished. The MFES died quickly, while the BFASS continued as an organization to run the annual fairs. Except for the fair, most female Garrisonians moved into the MASS.

89. BPL, Weston letter to May.

90. Ibid. In a letter to Chapman, Henry's wife Olivia Bowditch wrote that George Latimer, the fugitive slave whose freedom Bowditch had managed and who remained a close friend of the Bowditches, had offered to be involved in supporting the Fair in any way he could. Boston BPL, Olivia Bowditch letter to

Maria Weston Chapman, n.d. Hansen argues that Black women were less interested in the fair than White women because Blacks were more interested in projects that brought immediate aid to their community. See Hansen, "The Boston Female Anti-Slavery Society." People from throughout New England sent items or donations to the fair. See BPL, Henry Ingersoll Bowditch letter to Maria Weston Chapman, Oct. 23, 1847.

91. BPL, 1 Fanny Longfellow letter to Maria Chapman, n.d. Fanny arranged to have her brother send items from Europe to the fair. See also BPL, Henry Ingersoll Bowditch letter to Maria Weston Chapman, 1843. Bowditch assured Chapman that he could get highly salable items from his Paris friends.

92. BPL, Henry Chapman letter to Debra Weston, Nov. 26, 1841; see also Thomas Wentworth Higginson letter to Maria Weston Chapman, Nov. 9, 1857 offering to send more poems he wrote for the *Liberty Bell.* The 1841 Fair Committee included most of Boston's radical female abolitionists, Maria Weston Chapman, Mary Johnson, Thankful Southwick, Louisa Loring, Eliza Meriam, Ann Phillips, Mary Young, Caroline Weston, Abby Southwick, Lavinia Hilton, Mary Rogers, Emily Winslow, Hannah Tufts, Catherine Sargent, Lydia Maria Child, Mary Chapman, Eliza Follen, Henrietta Sargent, Susan Paul, Eliza Philbrick, Anne Warren Weston, Helen Garrison, Louisa Sewall, Cecilia Howard, Caroline Williams, Hannah Adams and Mary Willey. BPL, papers of Maria Weston Chapman, "Massachusetts Anti-Slavery Fair, 1841"; Sophia Thoreau letter to Maria Weston Chapman asking to add her and her mother's names to the "subscription list," of the *Bell,* BPL, January 24, n.d.

93. BPL, Samuel May letter to Mary Carpenter, Bristol, Dec. 29, 1843.

94. BPL, Eliza Lee Follen letter to Harriet Martineau, Nov., 21, 1844; see also Sarah Greene letter Chapman to Eliza Lee Follen, Dec., 31, 1844.

95. TWH, Houghton, Samuel May letter to Thomas Wentworth Higginson (580). See also BPL, Maria Weston Chapman Papers, notice for the 24th annual Anti-Slavery Bazaar. Among things advertised as available was a children's book by Harriet Martineau.

96. Julia Roy Jeffrey estimates that the Boston fair took in over $65,000 over its years of operation, Jeffrey, *The Great Army,* 108.

97. Hansen, "The Boston Female Anti-Slavery Society," 259–60.

98. BPL, Maria Weston Chapman Papers, notice for the 24th annual Anti-Slavery Bazaar. See also Henry Chapman letter to Deborah Weston, Nov. 26, 1841 for Olivia Bowditch's involvement. By 1844, being away most of the time, she felt her name was "a mere farce," since she wasn't actually doing any real work for the Fair. BPL, Henry Ingersoll Bowditch letter to Maria Weston Chapman, July 23, 1844. The Christmas tree was not the only event planned for children. Chapman also organized a summer outdoor festival so the children could "enjoy themselves." Higginson, *Part of a Man's Life,* 17.

99. BPL, Samuel May letter to Mary Carpenter, Bristol, Dec. 29, 1843.

100. BPL, William Lloyd Garrison letter to Oliver Johnson, July 3, 1861; TWH, Houghton, TWH letter to his mother, Jan. 1, 1857; TWH to his sister, Jan. 31, 1859; TWH to Maria Weston Chapman, Nov. 9, 1857; BPL, Caroline Weston letter to Samuel May, Oct. 21, 1871.

101. BPL, TWH letter to WLG, April 8, 1860. Sometimes people tried to exploit this transatlantic link. One person presented himself to Garrison as an abolitionist and Garrison wrote Webb that the person was going to England. Webb became suspicious of the visitor and asked Higginson about him; Higginson claimed he was not really part of the movement.

102. BPL, Samuel May letter to Richard Webb, Nov. 6, 1860.

103. Abolitionists used these international links and letters of introduction from one Abolitionist to another as they moved about the world. BPL, Richard Webb letter to WLG, March 1, 1854. On Caroline Weston's visits to "the older world. . . . [Webb] was always with me at every arrival and departure subsequently coming over on purpose from Dublin." When the Weston sisters traveled to Paris they took Webb with them and connected with "anti-slavery friends" on the Continent. BPL, Caroline Weston letter to Samuel May about Webb's death, Dec. 10, 1872. Weston also mentioned staying at the home of an English abolitionist in Devonshire. Webb also acted as an agent for American abolitionists; BPL, Samuel May letter to Richard Webb, March 9, 1860. Webb also contributed to a fund for John Brown; Samuel May letter to Richard Webb, Jan. 10, 1860.

See Robertson, *Parker Pillsbury* for a discussion of Pillsbury's enduring links to English abolitionists. In a letter to Mary Carpenter of Bristol Samuel May wrote of his friends on both sides of the Atlantic, including the Carpenter family, Dr. Esthin, Mr. Armstrong, and Mr. James. BPL, Samuel May letter to Mary Carpenter, Dec. 29, 1843.

104. May Goddard Collection, Schlesinger Library, Harvard University, Box 2, Abby May Journals, Summer, 1855, 1856, 1857. Garrison referred to Abby May as an old abolitionist comrade "signally consecrated to the cause of philanthropy." Mary Goddard Collection, Box 2 (35), WLG letter to Abby May, May 20, 1877.

105. Sarah Clarke also stayed with Philadelphia abolitionists. When the Motts rented a cottage in Newport for the summer she stayed with them. At other times she stayed with the Higginsons. TWH, Houghton (1073), TWH letter to his sisters, June 25, 1871.

106. On his travels Higginson stayed with other abolitionists exchanging information and gossip and enjoying good fellowship. On a speaking tour to the west, whenever possible, Higginson visited and stayed with abolitionists. He spent a night in Toledo, where much to his dismay there was "not a soul I knew—no abolitionists—no woman's rights people." TWH, Houghton, Box 4 (496), TWH letter to his mother, Feb. 1, 1855. For other cities where Higginson stayed with abolitionists see (495) TWH letter to [indiscernible], probably Jan. 22, 1855.

107. TWH, Houghton, Box 4 (457), TWH letter to his mother, January 16, 1854.

108. TWH, Houghton, Box 4 (378) TWH letter to his mother, Nov. 28, 1851.

109. TWH, Houghton, Box 4 (421), TWH letter to his mother, 1858.

110. TWH, Houghton, Box 4 (499), TWH letter to his mother, March 5, 1855.

111. See Friedman, *Gregarious Saints*, 55. Friedman does an excellent job of describing the social networks of nineteenth-century abolitionists. He identifies the inner circle of Garrisonians as the Boston Clique, in this group Garrison, the Chapmans, Maria Weston's sisters Deborah, Caroline, and Anne, Edmond Quincy, Ellis Gray Loring, Samuel Sewall, Arnold Buffum, Oliver Johnson, Charles Follen, George and Henry Benson, Francis Jackson, Wendell Phillips, Nathaniel Rogers, Samuel May, Parker Pillsbury, and Henry Wright. Abby Kelley, Stephen Foster, and Lydia Child were also part of the clique but not so central. Rogers left in a conflict over his militant anarchism. Although I believe Friedman is correct in his analysis of the different groups within abolitionism, I think he places too much distinction on the Boston clique. I think the groups

were more fluid than he allows, and that his focus on religious beliefs fails to account for many who came to abolitionism because of political beliefs and mingled with those with strong religious beliefs.

112. BPL, Caroline Weston Journal, Sept. 13, 1835–Jan. 13, 1836. For further evidence of social links and exchanging gifts between abolitionist families, see MHS, Caroline H Dall Papers, Lillian Clarke letter to Caroline Dall, Sept. 27, 1860; BFP, Peabody, Box 13, folder 5, from Lydia Maria Child letter to William Bowditch, Nov. 7, 1855. In this letter Child thanks Bowditch for all the support and kindness over the years and that his house was always open to her and a kind of refuge.

113. Anne Weston wrote to her sister Deborah that they had had a visit from Maria and others "as strong in the good cause as ever." Later Maria and Henry Chap dropped in for a visit and spent the evening. In the morning another Weston "went over to Cambridge" to visit abolitionist poet Longfellow. These visits involved socializing, exchanging gossip about other abolitionists, and talking strategy. Along with talking about "the good cause," the Westons exchanged gossip about Henry Ingersoll Bowditch. Having just heard about his engagement to "an English lady," Anne noted that the Chapmans "felt somewhat provoked at it, but Ann Terry [Green, soon to be the wife of Phillips] knew it all along." BPL, A. Weston letter to Deborah Weston, Dec. 6, 1836.

114. BPL, Caroline Weston letter to Deborah Weston, n.d.

115. BPL, Unknown, probably Maria Weston Chapman letter to Deborah Weston, n.d.

116. Quoted in Friedman, *Gregarious Saints*, 56.

117. TWH, Houghton, Box 4 (499), TWH letter to his mother, March 5, 1855.

118. BPL, Henry Ingersoll Bowditch letter to Maria Weston Chapman, July 23, 1844.

119. Bowditch, *Life*, 1: 160. Thomas Wentworth Higginson wrote that Douglass, despite all the trials and difficulties confronting him, had a humor that was infectious. Higginson, *Part of a Man's Life*, 20.

120. SGH, Houghton (852, 853), Samuel Gridley Howe letters to Theodore Parker, n.d. In the fishing party besides the Parkers and Howes were abolitionist poet James Russell Lowell and his wife and children. In another letter to Parker, Howe notes that John Whittier, "the heroic Quaker," had come to the house for a stay. SGH, Houghton (851), Samuel Gridley Howe letter to Theodore Parker, n.d.

121. Another case of conflict leading to splits involved Garrison's close friend Nathaniel Rogers. Rogers edited the anti-slavery *Herald of Freedom*. When he retired he appointed his son-in-law to be John French to run the paper. Anti-slavery people became concerned that French was using anti-slavery newspaper funds for other activities; Rogers defended him. When Parker, Abby Kelly, and Stephan Foster wanted French out Rogers attacked them and accused Garrison of being bureaucratic and losing his radical egalitarianism. Garrison countered that Rogers's anti-organizational views had gone so far as to undermine the very functioning of the New England Anti-Slavery Society. The conflict led to Rogers being removed from the organization. Although the two wrote privately about their sadness over the split, their friendship was lost.

122. BPL, Edmund Quincy letter to Maria Weston Chapman, Jan. 11, 1842. Bowditch used to joke about how his support of the Liberty Party was opposed by Chapman, Garrison, and Phillips, yet they remained friends and linked within the community of abolitionism. Ronald Walters, *The Antislavery Appeal:*

American Abolitionism After 1830 (Baltimore: Johns Hopkins Press, 1976) finds the conflicts between political abolitionists and moral suasionists more significant than I argue here. Certainly there was conflict, but except for the split with the "Clerical plotters," as the Garrisonians called them, the abolitionists were mostly able to find enough common ground and community to hold together. See Kraditor, *Means and Ends* for the strongest argument on this point. Despite the fact that Bowditch regularly visited the Westons, Anne Weston noted in a testy letter to Deborah a conflict with Bowditch's positions on some issues: "he can not reason for any length of time without straying from the point." BPL, Anne Weston letter to Deborah Weston, March 11, 1839.

123. BPL, Maria Weston Child letter to Miss Ball, n.d.

124. John Albion Andrew Papers, Houghton Library, Harvard University bMS AM 1569.7. (12), JAA letter to James Freeman Clarke, August 3, 1847; see also letters 17, 18.

125. Theodore Parkers Papers, BPL; see Parker letters to Matilda Goddard.

126. Henry Ingersoll Bowditch was on the ballot for the General Court as a Liberty Party Candidate in 1840 and garnered 20 votes. He continued on the ballot for each successive election, gaining votes each year. When the Free Soil Party was founded in 1848 the party wanted to nominate Bowditch for office, but realizing that the party might actually win, he withdrew his name. HIB, Harvard, Archives 6A9.20, Vol. 6, "Reunion of the Free Soilers, Aug. 9, 1877. See also Stewart, *Wendell Phillips*, 166.

127. Sanborn, *Dr. S. G. Howe*, 251, 252.

128. HIB, Harvard, MJ, May 18, 1846. Bowditch, an organizer of the event, claimed that 2,500 to 3,000 people attended and listed to Lovejoy, brother of the slain publisher, direct the sermon. Bowditch also mentions the younger Channing, Phillips, and James Russell Lowell being at the event. Caroline Weston claims the event occurred at Faneuil Hall. BPL, Caroline Weston letter to Anne Weston, n.d (1846).

129. Quoted in Elizabeth Rauh Bethel, *Roots of African American Identity: Memory and History in Antebellum Free Communities* (New York: St. Martin's, 1997), 23; see Bethel also for a description of the Commemorative Festival.

130. See Donald M. Jacobs, ed., *Courage and Conscience: Black and White Abolitionists in Boston* (Bloomington: Indiana University Press, 1993), particularly Jacobs's chapter, "David Walker and William Lloyd Garrison: Racial Cooperation and the Shaping of Boston Abolition," 1–20. Walker died in 1830 (under mysterious circumstances), the year before Garrison returned to New England to begin publishing the *Liberator*, but he read Walker when Garrison was working for Lundy's newspaper in Baltimore. The writings of Walker and Philadelphia's Black businessman James Forten attacked the ACS for its view of Blacks as inferior and needing to be removed from the country. See Goodman, *Of One Blood* for a discussion of Walker and Forten on abolitionist thinking.

131. BPL, Lucia Weston letter to Deborah Weston, n.d 1836; Lucia Weston to Deborah Weston, Jan. 22, 26, 1837. These centers also provided venues for young people to court. Lucia noted in her letter to Deborah, "Emma has fallen desperately in love with Dressor," an abolitionist "brethren."

132. J. Elizabeth Jones, *The Young Abolitionists, or Conversations on Slavery* (Boston: Anti-Slavery Office, 1848).

133. TWH, Houghton (625), TWH letter to his mother, Nov. 26, 1858. Holmes, who studied medicine with Bowditch in Paris and was the father of the jurist of the same name, was not in the abolitionist camp. In 1855 he argued

that the abolitionists were the "extreme party," and that although there was a logic in their position he rejected their equal rights argument, claiming "the White man must be the master." Instead of abolitionist rhetorical attacks against the South, Holmes called for love, understanding, and moderation. GFP, Oliver Wendell Holmes, MD, "Oration, 1855."

134. TWH, Houghton (638), TWH letter to his mother, July 10, 1859.

135. In 1877 Thomas Wentworth Higginson, a person also interested in parties and social events, noted that Howe was the spirit behind the social life of Newport. TWH, Houghton (1148), TWH letter to Fields, July 25, 1877.

Chapter 3. "All the Great Men and Men of Respectability Stood Aloof"

1. Thomas Wentworth Higginson, *Cheerful Yesterdays* (Boston: Houghton Mifflin, 1898), 125.

2. Oliver Wendell Holmes, Sr., coined this term to refer to Boston's leading families. Although trained in Paris, Holmes was the epitome of a New England provincial. He also was the author of the idea that Boston was the hub of the universe, that Boston society was the most cultivated and civilized and incorporated within it all the virtues of the modern world, intelligence, thoughtfulness, moderation, and tradition. Boston's leading families in Holmes's view were best situated to govern society because they carried within them the virtues he admired. They were more than just leaders, they were scholars and thinkers. Higginson's family, although not at the top of the social scale, were close enough, especially with their Harvard connection, to be included within Holmes's pantheon of virtue.

3. Higginson's aunt was a Storrow and the Channings his cousins. TWH, Houghton (620).

4. Higginson, *Cheerful Yesterdays*, 124–25.

5. Thomas Wentworth Higginson, *Part of a Man's Life* (Boston: Houghton Mifflin, 1905), 17.

6. For a discussion of Holmes's views on abolitionism and race, see Louis Menand, *The Metaphysical Club* (New York: Farrar, Straus, and Giroux, 2001), chap. 1.

7. Recent scholarship on abolitionists has argued that they were primarily Victorian paternalists seeking religious purity and self-discovery rather than activists attempting to organize a social struggle movement. Although it is true that many abolitionists were seeking individual religious purity, this characterization misses more than it captures. For one it ignores those such as Phillips, Bowditch, Andrews, Dana, Sumner, Howe, and others who came into abolitionism not from a religious orientation but from a rights and social justice concern. It also fails to account for much of the work being done by those who were religious possessive individualists. Chapman, Garrison, Sewell, Johnson, and others did reject party politics, but they also sent organizers out to win converts to the movement. For historians' views of abolitionists, see Louis Filler, *The Crusade Against Slavery, 1830–1860* (New York: Harper and Row, 1960); James Brewer Stewart, *Holy Warriors: The Abolitionists and American Slavery* (new York: Hill and Wang, 1976); and Ronald Walters, *The Antislavery Appeal: American Abolitionism After 1830* (Baltimore: Johns Hopkins University Press, 1976).

8. Quoted from Aileen S. Kraditor, *Means and Ends in American Abolitionism:*

Garrison and His Critics on Strategy and Tactics, 1834–1850 (New York: Panteon, 1967), 5.

9. Anti-Slavery Collection, Boston Public Library, Lucia Weston letter to Deborah Weston, March 3, 1836. Lucia noted that at a Boston Female Anti-Slavery Society meeting "There were about a thousand mobbers present. Mrs. Southwick confronted the men. The men were called by handbills put out in the street and an editorial in the *Herald*."

10. In letters to other abolitionists, William Lloyd Garrison refers to open attacks or threats of attacks. See BPL, WLG letter to Oliver Johnson, Jan. 19, 1861 and WLG to Edmund Quincy, Jan. 24, 1861. For attacks against anti-slavery speakers outside Boston, see Stacey Robertson, *Parker Pillsbury: Radical Abolitionist, Male Feminist* (Ithaca, N. Y.: Cornell University Press, 2000), 88–90.

11. Quoted in Harold Schwartz, *Samuel Gridley Howe: Social Reformer, 1801–1876* (Cambridge, Mass.: Harvard University Press, 1956), 192.

12. Ibid.

13. HIB, Harvard, MJ, April 13, 1851. Because of his outspoken views against slavery Bowditch also was challenged to a duel by Virginian E. S. Gaillard. Papers of S. L. M. Iatromachia, Countway Library, Harvard University, manuscript not published, 1866.

14. Bowditch, *Life*, 1: 128.

15. Higginson, *Part of a Man's Life*, 19.

16. Franklin Sanborn, *Dr. S. G. Howe, the Philanthropist* (New York: Funk and Wagnalls, 1891).

17. GFP, newspaper clipping in Douglass file.

18. Phillips also called his enemies "Cotton Whigs." See James Brewer Stewart, *Wendell Phillips: Liberty's Hero* (Baton Rouge: Louisiana State University Press, 1986). When mobs attacked Phillips's home, a bodyguard was formed composed of militant blacks, radical German artisans, Higginson, George Smalley, who married Phillips's adopted daughter, Samuel May, and John Brown's brother Frederick Brown. May Goddard Collection. Box 2, Schlesinger Library, Harvard University, Abby May's Journal, 1860.

19. Quoted in Leonard W. Levy, *The Law of the Commonwealth and Chief Justice Shaw* (Cambridge, Mass.: Harvard University Press, 1957) 86.

20. JFC, Houghton (519), JFC letter to Samuel Gridley Howe, Aug. 24, 1851.

21. Bowditch, *Life*, 1: 178.

22. Julia Ward Howe, *Reminiscences, 1819–1899* (Boston: Houghton Mifflin, 1899), 218, 252. She also argued that Webster, who the abolitionists felt sold out to the slave powers, was the "political idol of the Massachusetts aristocracy" (218).

23. See Stewart, *Wendell Phillips*; see also letters of Elizabeth Buffum Chace, GFP; letters of Lydia Child and the Weston sisters, BPL. See also Russel B. Nye. *Fettered Freedom: Civil Liberties and the Slavery Controversy 1830–1860* (East Lansing: Michigan State University Press, 1949) for a discussion of how concern for basic liberties informed abolitionists. See also Fredrickson, *The Inner Civil War*, and Lewis Perry, *Radical Abolitionism: Anarchy and the Government of God in Antislavery Thought* (Ithaca, N. Y.: Cornell University Press, 1973) for views of the different reasons intellectuals came into the abolitionist camp. Perry focuses more on religious motivations while Fredrickson also sees nonreligious influences.

24. Higginson, *Cheerful Yesterdays*, 114.

25. JFC, Houghton (519), JFC letter to Samuel Gridley Howe, Aug. 24, 1851.

26. HIB, Countway, MJ, May 18, 1846. "All the great men and men of respectability stood aloof."

27. Abolitionists did not help matters by their seeming indifference to the conditions of free labor and their close ties to aristocratic England. See Donald M. Jacobs, ed., *Courage and Conscience: Black and White Abolitionists in Boston* (Bloomington: Indiana University Press, 1993), 117, 118.

28. The term "Hunkers" for Northern pro-slavery supporters is a constant reference by abolitionists; see the papers of the abolitionists in the Abolitionists Papers, BPL. Higginson, TWH, Houghton, Box 4 (360), calls the pro-slavery position of Northerners "Hunkerism."

29. Quoted in Schwartz, *Samuel Gridley Howe*, 181, 183.

30. BPL, Theodore Parker Sermons, Sermon 5, "The Chief Sins of a People," April 10, 1851.

31. Ibid., Sermon 14.

32. GFP.

33. BPL, Parker, Sermon 12, "The New Crime Against Humanity," June 4, 1854.

34. Theodore Parker, *The Boston Kidnapping: A Discourse to Commemorate the Rendition of Thomas Simms, Delivered on the First Anniversary Thereof, April 12, 1852* (Boston: Crosby, Nichols, 1852), 44.

35. HIB, Harvard, Seq., Sept. 16, 1886.

36. HIB, MHS, Box 2, Scrapbook; C. F. Folsom, "Henry Ingersoll Bowditch," *Proceedings of the American Association of Arts and Sciences* 28; see also Bowditch, *Life*, 100 for his feelings of being rejected and no longer invited to "fashionable parties."

37. Quoted in Schwartz, *Samuel Gridley Howe*, 190.

38. BFP, Peabody, Box 13, folder 1, William Bowditch letter to Ingersoll, March 1846.

39. HIB, Countway, Seq., Sept. 16, 1886.

40. Bowditch, *Life*, 134. Nov. 11, 1842.

41. HIB, Countway, Seq., Sept. 17, 1886. In 1885 Bowditch claimed in a letter to the newspaper that Emerson was not an abolitionist. This stirred up a hornets' nest of protest by Emerson's supporters. William Potter argued that Emerson was an abolitionist, but that because he was a scholar and intellectual he could not get involved in the give and take of abolitionism. Bowditch contemptuously replied that being an intellectual was not an excuse to avoid political involvement in the major justice issue before the nation. HIB, Countway, Seq., Nov. 19, 1885.

42. Ibid.

43. Bowditch did claim that when Emerson finally spoke out in the Senate against the beating of Sumner and Brown's killing, "Emerson spoke bravely and well." But until he publicly used his position to attack slavery, Bowditch saw Emerson as "limited as others are." Ibid., Nov. 19, 1885, Sept. 17, 1886.

44. HIB, Harvard, Seq., July 28, 1885.

45. BPL, Maria Weston Chapman Papers, MWC letter to unknown, Nov. 1842.

46. JWH, Houghton (320), "Women's Rights Question." Her criticism of abolitionists in the 1850s has been seen as an indication of her hostility to abolitionism. It must be remembered that Howe was at the time in constant bitter conflict with her husband, who threatened to divorce her and take away her children. Sumner, her husband's closest friend and an active abolitionist, supported her husband. Howe's attacks on abolitionists may have been linked to

that conflict. Her private letters reflect this ambivalence; attacking abolitionists but expressing solidarity with the cause and close personal attachment to the Parkers and Clarkes. She identified herself with the abolitionists, as her offer to be part of Phillips's bodyguard indicates.

47. Howe, *Reminiscences*, 218.

48. Laura Howe Richards and Maud Howe Elliot, *Julia Ward Howe, 1819–1910* (Boston: Houghton Mifflin, 1925), 260.

49. JFC, Houghton (519), JFC letter to Samuel Gridley Howe, Aug. 24, 1851.

50. Parker, Sermon 12.

51. Parker, *The Boston Kidnapping*, 38.

52. Abolitionists "sought to establish a principle, the rights of human nature." GFP, Wendell Phillips, letter to the "Commemoration of the 50th Anniversary of the Organization of the Anti-Slavery Society," Philadelphia, 1884. Chace noted that the "long-tried Abolitionists saw the necessity of all removal of race prejudice, and the establishment of the principle of a common humanity."

53. BPL, Theodore Parker Sermons, "Some Thoughts on the New Assault upon Freedom in America and the General State of the Country," Monday Feb. 12, 1854, BPL.

54. See *Pierson v. Post* (New York Supreme Court, 1805). The superior court judge ruled that to obtain possession a person needs to extend labor and bring something that is wild into "certain control." Locke argued that property came about as one put one's labor to improving what is wild. Once labor has been incorporated in, for example, land, the land becomes the property of the persons who improved it with their labor. They then can sell or transfer that property. The state has the responsibility of protecting that incorporated labor. Hence Locke argued that states are created to protect basic rights, among which are the rights of life, liberty, and property.

55. Higginson claimed that one of the first anti-slavery books, David Walker's 1829 *An Appeal to the Colored Citizens of the World*, was "based absolutely on the Declaration of Independence and on the theory that the Negro was a man." Higginson, *Part of a Man's Life*, 116.

56. Parker, *The Boston Kidnapping*, 41. See Parker, Sermon, "Some Thoughts on the New Assault upon Freedom in American and the General State of the Country, Feb. 12, 1854." He argued that the basic principles of New England were equal rights. He used the "truths of the Declaration of Independence" as the basis for progress of "mankind."

57. Henry Ingersoll Bowditch, *An Address on the Life and Character of James Deane, M.D., of Greenfield, Mass., Aug. 4, 1858* (Greenfield, Mass.: H.D. Mirick, 1858), Library of Congress Collection.

58. The abolitionists argued that the problem of slavery was not only in its brutality but also at its base. Their critique of slavery was both institutional, that the institution itself was corrupt, and ideological, that it violated the fundamental premise of absolute human equality. See Ellen Dubois, "Women's Rights and Abolition: The Nature of the Connection," in Lewis Perry and Michael Fellman, eds., *Antislavery Reconsidered: New Perspectives on the Abolitionists* (Baton Rouge: Louisiana State University Press, 1979).

59. GFP, Wendell Phillips, Letter to the "commemoration of the 50th Anniversary." Chace noted that the "long-tried Abolitionists saw the necessity of all removal of race prejudice, and the establishment of the principle of a common humanity."

60. Bowditch responded to the claim that the war concerned state's rights, that "state's rights were dear to Massachusetts." HIB, Harvard, Seq., July 6, 1886.

61. BPL, Parker, Sermon 12.

62. Bowditch, *Life*, 175.

63. BPL, letters of Lydia Child and the Weston sisters.

64. In the conflict of 1838–40, one of the issues thrown against the Garrisonians was their resistance to letting the MASS get behind the Liberty Party. This created discord, but was secondary to the conflict over women's role in the movement and the anti-clerical tone of the Garrisonians. Although Bowditch's and Whittier's involvement in the Liberty Party brought on Maria Weston Chapman's wrath, the split was less significant in New England than is often depicted. William Bowditch, who sided with the position of Garrison, Quincy, and Johnson that involvement in electoral politics was corrupting and was a non-voter, nonetheless supported the Free Soil Party and helped by publicizing its candidates. See WBP, Peabody, Bound Vol. 4, 88. Bowditch's non-voter position did not prevent him from being a close friend and advisor to Sumner, who address letters "my dear Bowditch." See BFP, Peabody, Box 13, folder 5, Charles Sumner letters to William Bowditch, April 2, April 30, June 12, 1852; April 5, April 17, 1854; June 7, 1860. Bowditch was also a close friend of politically active Richard Dana; Jan. 18, 1853. The Buffum family of Fall River is another example of how this conflict less significant than historians have made it appear. Elizabeth Buffum Chace and her husband were nonvoters, while her father, an intimate friend of Garrison, was a supporter and activist in the Liberty Party. GFP, Chace, *Reminiscences*.

65. HIB, Harvard Seq., Sept. 16, 1886.

66. Anger over the war with Mexico was intense in New England. Sumner proclaimed that the war stained those whose representatives voted for war appropriations, and that the army should be allowed to perish "like the legions of Varus. Their bleached bones, in distant valleys where they were waging an unjust war, would not tell such a tale of ignominy to posterity as this lying act of Congress." Quoted in Schwartz, *Horace Gridley Howe*, 159. Until 1845 Sumner had been a "passive Whig."

67. Sumner and Howe were actively working against the "Cotton Whigs" by fall 1846, when Howe accepted the Conscience Whig nomination to run against Winthrop. Franklin Sanborn claimed that Winthrop became an early leader of the "Cotton Whigs." He was chosen Speaker of the House in 1847 and went on to the Senate before being defeated by Free Soil (then Republican) Henry Wilson in 1855. Sanborn, *Dr. S. G. Howe*, 211–30.

68. Higginson claimed Whittier tricked him into running. TWH, Houghton (360), TWH letter to Waldo, 1850.

69. HIB, Harvard, Archive 6a9.20, Vol. 6. "Reunion of the Free Soilers, Aug. 9, 1877.

70. TWH, Houghton, (360), TWH letter to Waldo, 1850.

71. See Kraditor, *Means and Ends*, 141–77, on this issue.

72. TWH, Houghton (318–350), TWH letter to his mother, Jan. 3, 1850; TWH letter to Waldo, June 4, 1850.

73. SGH, Houghton (1131), SGH letter to Sumner, 1854.

74. Sanborn, *Dr. S. G. Howe*, 250.

75. Higginson was surprised that John Palfrey supported the coalition with Massachusetts Democrats. TWH, Houghton (367), TWH letter to Waldo, Sept. 13, 1851; (371), TWH letter to his mother, Oct. 5, 1851.

76. TWH, Houghton (474), TWH letter to his mother, Dec. 28, 1854. See also Schwartz, *Horace Gridley Howe*, 188. Wilson's commitment to the cause continued to be a problem for the more principled abolitionists. In 1857 Higginson noted that, although Wilson had anti-slavery feelings, "he is a politician in grain and is weak among stronger personals." Higginson thought Wilson needed Sumner's presence to keep from compromising too much. TWH, Houghton (593), TWH letter to Curtis, Jan. 25, 1857.

77. TWH, Houghton (393), TWH letter to Mary, April 16, 1852. For a description of theologically trained ministers moving to radical positions in opposition to the clerical establishment, see Robertson, *Parker Pillsbury*; Ronald Walters, *The Antislavery Appeal: American Abolitionism After 1830* (Baltimore: Johns Hopkins University Press, 1976); Perry, *Radical Abolitionism*. The term "come-outer" originally came from the evangelical awakening, but by the late 1830s and 1840s it was used for radical abolitionists who believed that the existing churches had become too corrupted by their failure to oppose slavery and argued that members should "come out" of the church.

78. TWH, Houghton (365), TWH letter to Sam, June 29, 1851. See Perry, *Radical Abolitionism*, for a discussion of the come-outers.

79. For this split from the Garrisonian point of view, see Chapman. *Right and Wrong in Massachusetts*.

80. Bowditch noted ironically that in "Catholic France I imbibed ideas of liberty unknown in Republican and Protestant America." HIB, Harvard, Seq., Sept. 16, 1886.

81. Bowditch, *Life*, 1: 117.

82. Ibid., 114.

83. GFP, MS group 69, folder 1154, William Bowditch letter to Garrison's son, April 3, 1886.

Chapter 4. "To Do Battle for Justice and the Oppressed"

Epigraph: BPL, Theodore Parker Sermons, Sermon 12, "The New Crime Against Humanity," June 4, 1854.

1. See Leonard W. Levy, *The Law of the Commonwealth and Chief Justice Shaw* (Cambridge, Mass.: Harvard University Press, 1957), 72–77.

2. Nonresistant abolitionists were concerned that Latimer's capture would lead to violent action. William Channing in a letter to Francis Jackson noted that "some colored men and others among ourselves . . . are inclined to extreme measures." BFP, Peabody, Box 13, folder 8, William Channing letter to Francis Jackson, Nov. 4, 1842.

3. Quoted in Levy, *Law of the Commonwealth*, 81.

4. Phillips denounced not only the Constitution but all those who used it to defend slavery, judges, court officers, and jailers and lawyers. But he also denounced all those in the North who did not stand up against slavery as "guilty ones . . . the white slaves of the North." Quoted in William M. Wiecek, "Latimer: The Problem of Unjust Laws," in Lewis Perry and Michael Fellman, eds., *Antislavery Reconsidered: New Perspectives on the Abolitionists* (Baton Rouge: Louisiana State University Press, 1979), 233.

5. BFP, MSH, Box 2, Scrapbooks, 1894, Vincent Yardley Bowditch, Memoir of Henry I. Bowditch and Olivia Bowditch. See also *Latimer Journal*, HIB, MHS; this journal was Bowditch's collection of material on the Latimer case.

6. BPL, letter to subscribe money for George Latimer freedom. This call to raise money to buy Latimer's freedom also denied the legitimacy of slavery.

7. HIB, Harvard, 134, Nov. 11, 1842.

8. BPL, Henry Ingersoll Bowditch letter to John Quincy Adams, Feb. 12, 1843; HIB, Harvard, Seq., Sept. 16, 1886.

9. BFP, MHS, Scrapbook, 1894.

10. HIB, Harvard, MJ, Autobiographical Note.

11. Quoted in Louis Menand, *The Metaphysical Club* (New York: Farrar, Straus, and Giroux, 2001), 27.

12. HIB, Harvard, MJ, Oct. 31, 1846.

13. BFP, Peabody, Box 13, folder 11, Documents of the Vigilance Committee of the Massachusetts Anti-Slavery Society. Bowditch hoped the meeting would lead to "a national league" to oppose the capture of slaves. HIB, Harvard, MJ, Oct. 31, 1846.

14. Quoted in his biography by his daughter Laura Richards, *Samuel Gridley Howe* (New York: Appleton-Century, 1935), 191.

15. SGH, Houghton, Committee of Vigilance Subscription Book.

16. BFP, Peabody, Box 13, folder 11, Documents of the Vigilance Committee of the Massachusetts Anti-Slavery Society. Louisa Loring's husband Ellis Loring was treasurer of the committee. One of those paid by the committee was deputy sheriff Jacoby Pratt.

17. Theodore Parker, *The Boston Kidnapping: A Discourse to Commemorate the Rendition of Thomas Simms, Delivered on the First Anniversary Thereof, April 12, 1852* (Boston: Crosby, Nichols, 1852), 25, 26. Vigilance Committees also formed in other towns throughout New England.

18. For a list of the Boston members of the Vigilance Committee see the first few pages of Austin Bearse, *Reminiscences of Fugitive-Slave Law Days in Boston* (Boston: Warren Richardson, 1880).

19. At that meeting and a follow-up one, leading black abolitionists urged the black community to prepare to resist the law. Abolitionist printer William Nell, lawyer Robert Morris, and Salem abolitionist Charles Lenox Remond called on the community in the name of Crispus Attucks to fight for their freedom. Joshua Smith advised those in attendance to buy Colt revolvers. Gary Collison, *Shadrach Minkins: From Fugitive Slave to Citizen* (Cambridge, Mass.: Harvard University Press, 1997).

20. GFP; Bearse, *Reminiscences of Fugitive-Slave Law Days*, 8.

21. At another point a crowd of several hundred Vigilance Committee members and activists from the Boston black community found Hughes on the street and attempted to attack him. Hughes escaped in a carriage only to be arrested for driving too fast and not stopping to pay a toll on the Cambridge bridge. Collison, *Shadrach Minkins*, 96–98.

22. U.S. district marshal Charles Devens was a boyhood friend of Higginson. When the Fugitive Slave Bill was passed, Higginson wrote to Devens that the "cruel and unrighteous" Fugitive Slave Law that "strikes down all the essential safeguards of that liberty" made Devens as a marshal potentially complicitous in the immoral slave system. He called on Devens, "for God's sake let us have some men in Massachusetts who can do right. . . . There is no plea of official duty to bind you." TWH, Houghton (340).

23. BFP, MHS, Box 3, John, Everett, and Theodore Cabot letter to Vincent Bowditch, Dec. 27, 1902.

24. Richards, *Samuel Gridley Howe*, 197.

25. TWH, Houghton (383), Loring letter to TWH, n.d.

26. Bearse, *Reminiscences of Fugitive-Slave Law Days*, 15.

27. For a description of the rescue see Collison, *Shadrach Minkins*, 110–30.

28. John Albion Andrews Papers, Houghton Library, Harvard University, bMS AM 1569.7 (21), JAA letter to James Freeman Clarke, March 1, 1851.

29. Ibid.

30. Bowditch also noted that one of the rescuers hid at his house. Bowditch felt that his home was "ennobled" by being the hiding place of someone willing to die for the "cause of liberty." HIB, Harvard, MJ, Feb. 16, 1851.

31. Parker, *The Boston Kidnapping*, 30.

32. Ibid., 34.

33. Ibid.

34. TWH, Houghton (375), TWH letter to his mother.

35. Ibid. (486), Franklin Sanborn letter to TWH, March 4, 1897. Bigelow's wife ran an underground railroad station, and Minkins stayed at their home. Also on the jury was Hartwell, another anti-slavery person. Neither Hartwell nor Bigelow was going to find them guilty.

36. Essex County Abolitionists, particularly Lynn shoe workers, had openly announced they would prevent the law from being enforced. An attempted capture of a fugitive slave in New Bedford had been thwarted by the Vigilance Committee there. Parker, *The Boston Kidnapping*, 35, 36.

37. HIB, Countway Library, Harvard, MJ, April 8, 1851.

38. Ibid., April 13, 1851.

39. TWH, Houghton (382), TWH letter to Mary, 1851; BPL, TWH letter to the editor, *Newport Union*.

40. TWH, Houghton, Journal, June 11, 1850.

41. Thomas Wentworth Higginson, *Cheerful Yesterdays* (Boston: Houghton Mifflin, 1898), 140.

42. TWH, Houghton, Journal, June 11, 1850.

43. HIB, Harvard University, MJ, April 8, 1851. Higginson noted that "it is worth coming to Boston occasionally to see that there are places worse than Newburyport; there is neither organization, resolution, plan, nor popular sentiment." TWH, Houghton (382), TWH letter to Mary, 1851.

44. James Brewer Stewart, *Wendell Phillips: Liberty's Hero* (Baton Rouge: Louisiana State University Press, 1986), 155.

45. BPL, Narrative of Thomas Wentworth Higginson on the Burns Case, n.d.

46. BPL, Francis Jackson letter to Maria Child, Sept. 9, 1860.

47. Parker, *The Boston Kidnapping*, 42. HIB, Harvard, MJ, April 13, 1851.

48. HIB, Harvard, MJ, April 13, 1851.

49. BFP, Peabody, William Bowditch Papers, Bound Vol. 5.

50. Ibid., April 20, 1851.

51. Parker, *The Boston Kidnapping*, 42–44.

52. Ibid., 9.

53. Ibid., 43–44.

54. Quoted in Stewart, *Wendell Phillips*, 191–92.

55. Parker, *The Boston Kidnapping*, 14, 19.

56. Ibid., 24.

57. Ibid., 27. Parker originally believed that New England's tradition of resistance to injustice of the Adamses and Otises would prevent the Fugitive Slave Law from being implemented in the region (54).

58. Ibid., 33.

59. Ibid., 41.

60. Ibid., 46. Parker noted Boston sent back the "first man she ever stole since the Declaration of Independence" (31); BPL, Theodore Parker Sermons, Sermon 12, "The New Crime Against Humanity," June 4, 1854.

61. BPL, Theodore Parker Sermons, Sermon 5, "The Chief Sins of a People," April 10, 1851.

62. Ibid.

63. TWH, Houghton (382), TWH letter to Mary, 1851.

64. Parker, *The Boston Kidnapping*, 44.

65. SGH, Houghton (314), SGH letter to Theodore Parker, n.d.

66. BPL, Parker Sermon 5.

67. Parker, *The Boston Kidnapping*, 10.

68. BPL, Parker Sermon 5.

69. Francis Jackson wrote of the conscious Whigs that they struggled "manfully" against the party regulars. BPL, Francis Jackson letter to William Lloyd Garrison, Sept. 30, 1846. We also must be careful not to read too much into the language used in the nineteenth century. The repeated use of the word "manly" by abolitionists indicates a growing gender division in the 1850s; yet it must also be remembered that the word despite its being obviously gendered may not have had that implication for those who used it despite its seeming self-evidence. The indication of this is a letter to James Freeman Clarke from Lydia Maria Child. Child recommended to Clarke that he ask Eliz: "She has a *manly* intellect and clear moral vision. Her pen is powerful." JFC, Houghton (109), Lydia Maria Clarke letter to JFC, Feb. 16, 1863.

70. Henry Ingersoll Bowditch, *An Address on the Life and Character of James Deane* (Greenfield, Conn.: J.D. Mirick, 1858), Library of Congress. Bowditch also claimed that by his act to "stand a man besides those . . . heroes who though few in number first fell into the ranks of the grand phalanx of humanity" he found his virtue. BPL, HIB letter to Maria Weston Chapman, Aug. 6, 1843.

71. HIB, Harvard, Seq.

72. Stacey Robertson, *Parker Pillsbury: Radical Abolitionist, Male Feminist* (Ithaca, N.Y.: Cornell University Press, 2000), 27.

73. HIP, Harvard, MJ, Feb. 16, 1851.

74. Parker, *The Boston Kidnapping*, 60, 62, 64.

75. See Robertson, *Parker Pillsbury*, for a discussion of the issue of manhood among abolitionists. The tendency to see the struggle against slavery in gendered terms was particularly true in the South. Southerners called northern abolitionists effeminate; they particularly accused Phillips of being cowardly and unmanly and depicted him as needing women to protect him. See Stewart, *Wendell Phillips*, 193.

76. BFP, MHS, William I. Bowditch, *The Rendition of Anthony Burns* (Boston: Robert F. Wallcut, 1854), pamphlet. Bowditch argued that sending Burns back to Virginia was a violation of Massachusetts law, because under the Massachusetts Declaration of Rights, Article 1, "On Massachusetts soil, all men, without regard to complexion are presumed to be free until the contrary is established beyond a reasonable doubt." Bowditch believed there was reasonable doubt as to whether Burns was in fact the person owned by the Virginian, hence Commissioner Loring should have freed Burns.

77. BPL, Samuel May letter to TWH, n.d. May wrote that Bowditch told him to write to Higginson and ask him to bring Worcester to Boston to stop Burns's

return. "The country must back the city, and if necessary lead it. We shall summon all the country friends. Come strong."

78. HIB, Harvard, MJ, June 10, 1854. Bowditch noted that at the meeting "each man wanted to talk and mourn entirely with his neighbor and himself apparently. This was the bane of everything—no leader, no head—and consequently anarchy was the result. Every plan failed to be fully carried out." BPL, Narrative of Thomas Wentworth Higginson on the Burns Case, n.d.

79. HIB, Harvard, MJ, June 10, 1854.

80. BPL, Narrative of Thomas Wentworth Higginson on the Burns Case, n.d.

81. Higginson, *Cheerful Yesterdays*, 151.

82. Who actually killed Batchelder remains a mystery. Thomas Drew, an abolitionist from Worcester, claimed it was Martin Stowell and that he purchased the gun for Stowell. Other evidence indicates that Hayden fired the fatal shot. TWH, Houghton, Box 4, William Channing letter to TWH, n.d., 1874.

See also BPL, Thomas Drew letter to TWH, April 16, 1888.

83. HIB, Harvard, MJ, June 10, 1854.

84. Higginson, *Cheerful Yesterdays*, 158. See BPL, *Boston Advertiser* clipping, n.d.

85. Ibid. See also BPL, Samuel May letter to unknown probably Higginson or Hayden, n.d. May believed that if the rush on the Court House had been coordinated with the crowd coming from Faneuil Hall "it might have succeeded." May also warned, "a warrant for your arrest is in preparation, but not yet issued."

86. HIB, Harvard, MJ, June 4, 1854.

87. Worcester alone sent over 900 in a special train. BPL, *Boston Advertiser* clipping, n.d.

88. HIB, Harvard, Seq., Sept. 16, 1886.

89. In letters to friends not in Boston at the time of Burns's return to slavery, abolitionists told again and again of the horror of federal troops rushing at the crowd with drawn swords, guns, and bayonets. Behind the cavalry were troops with cannons pointed at the crowd. The writers also noted the booing and hissing of the crowds and the cries of shame as Burns moved passed Revolutionary icons. BPL, Samuel May letter to TWH, June 2, 1854; Osgood letter to TWH, June 6, 1854. HIB, Harvard, MJ, June 4, 1854.

90. Ibid.

91. BPL, Parker Sermon 12, "The New Crime Against Humanity," June 4, 1854. The impact of the Burns affair is reflected in the Journal of Caroline Wells Headley Dall. Although she notes in January 1853 that she went to her first abolitionist meeting and was "rather disgusted by the violence" of the rhetoric, by May she was more "aroused by some of the remarks." By April she was attending James Freeman Clarke's sermons and becoming more sympathetic toward abolitionism. After the Burns rendition she was now thoroughly discussed with the fact that northerners seemed to be "controlled by a miserable set of Southerners," and in support of those who attempted to rescue Burns despite the violence. By 1855 she was attending Parker's as well as Clarke's sermons. Caroline Wells Healey Dall Papers, Schlesinger Library, Harvard University 1832 Box 1, 8, Journal.

92. TWH, Houghton, Box 4, William Channing letter to TWH, n.d. 1874.

93. Initially Lewis Hayden, the man who actually shot the guard, was a target of police suspicion. Ironically Marshal Tukey, a Mason, warned fellow Mason Hayden that he was under suspicion, and Hayden with the support of Sewall and other abolitionists left town. Tukey was a white Mason and Hayden was a

member of the Black Prince Hall Masonic Lodge. Despite their racial segregation, obviously Tukey felt fraternal enough to warn Hayden.

94. BPL, Samuel May letter to TWH, June 10, 1854. Francis Jackson offered to buy Higginson tickets on a packet to Canada; Higginson declined. Garrison, who was critical of the attack, wrote to Higginson offering advice and aid. BPL, William Lloyd Garrison letter to TWH, June 1, 1854. Lucy Stone suggested ironically that it would be best for the cause if they hung Higginson. Tilden Edelstein, *Strange Enthusiasm: A Life of Thomas Wentworth Higginson* (New Haven, Conn.: Yale University Press, 1968) 171.

95. BPL, TWH letter to his mother, May 29, 1854. Mary Higginson jokes that Higginson's letters from prison will be read by the jailer; his niece jokes that the jailer wouldn't be able to read them.

96. BPL, Account of those who offered support to Higginson.

97. TWH, Houghton (465), TWH letter to his mother, June 24, 1854; (466), TWH letter to his aunt, July 25, 1854.

98. TWH, Houghton, bMs Am 784, TWH letter from his mother, June 15, 1854. See also BPL, TWH letter to his mother, May 29, 1854.

99. Edelstein, *Strange Enthusiasm*, 162, 166.

100. TWH, Houghton, clippings on the Burns riot and Higginson arrest. See also (470), TWH letter to unknown, Nov. 9, 1854; (471), TWH letter to his mother, Nov. 20, 1854.

101. BPL, William Bowditch letter to TWH, n.d.

102. BPL, TWH letter to Theodore Parker, Feb. 12, 1855. Higginson consulted with William Bowditch to put together a defense team. BPL, William Bowditch letter to TWH, June 13, 21, 1854. Bowditch recommended John Andrew and Henry Durant as Higginson's lawyers. Higginson's brother sent $100 to help with the cost of the trial, not because they were brothers but because "it is the only way you know that we traders can show any sympathy with our own dignity." BPL, Charles Higginson letter to TWH, June 10, 1854.

103. HIB, Harvard, MJ, Dec. 10, 1857.

104. BPL, William H. Channing letter to TWH, July 4, 1854.

105. BFP, MHS, Scrapbook; C. F. Folsom, Memorial, *Proceedings of the American Academy of Sciences* 28.

106. BPL, HIB letter to TWH, Aug. 10, 1854.

107. BPL, HIB letter titled "confidential," unknown person, Aug. 10, 1854.

108. BPL, George Fisher letter to TWH, June 4, 1855. The code was a simple number for letter substitution. People were not brought into the League until they were vetted by local councils of the league. It was to be a "military organization." See also HIB, Harvard, Seq., Sept. 16, 1886.

109. Ibid.; see also Hudson Papers, Sophia Smith Collection, Smith College, WIB letter to E. D. Hudson, Feb. 20, 1855. Bowditch wanted Hudson to form a cell in the Springfield area, "to prevent the return of another fugitive from this state." See SGH, Houghton (826), SGH letter to Theodore Parker, n.d.

110. The lodges continued military training until the Civil War. See "Notes of the Class of 1828," Harvard College. Despite extensive plans and training the league never had an opportunity to go into action because Burns was the last fugitive removed from Massachusetts. Bowditch, *Life*, 1: 273–79.

111. Quoted in Edelstein, *Strange Enthusiasm*, 162.

112. BPL, TWH letter to Anne Weston, Sept. 13, 1854.

113. BPL, J. H. Fowler, letter to TWH, June 30, 1854.

114. Sumner's abolitionist militancy was unquestioned. During the Mexican-

American War he gave a speech in which he proclaimed "the war stained those whose representatives voted for war appropriations and the American Army should be allowed to perish "like legions of Varus their bleached bones in distant valleys where they were waging an unjust war, would not tell such a tale of ignominy to posterity as their lying act of congress." Harold Schwartz, *Samuel Gridley Howe: Social Reformer 1801–1876* (Cambridge, Mass.: Harvard University Press, 1956), 159.

115. Sanborn, *Dr. S. G. Howe*, 247–48.

116. Higginson, Parker, and Samuel Gridley Howe focused much of their energy on Kansas, which they saw as a heroic battle between the forces of slavery and freedom. Parker's involvement in these activities declined in the late 1850s with his failing health. He and his wife traveled to Italy in hopes the weather would improve his health. It failed, and Parker died in 1860.

117. TWH, Houghton (563), TWH letter to his mother, Aug. 29, 1856; see also (565), (566), Sept. 3, 12, 1856.

118. TWH, Houghton (568), TWH letter to his mother, Sept. 24, 1856; see also (560), TWH letter to his mother, June 26, 1856. Although Henry and William Bowditch worked feverishly for abolition, their brother Ingersol refused to support abolitionism or give money to Kansas, something even some conservative merchants were willing to do. See TWH, Houghton (560), TWH letter to his mother, June 26, 1856.

119. Sanborn, *Dr. S. G. Howe*, 254.

120. TWH, Houghton (563), TWH letter to his mother, Aug. 29, 1856; see also (565), (566), Sept. 3, 12, 1856.

121. BPL, TWH letter to Samuel May, June 7, 1857. See also TWH, Houghton, (594), TWH letter to his mother, Jan. 27, 1857. Phillips and Garrison argued that the Constitution would forever bind New England to slavery and the only answer was to break from the union. BPL, Draft of 1846 Statement by Francis Jackson and William Lloyd Garrison on disunion. The disunion option had supporters among the leadership of the Massachusetts and American Anti-Slavery Societies, but it was never a monolithic idea. Henry Ingersoll Bowditch, a vice president of the MASS, never endorsed disunion. See HIB, Harvard, MJ, March 20, 1849.

122. TWH, Houghton (580), Samuel May letter to TWH, Dec. 18, 1856; (586), May to TWH, Feb. 7, 1857; see also (581), Daniel Mann, "a small farmer," letter to TWH. May wrote to Higginson that May wanted his name on the call for the disunion convention. TWH, Houghton (580), Samuel May letter to TWH, n.d.

123. Ibid. (592), TWH letter to his mother, Jan. 27, 1857.

124. Ibid. (587), Statement of the Worcester Committee of Disunion. BPL, TWH letter to WLG, June 23, 1857.

Chapter 5. "The Issue Is Universal Justice"

Epigraphs: Wendell Phillips Garrison and Francis Jackson Garrison, *William Lloyd Garrison, 1805–1879: The Story of His Life Told by His Children* (1885–89; New York:Negro Universities Press, 1969), 4: 157–59; BFP, MHS, Scrapbooks, Memorial to Lt. Nathaniel Bowditch, Vol. I, AAAG, First Cavalry Brigade, 2nd Division, Army of the Potomac.

1. WBP, Peabody, Bound Vol. V, Autobiographical Sketch.

2. BPL, Will of Francis Jackson, Jan. 28, 1861. He gave $5,000 to a trust for "women's rights to vote, hold office, manage and desire property and all other rights enjoyed by men." Lucy Stone, Wendell Phillips, and Susan B. Anthony were to administer this trust. He also put money into a trust for Elizabeth Eddy and Lizzie Bacon, a significant amount of which was supposed to go into the fund for woman's rights when Eddy and Bacon died. This will was later revised to place $10,000 in trust for anti-slavery work; see discussion below.

3. Ibid.; BFP, Peabody, Box 13, folder 9, Wendell Phillips letter to Francis Jackson, Aug. 26, 1860. Phillips recommended to Jackson that William Bowditch advise him. Bowditch was by this time focusing most of his legal work on trusts and wills.

4. WBP, Peabody, Bound Vol. V, Autobiographical Sketch.

5. WBP, Peabody, Bound Vol. V, WLG letter to William Bowditch, March 28, 1868.

6. BPL, Minutes of the Trustees of the Jackson Trust. The heirs to the Jackson estate challenged the will, particularly the money to be given to women's rights. From 1862 to1867 the estate was tied up in court. Once the heirs' issue was settled, the conflict between Garrison, May, and Quincy and Phillips, Bowditch, Jackson, and Whipple tied up the funds for another two years. Finally in March 1869 the court removed the four trustees who opposed Garrison and the heirs turned over $9,000 to be quit of any further claim on the estate. In April the trustees paid a total of $18,475.43 to the New England branch of the Freedman's Bureau. Garrison and Garrison, *William Lloyd Garrison*, 4: 237–38.

7. BPL, Samuel May letter to Samuel Joseph May, March 26, 1869. See also WBP, Peabody, Bound Vol. V, Autobiographical Sketch. See also WLG, letter to William Bowditch, March 28, 1868.

8. Thomas Wentworth Higginson, *Part of a Man's Life* (Boston: Houghton Mifflin, 1905).

9. BPL, Samuel May letter to Samuel Joseph May, March 26, 1869.

10. WBP, Peabody, Bound Vol. V, WLG letter to William Bowditch, March 28, 1868.

11. BFP, Peabody, Box 13, folder 4, Wendell Phillips letter to William Bowditch, n.d. See also BPL, Thomas Wentworth Higginson letter to Honorable Charles Allen, Feb. 23, 1869. In a letter to James Freeman Clarke, a close family friend as well as a friend of Garrison, Quincy, and May, Higginson wrote that he supported Phillips and Bowditch and believed their position pushing for continued political equality should be supported. Higginson saw splitting the money as the most politic and just means of ending the feud. Clarke agreed. TWH, Houghton, TWH letter to James Freeman Clarke, Feb. 20, 1869; also James Freeman Clarke letter to TWH, March 2, 1869.

12. GFP; Elizabeth Buffum Chace, *Anti-Slavery Reminiscences* (Central Falls, R.I.: E.L. Freeman, 1891)16; Massachusetts Anti-Slavery Society, *Annual Reports*, vols. 11–22.

13. James Brewer Stewart, *Wendell Phillips: Liberty's Hero* (Baton Rouge: Louisiana State University Press, 1986), 72.

14. See Stewart, *Wendell Phillips*, for examples of racial paternalism on the part of some of the Garrisonians, particularly Quincy and Chapman. Black abolitionists were particularly put off by the paternalism of upper-class abolitionists, particularly the tendency to preach to black abolitionists about self-discipline who many found patronizing. To be fair, many of these Brahmans acted paternalistically to most of their contemporaries. Much has also been made of Gar-

rison's opposition to Frederick Douglass's desire to start his own newspaper. Garrison objected not because Douglass was black, but because Garrison's always financially tenuous *Liberator* was dependent on black subscribers. Rightly afraid that Douglass's *North Star* would take subscribers from his paper, he attempted to browbeat Douglass into giving up the idea. But this treatment was not unique to Douglass: Garrison tended to browbeat all those who opposed him, black or white. Lawrence Friedman, *Gregarious Saints: Self and Community in American Abolitionism, 1830–1870* (Cambridge: Cambridge University Press, 1982), 187–88.

15. BPL, Samuel May letter to WLG, Oct. 15, 1873.

16. Quoted in Friedman, *Gregarious Saints*, 174. Friedman notes that abolitionists struggled against the "cord of prejudice" within themselves (172).

17. Ibid., 174.

18. GFP, Chace, *Anti-Slavery Reminiscences*, 14–16.

19. See Stewart, *Wendell Phillips*, 99.

20. Bowditch, *Life*, 130.

21. BPL, Maria Weston Chapman Papers, note, n.d. Abolitionist speakers boycotted the old Lyceum, and the new one effectively took over in New Bedford. Although Chapman championed equal rights for blacks, she also expressed the paternalism that alienated many black abolitionists. "Segregation policy was inhuman and wrong. It virtually excludes from its advantages those who most need them. It takes the colored population those whom the undeserved contempt and ill usage of society has degraded—those whom cruel prejudice has condemned to ignorance and increased their discrimination by adding its own might to them by proscription."

22. Friedman, *Gregarious Saints*, 162.

23. TWH, Houghton (575), TWH note to unknown, n.d.

24. GFP, Chace, *Anti-Slavery Reminiscences*, 44.

25. Ibid.

26. Quoted in Friedman, *Gregarious Saints*, 184.

27. Thomas Wentworth Higginson was also known for regularly having black houseguests. In 1859 he wrote to his mother that "the greatest heroine of the age, Harriet Tuckman (sic)," whom the "slaves call . . . Moses," was a guest at his home. TWH, Houghton (636), TWH letter to his mother Louisa, June 17, 1859.

28. Garrison argued that with the war rushing forward there should be no more anti-slavery meetings or even meetings for women's rights. BPL, WLG letter to Oliver Johnson, n.d.

29. Initially Phillips responded to Southern secession with a good riddance attitude. See Thomas Wentworth Higginson, *Contemporaries* (Boston: Houghton Mifflin, 1899), 274–76. Higginson was also slow to warm to the war.

30. Once blacks were enlisted, several abolitionists came forward to lead those troops. Besides Higginson, several veterans of the Kansas campaign and even some involved with Brown's Harper's Ferry attack led black units during the war. John McKivigan, "His Soul Goes Marching On: The Story of John Brown's Followers After the Harpers Ferry Raid," in McKivigan and Stanley Harrold, eds., *Antislavery Violence: Sectional, Racial, and Cultural Conflict in Antebellum America* (Knoxville: University of Tennessee Press, 1999), 288–89.

31. BFP, MHS, Scrapbooks, Memorial to Lt. Nathaniel Bowditch, Vol. I, AAAG, First Cavalry Brigade, 2nd Division, Army of the Potomac.

32. See Stewart, *Wendell Phillips*, 248.

33. Quoted in ibid., 265.

34. Garrison, *William Lloyd Garrison*, 6: 157–59..

35. Quoted in Stewart, *Wendell Phillips*, 244.

36. GFP, Chace, *Anti-Slavery Reminiscences*, 44.

37. TWH, Houghton (575), TWH note to unknown, n.d.

38. JWH, Houghton (320), Box 12, Address.

39. But if Chapman, Garrison, Quincy, May, and Johnson disagreed with Phillips, Bowditch, Foster, Douglass, and others on what to do after the war, they all agreed that central to the struggle against slavery was the struggle for human rights. Chapman said it was not a local affair but a "struggle for the welfare and rights of mankind." BPL, Maria Weston Chapman Papers, note, n.d.

40. Samuel May, who supported Garrison, noted in a letter to Samuel Joseph May that Phillips and his friends should have "terminated the anti-slavery agitation and cause as such when slavery was abolished by National Decree. It could have been done then with eminent propriety, justice, and effectiveness and the country and the world would have been forced to bear witness to the true dignity and splendid success of that 35 year moral war." May went on to argue that there was a new world and changed "social and political conditions in the South." BPL, Samuel May letter to Samuel Joseph May, March 26, 1868.

41. Quoted in Stewart, *Wendell Phillips*, 254.

42. Ibid., 285; Friedman, *Gregarious Saints*, 269.

43. Quoted in Mary Hetherington Grant, *Private Woman, Public Person: The Account of the Life of Julai Ward Howe from 1819–1868* (New York: Carlson Press, 1994), 161.

44. May Goddard Collection, Schlesinger Library, Harvard University, Box 2, Julia Ward Howe letter to Samuel May, May 14, 1890. See James McPherson, *The Struggle for Equality: Abolitionists and the Negro in the Civil War and Reconstruction* (Princeton, N.J.: Princeton University Press, 1964); McPherson, *The Abolitionist Legacy: From Reconstruction to the NAACP* (Princeton, N.J.: Princeton University Press, 1975); and George Fredrickson, *The Inner Civil War: Northern Intellectuals and the Crisis of the Union* (New York: Harper and Row, 1965) for abolitionists' views of the post-Civil War struggle for equality. See also Aileen S. Kraditor, *Means and Ends in American Abolitionism: Garrison and His Critics on Strategy and Tactics, 1834–1850* (New York: Pantheon, 1969).

45. Barnett Papers, London Metropolitan Archives, American Diary, 1867.

46. Quoted in McPherson, *The Abolitionist Legacy*, 19.

47. BFP, MHS, Memorial to Nathaniel Bowditch, "Introduction."

48. Franklin Sanborn, *Dr. S. G. Howe, the Philanthropist* (New York: Funk and Wagnalls, 1891), 288.

49. McPherson, *The Abolitionist Legacy*, 57.

50. This is not to say that the abolitionists were enthusiastic states rights federalists. They lived in a world where the location of power was in flux. Central to their concern was how that power was exercised, not where it was located. When the federal government was in the hands of the slave powers and was using its power to capture slaves in free states and return them to slavery, the abolitionists fought that power. When local governments were using their power to thwart the protection of basic rights, as in the case of southern state governments, the abolitionists looked to the federal government to step in and protect those rights.

51. See Stewart, *Wendell Phillips*, for a discussion of Phillips's vision of the reconstructed South. See also Friedman, *Gregarious Saints*, 269.

52. See McPherson for a discussion of Higginson's inconsistent position of

Black rights. See also Tilden G. Edelstein, *Strange Enthusiasm: A Life of Thomas Wentworth Higginson* (New Haven, Conn.: Yale University Press, 1968), 324. Higginson attacked E. L. Godkin, editor of the original abolitionist *Nation*, for his increasingly racist attacks against reconstruction. Ironically Garrison's son as an associate of Godkin also came to repeat these views.

53. Ibid., 333–35.

54. JWH, Houghton (310), Speeches, Box 12, n.d.

55. Higginson, *Part of a Man's Life*, 120.

56. WBP, Peabody, Bound Vol. 5, William Bowditch letter to Senator Hoar, Jan. 31, 1889.

57. HIB, Harvard, B MSc11.2 fd 1, HIB letter to Edward Jarvis, Oct. 1873.

58. Higginson, *Part of a Man's Life*, 120.

59. JWH, Houghton (320), Box 12, address.

60. TWH, Houghton (1107), TWH letter to his sisters, April 19, 1874.

61. HIB, Harvard, Seq., HIB letter to Olivia, n.d.

62. TWH, (491), TWH draft of a letter to unknown. probably an editor, n.d.

63. TWH, Houghton 1162.10 (75, 76, 77), William Jennings Bryan letter to TWH, Nov. 15, 1900; TWH letter to William Jennings Bryan, Dec. 3, 1901. Bryan allowed that, although he sent money to Booker T. Washington, he objected to Theodore Roosevelt inviting Washington to the White House for dinner as a social equal.

64. GFP, Chace, *Anti-Slavery Reminiscences*, 17.

65. WFP, Peabody, Box 13, folder 18.

66. It was this commitment to the principles of the Declaration of Independence that led to the abolitionists' ambivalence toward Lincoln's original call to arms. Abolitionists believed a people had the right to government of their consent. Many had for years advocated disunion of the North from the nation because that basic principle was corrupted by the 3/5 clause of the Constitution and the fugitive slave laws. When the South seceded and Lincoln did not make emancipation part of the northern war aims, many abolitionists felt good riddance. It was only as they came to realize that a successful South would mean a continuation of slavery for millions of blacks, and especially after the emancipation acts of northern generals. that abolitionists fully joined the war camp, although many still had civil liberties concerns. See Fredrickson, *The Inner Civil War* for the issue of disunion and secession.

Abolitionists were not necessarily consistent. Samuel Gridley Howe championed women's right to vote, but opposed his wife speaking in public and wanted her to remain within the traditional bounds of womanhood, a conflict that haunted their unhappy marriage. In 1852 Howe aligned himself with the state's factory owners by opposing the ten-hour day law, believing that the laws would undermine workers' autonomy; by 1866 he was advocating laws to protect workers from long exhausting work and low pay. See Samuel Gridley Howe, *Letters and Journals of Samuel Gridley Howe*, ed. Laura Howe Richards (Boston: D. Estes, 1906), 2: 343; Massachusetts Public Documents, Fifth Annual Report of the State Board of Charities (1869). Like Howe's, Phillips's position on labor and the role of the state was not consistent. See Stewart, *Wendell Phillips*. William Bowditch took a strong position favoring labor and opposing what he felt was the tendency of capitalism to exploit workers. See Jonathan Glickstein, "Abolitionists and the Labor Market," in Lewis Perry and Michael Fellman, eds., *Antislavery Reconsidered: New Perspectives in the Abolitionists* (Baton Rouge: Louisiana State University Press, 1979) for Bowditch's and other abolitionists' positions toward labor. Glickstein gives them too much credit for clear consistent thinking; even their views of racial equality fluctuated over time. What we need to remember is that these people were writing at a time in which industrial capitalism was in its infancy and a clear analysis of the nature of that system was not readily available anywhere.

67. Quoted in Stewart, *Wendell Phillips*, 282.

Chapter 6. "Blessed Are They Who When Some Great Cause . . . Calls Them . . . Come"

Epigraphs: Elizabeth Buffum Chace, *Anti-Slavery Reminiscences* (Central Falls, R.I.: E.L. Freeman, 1891), 47, 44, 47.

1. Julia Ward Howe, *Reminiscences: 1819–1899* (Boston: Houghton Mifflin, 1899), 375.

2. Although Henry Blackwell pledged equality when he married Lucy Stone, in practice he often resented her repeated absences from home and did not eagerly embrace equal child rearing. See Ellen Carol DuBois, *Feminism and Suffrage: The Emergence of an Independent Women's Movement in America, 1848–1869* (Ithaca, N.Y.: Cornell University Press, 1978), 27. Julia's husband's hostility to an egalitarian marriage was up-front and nasty. As late as July 1875, only six months before his death, Samuel Gridley Howe was still complaining about Julia's support of women's rights and the impact of the movement on gender relations. In a letter to his old friend Frank Bird, Howe whined, "I have fearful and useful teachings of the ill-effects of this woman's movement and concern in public affairs upon domestic duties, relations and affections." Letter reprinted in F. B. Sanborn, *Dr. S. G. Howe, the Philanthropist* (New York: Funk and Wagnalls, 1891), 339.

3. TWH, Houghton (433), TWH letter to his mother, Jan. 30, 1853.

4. Ibid. Higginson mentions in several letters to his mother the radical habit of wearing bloomers.

5. BPL, Lucy Stone letter to Friend May, Aug. 5, 1851.

6. Ibid., Aug. 14, 1851.

7. Also testifying were Higginson, Parker, and Phillips. See Tilden G. Edelstein, *Strange Enthusiasm: A Life of Thomas Wentworth Higginson* (New Haven, Conn.: Yale University Press, 1968), for Higginson's involvement in woman's rights.

8. TWH, Houghton (502), TWH letter to his mother, April 27, 1855.

9. Ibid. Lucy had to have a male trustee, James Buffum, whom she constantly berated because of the indignity of having to have him in the first place.

10. Ibid. (503), TWH letter to his mother, May 1, 1855.

11. It is unclear from how Higginson writes up the event whether Lucy said "not obey," or just did not say "obey."

12. See note 2.

13. GFP, Lucy Stone letter to James Buffum, Oct. 6, 1856.

14. Ibid., Lucy Stone to Buffum, July 4, 1857.

15. BPL, Lucy Stone letter to Friend May, Aug 14, 1851.

16. Chace, *Anti-Slavery Reminiscences*, 44.

17. BPL, Amenia White letter to Lucy Stone, Oct. 20, 1878.

18. Thomas Wentworth Higginson, *Cheerful Yesterdays* (Boston: Houghton Mifflin, 1898), 121.

19. The movement from abolition to suffrage has been well documented by

historians beginning with Aileen S. Kraditor, *The Ideas of the Woman Suffrage Movement, 1890–1920* (New York: Columbia University Press, 1965). Kraditor argued that the suffrage movement abandoned abolitionists' natural rights doctrine; she nonetheless accepts the position that abolitionists were crucial in the early years of suffrage. Ellen DuBois, whose work on early suffrage remains the standard to which all others refer, establishes clearly the link between early suffrage and abolition. Ellen Carol DuBois, *Feminism and Suffrage: The Emergence of an Independent Women's Movement in America, 1848–1869* (Ithaca, N.Y.: Cornell University Press, 1978). See also Lori D. Ginzberg, *Untidy Origins: A Story of Woman's Rights in Antebellum New York* (Chapel Hill: University of North Carolina Press, 2005) and Nancy Hewitt, *Women's Activism and Social Change: Rochester, New York, 1822–1872* (Ithaca, N.Y.: Cornell University Press, 1984).

20. *Commemoration of the 50th Anniversary of the Organization of the American Anti-Slavery Society in Philadelphia, 1884* (Philadelphia: Donald Publ., 1884).

21. Lydia Maria Child's husband David was a bit of a ne'er do well. Lydia was constantly trying to negotiate a position for him, but he would rather only work a few hours a day and putter around the garden the rest of the time. Lydia used her contracts to procure work for him in publishing and translating, but his laziness was frustrating for her. BFP, Peabody, Box 13, folder 5, Lydia Maria Child letter to Francis Jackson, Oct. 14, 1860.

22. BPL, A. Weston letter to Deborah Weston, March 11, 1839.

23. Phelps argued that by accepting women as equal members of the organization the Massachusetts Anti-Slavery Society "in its principles and modes of action had become a women's rights . . . society. He objected to women speaking to "promiscuous assemblies," meaning mixed sex audiences. Phelps noted that Kelley and the Grimkes were commonly talking to "promiscuous assemblies" and distracting people from anti-slavery. He also objected to Maria Weston Chapman's dominant role in the MASS. GFP, Ninth Annual Report, MASS, 1841.

24. GFP, Maria Weston Chapman's pamphlet *Right and Wrong in Massachusetts* (Boston: Dow & Jackson, 1840), 53.

25. Ibid. Chapman claimed that the issue was about freedom and rights. To deny women equal rights was to "act against freedom . . . and any act against freedom is treason to the slave. . . . Men whose principles, thus imperfectly developed are at war with each other, will, in all probability become worse in their last state than in their first" (156).

26. Ironically, a leading traditionalist opposed to women's equal participation in the AASS was Henry Stanton, husband of Elizabeth Cady Stanton.

27. GFP, "Ann Phillips: A Memorial Sketch," 1886. See also Wendell Phillips Garrison, *William Lloyd Garrison, 1805–1879* (New York: Negro Universities Press, 1969), all four volumes for letters about these controversies.

28. This break from traditional roles was not easy for either Abby or Stephan. During the early years of their marriage her salary and constant traveling bothered him, whose own career as an organizer effectively ended with his new role as child care provider and work on the farm. Abby also was concerned that being constantly on the road would prove stressful for their marriage, but as she adjusted her speaking schedule to bring her closer to home things improved.

29. TWH, Houghton (435), TWH letter to his mother, May 15, 1853; (440), TWH letter to Mary, Sept. 4, 1853; (477), TWH letter to Molly, n.d. Higginson's mother Louisa did not approve of women voting. "Exactly how far you go on the woman's rights question, I have more doubts you don't want them to vote

do you?" she asked him in 1852 (395), Louisa Higginson to TWH, April 22, 1852. In a letter to William Bowditch, her son-in-law, Louisa allowed that he had convinced her that women who wanted to vote should be allowed to, but she did not care to, because if women "attend to their own special duties as they require they will not have the time or opportunity to become sufficiently instructed in public matters whether of political or financial to be intelligent voters. Some few may be fitted we will leave it to them." BFP, Peabody, Box 13, folder 3, Louisa Higginson letter to WIB, n.d.

30. Quoted in Edelstein, *Strange Enthusiasm*, 148–49.

31. BPL, Lucy Stone letter to TWH, July 15, 1854. Antislavery agitation and women's rights went hand in hand. In the same letter that he talked about his and Parker's trial around the Burns case, and his around the Butman incident in Worcester, Higginson talked about the importance of the women's rights movement and how they needed to get Parker's sermon on "Woman and Her Wishes" out to the public along with Elizabeth Cady Stanton's "Appeal to the New York Legislature"; ibid., TWH letter to Maria Weston Chapman, Nov. 30, 1854. See also Samuel May letter to TWH, June 2, 1854. May noted that the Woman's Convention was "crowded to excess."

32. BPL, Lucy Stone letter to Friend May, Aug. 14, 1851.

33. BPL, Lucy Stone letter to Friend May, June 28, 1853.

34. TWH, Houghton (461), TWH letter to Samuel Johnson of Salem. See Johnson's reply, March 22, 1854. See also BPL, TWH letter to Mary, May 27, 1854; the letter was written on the back of the flyer "To the Friends of the Cause of Woman."

35. Lori Ginzberg also argues that women saw reform as a broad movement to transform society. Unlike this work, which emphasizes the community of social links and natural rights, Ginzberg focuses on the emergence of an ideology of domesticity and female benevolence. Lori D. Ginzberg, *Women and the Work of Benevolence: Morality, Politics, and Class in the Nineteenth-Century United States* (New Haven, Conn.: Yale University Press, 1990); see also Hewitt, *Women's Activism*. See Nancy Isenberg, *Sex and Citizenship in Antebellum America* (Chapel Hill: University of North Carolina Press, 1998) for the broad rights discussion that informed the early feminist movement.

36. Quoted in Higginson, *Cheerful Yesterdays*, 120. He referred to women's rights as one of the "sisterhood of reforms."

37. Thomas Wentworth Higginson, *Common Sense About Women* (Boston: Houghton Mifflin, 1881), 77.

38. BPL, Theodore Parker Sermons, "Some Thoughts on the New Assault upon Freedom in American and the General State of the Country," Feb. 12, 1854.

39. BFP, Peabody, Box 13, folder 5, Lydia Maria Child letter to "honored friend," probably Francis Jackson, Oct. 14, 1860.

40. BPL, Theodore Parker Sermons, Sermon 8, "Public Function of Woman," March 27, 1853.

41. Ibid., 5.

42. Ibid., 12.

43. Their children remembered their father's objection to women speaking out in public, particularly Julia. Laura Richards and Maude Howe Elliot, *Julia Ward Howe, 1819–1910* (Boston: Houghton Mifflin, 1925), 115.

44. Deborah Pickman Clifford, *Mine Eyes Have Seen the Glory: A Biography of Julia Ward Howe* (Boston: Little Brown, 1979), 160.

45. Richards and Elliot, *Julia Ward Howe*, 134.

46. Ibid., 115.

47. Ibid., 123.

48. Howe, *Reminiscences*, 372.

49. Ibid.

50. JWH, Houghton (320), Box 10, manuscript.

51. Quoted in Clifford, *Mine Eyes Have Seen the Glory*, 174.

52. Women suffrage supporters of the Fourteenth and Fifteenth Amendments were afraid Anthony, Stanton, and Pillsbury would lead woman's suffrage away from the Republican Party and into what they felt would be a disastrous alliance with pro-woman suffrage racist Democrats that would alienate Republican women. To counter Stanton and Anthony they formed the NEWSA. See DuBois, *Feminism and Suffrage*, 164–69 for the anti-Stanton, Anthony, Pillsbury motive behind the NEWSA.

53. See DuBois, *Feminism and Suffrage*, 71–74 for the conflict over the Fourteenth and Fifteenth Amendments among suffrage supporters. At one point Phillips argued for approaching suffrage for black males and females "one thing at a time" (63).

54. BPL, Samuel May letter to Samuel Joseph May, March 26, 1868.

55. The ironies in this debate abound. Elizabeth Cady Stanton, whose husband bolted from the AASS because it supported women's rights, argued that the AASS had to take a principled position for women's right to vote and not accept any compromise, or women should leave the organization. Phillips, who had strongly supported women's rights through the 1830s, '40s, and '50s and defended women's equal role in the AASS and the propriety of the AASS defending women's rights, now claimed that the AASS should not make support of women's suffrage a touchstone for supporting black rights.

56. DuBois, *Feminism and Suffrage*, 91–102. DuBois argues that Stanton and Anthony joined Train in anger at and disgust with the Republican Party, which they felt had betrayed women, and in a pragmatic attempt to break off dependence on the Radical Republicans to chart an independent course. This work argues that her analysis underplays the significance of this opportunism on the sensibilities of committed woman's suffrage supporters who had come through the abolitionist campaign and years of struggle against racism, their own as well as society's. Although it is true that Stanton, Anthony, and Pillsbury had abolitionist credentials, for many their links with Train's racist diatribes canceled those credentials. The appeal to racism may have been opportunistic in 1868, but it fed into a racism deeply ingrained in American culture and soon entwined women's suffrage with the ideals of white womanhood. DuBois points out that Henry Blackwell was capable of putting aside his egalitarian principles for opportunism (96, 100). See Newman, *White Women's Rights*, 62–65 for the campaign for women's rights and the racial assumptions that increasingly came to infect it. See also Kraditor, *The Ideas of the Woman's Suffrage Movement*, 185–90 for how white women increasingly abandoned equal rights for white privilege. By the 1880s the NWSA attacked both Republicans and Democrats and advocated independence from both parties. May Goddard Collection, Schlesinger Library, Harvard University, Box 2, Lucy Stone letter to Abby May, Sept. 17, 1872.

57. BPL, Samuel May letter to Samuel Joseph May, March 26, 1868. May wrote that he supported Stone in "oppos[ition]" to the Train-Anthony-Stanton-Pillsbury doings."

58. Wendell Phillips Garrison and Francis Jackson Garrison, *William Lloyd Garrison, 1805–1879: The Story of His Life Told by His Children* (New York: Negro Universities Press, 1969), 4: 242–43. Ironically, given its old abolitionist editor, Parker Pillsbury, the *Revolution* soon adopted overtly racist arguments, juxtaposing white women's intelligence and morality against "black ignorance and corruption." Quoted in DuBois, *Feminism and Suffrage*, 108.

59. Eventually money from this fund was divided between Susan B. Anthony, who used it to publish the "History of Women," and Lucy Stone, who supported the *Women's Journal.* WBP, Bound Vol. 5; see particularly Alice Stone Blackwell letter to WIB, July 11, 1893.

60. BFP, Peabody, Box 13, folder 19, Susan B. Anthony letter to Wendell Phillips, Nov. 14, 1867.

61. BFP, Peabody, Box 13, folder 10, Lucy Stone letter to Wendell Phillips, May 2, 1869; Susan B. Anthony letter to WP, May 2, 1869; LS letter to WP, May 6, 1869; SBA letter to LS and WP, June 1, 1870.

62. BFP, Peabody, Box 13, folder 10, LS to WP, July 8, 1871. Stone was willing to consider giving Anthony $150, but she demanded a full third of the fund. LS letter to WP, April 15, 1870; LS letter to WP June 2, 1870. WBP, Peabody, Bound Vol. 5, SBA letter to WP, April 28, 1870.

63. BPL, LS letter to TWH, Jan. 9, 1873.

64. While Pillsbury, Anthony, and Stanton publicly attacked Republican Reconstruction for failing to address the interests of women, Stone, Howe, Higginson, Bowditch, and Blackwell argued that public attacks against Republicans would alienate potential women's rights supporters. Privately they were also disappointed with the failures of the Republicans to support suffrage more aggressively. TWH, Houghton (1077), TWH letter to his sisters, Dec. 15, 1871.

65. JWH, Houghton (320), Speeches, Box 12.

66. Tactically the NEWSA argued for support of the Fourteenth and Fifteenth Amendments, while pushing for women's suffrage, first in the District of Columbia, then in the territories, and finally through a general amendment. How historians have understood this conflict partly depends on their focus of concern. For the most part, historians of women's history see Anthony's and Stanton's opposition to the amendments as an indication of the movement toward an independent, women-centered movement, while Stone's and Howe's position has been seen as keeping women subordinate to other concerns. This work does not so much disagree with that understanding as try to view the split from the perspective of the time. In looking back from what happened to woman's suffrage after this period, certainly Stanton's and Anthony's independent course led to an independent and vibrant women's movement. But it was not at all clear in 1868 that this was where that division was heading. For committed feminists such as Stone, Anthony and Stanton were heading toward not an independent women's movement but a capitulation to racism and exclusionism. Indeed, even historians who support the Stanton-Anthony version of events have noted its costs in class and race exclusivity. Besides DuBois and Kaditor, see Jean Fagan Yellin, *Women and Sisters: The Anti-Slavery Feminists in American Culture* (New Haven, Conn.: Yale University Press, 1989).

67. See Eleanor Flexner, *Century of Struggle: The Woman's Rights Movement in the United States* (Cambridge, Mass.: Harvard University Press, 1975), 154–56. See DuBois, *Feminism and Suffrage,* for the controversy at the Equal Rights Convention.

68. Quoted in Stacey M. Robertson, *Parker Pillsbury: Racial Abolitionist, Male Feminist* (Ithaca, N.Y.: Cornell University Press, 2000), 148.

69. See James Brewer Stewart, *Wendell Phillips: Liberty's Hero* (Baton Rouge: Louisiana State University Press, 1986), 285.

70. JWH, Houghton (320), Speeches, Box 15.

71. Richards and Elliot, *Julia Ward Howe*, 198.

72. Julia's daughters writing sixty years after the event claim that one reason for the split was that the American Woman's Suffrage Association was not so radical and accepted men into the organization. Eleanor Flexner and Ellen DuBois, following Richards and Elliot, argue that the NWSA was more radical than the AWSA, basing their assessment partly on the fact that the latter accepted males, even into leadership positions. Flexner also argues that the NWSA took positions on divorce, religion, and other controversial issues while the AWSA did not. I am not convinced this was the case. Pillsbury and Stanton took free-thinking positions in the organization's paper, *Revolution*, but among the AWSA there were just as radical positions on religion and divorce. Also it has been noted that the AWSA distanced itself from Victoria Woodhull, condemning her doctrines of sex at their 1871 convention; it should be noted that although Stanton remained loyal to Woodhull through most of her controversies, the NWSA due to Anthony's influence attempted to distance itself from Woodhull.

When Alice Stone Blackwell took over the *Woman's Journal*, she established an editorial policy that the journal should not address issues outside suffrage and issues concerning women, such as "dress reform, cooperative housekeeping, the servant question, the general subject of the employment of women." She argued that other reform issues such as labor rights or immigration would only alienate potential supporters, using the example that the *Journal*'s support of immigrant that led supporters in California to refuse to distribute it. But this was not until the mid-1880s, when Alice was already trying to move the AWSA into merger with the NWSA. GFP, Box, 21, folder 43, Alice Stone Blackwell letter to Eva, July 28, 1886. The fundamental difference between the two organizations was the AWSA's continued commitment to black rights and the belief that suffrage was part and parcel of a natural rights position, and its willingness to work with Radical Republicans, although in 1872 both organizations joined with Republicans in support of Grant. See Flexner, *Century of Struggle*, 154–56. Although it is true that men were prominent members of the AWSA (Higginson was president at one time, and Garrison was elected president two years before his death), this was not the issue that divided the two organizations. Stone, Howe, Higginson, Bowditch, and others in the AWSA were militantly committed to promoting women's suffrage as a campaign for human rights and part of the general campaign for equal rights to all. Stanton and Anthony increasingly oriented the NWSA as a woman-centered organization. BPL, LS letter to WLG, Dec. 3, 1876.

73. BPL, LS letter to WLG, Feb. 27, 1869.

The NWSA created a Committee of Correspondence to build support for the new national organization, which was "at once more comprehensive and more widely representative than any [existing organizations]. Support was quickly rounded up among old abolitionists; Garrison, Hoar, and Clarke lent their names to the new movement. TWH, Houghton Box 6 (1042). See also "Dear . . ." letter issued Aug. 15, 1869; BPL, Mary Livermore letter to WLG Aug. 16, 1869.

74. BPL, LS letter to WLG, Aug. 22, 1869.

75. JWH, Houghton (320), Speeches, Box 14.

76. Ibid.

77. Ibid., Box 15.

78. Ibid. (320), "Talk Before Concord," 1870.

79. Ibid. Julia told the people of Concord that when the women's movement began twenty years earlier she was not "in their ranks," but listening to Theodore Parker's sermons, she finally came to realize, "we could not take the husband, with his absolute authority." Ironically Julia's own husband continued to try to assert "his absolute authority," but by 1870 Julia had come to ignore him and find new fellowship among women and those men, such as Higginson and Wendell Phillips, who "brought with him the breath of that freer air, the power of that larger effort," who supported women's rights.

80. William Bowditch, *Woman Suffrage, a Right Not a Privilege* (Cambridge, Mass.: University Press, 1872), 40 (Library of Congress collection). noted that in Massachusetts the founding document claims that the right to govern rests in the "people of the Commonwealth," not men but "all people." Bowditch followed this with a shorter (*Woman Suffrage* was 51 pages) "The Right to Govern Ourselves," which again stressed that the right of suffrage was a natural right. Julia Ward Howe told her daughter that in speeches she stressed that women's suffrage was an "individual right, integral to humanity, ideal justice." Richards and Elliot, *Julia Ward Howe*, 278.

81. Bowditch, *Taxation of Women in Massachusetts*. WBP, Peabody, Box 13, folder 3, Abby Foster to WIB, March 20, 1875. Foster also noted in her letter that Senator Hoar has lost his backbone. She saw him as having abandoned the "Negro... but the rebellious old slaveholders and their now rebellious sons must have charity," by strengthening elite schools and doing nothing to protect the black schools. See also Davis letter to WIB, April, 9, 1875. Bowditch's "The Right to Govern Ourselves" and "How Long Shall We Rob and Enslave Women" were major pamphlets in the campaign for women's rights. WBP, Peabody, Bound Vol. 5.

82. BFP, Peabody, Box 13, folder 3, WLG to WIB April 3, 1873.

83. Schlesinger Library, Harvard University, William Bowditch letter, 1879. The names on these petitions read like a who's who of the region's abolitionists and their children. See also BFP, Peabody, Box 13, folder 4, Samuel May letter to WIB, Oct. 18, 1874.

84. May Goddard Collection, Schlesinger Library, Harvard University, Box 2, Nov. 2, 1869, Dec. 1873, Sept. 1879.

85. JWH, Houghton (323), Box 19, "notebooks, 1880s."

86. BFP, MHS, Box 2, *Woman's Journal*, Boston, 1892.

87. May Goddard Collection, Schlesinger Library, Harvard University, Box 2, Lydia Maria Child letter to Abby May, Aug. 15, 1874.

88. Bowditch, *Woman Suffrage, a Right Not a Privilege*, 22.

89. TWH, Houghton (1077), TWH letter to his sisters, Dec. 15, 1871. Sumner also supported Hoar's position on equal representation on juries.

90. May Goddard Collection, Schlesinger Library, Harvard University, Box 2, Lucy Stone letter to Abby May, Sept. 17, 1872.

91. GFP, Box, 46, MS group 69, folder 1154, WIB letter to WLG II, March 17, 1885.

92. BFP, Peabody, Bound Vol. 5, WIB letters to Senator Hoar, Jan. 31, 1889, Feb. 11, 1889.

93. Richards and Elliot, *Julia Ward Howe*, 275.

94. JWH, Houghton (320), "Speeches," Box 15.

95. JWH, Houghton (320), Box 13, "Lecture on Divorce and Marriage, 1884." See also Richards and Elliot, *Julia Ward Howe*, 259, for Julia's petition to reform Massachusetts divorce laws.

96. In an early 1860s essay Julia pointed to "the equality, the dignity and the eternal dissimilarity of the two sexes." JWH, Houghton (322), no date. See also her justification for her campaign for Mother's Day for Peace, *Reminiscences.*

97. Besides Lucy Stone's daughter Alice Stone Blackwell, who took over the *Woman's Journal* and the leadership of the AWSA, also active were Abby Kelley Foster's daughter Abby and the children of Henry and William Bowditch, particularly William's daughter Susan and Henry's daughter Lucy. WBP, Peabody, also Bound Vol. 5.

98. JWH, Houghton (320), Box 13, "Draft of address to Association for the Advancement of Women, 1890." Julia was not the only one concerned. Blackwell, although pushing the merger, privately was concerned that "Miss Anthony and 2 or 3 of her special friends in whom the old 'National vs. American spirit' is still strong" would dominate the new organization. WBP, Peabody, Bound Vol. 5.

99. Stanton embraced the idea of limited franchise in the 1860s conflict. She increasingly talked about ignorant "Sambo" and the horror of enfranchisement of "Africans, Chinese, and all the ignorant foreigners the moment they touch our shores." Quoted in Flexner, *Century of Struggle*, 1975, 147. See Yellin, *Women and Sisters* and Newman, *White Women's Rights* for a discussion of the increasing importance of white women's privilege in the campaign for suffrage.

100. GFP, Elizabeth Cady Stanton to WLG II, Dec. 5, 1899.

101. JWH, Houghton (320), box 13, "Draft of address."

102. TWH, Houghton (1131), TWH letter to Anne, Nov. 12, 1891. Many members of the New England Woman's Club were old abolitionists or children of abolitionists. See Clifford, *Mine Eyes Have Seen the Glory*, 251–53 for a discussion of Julia's opposition to the Federation and her involvement in the AAW.

103. Richards and Elliot, *Julia Ward Howe*, 206. The AAW brought women together from various parts of the country to talk about issues of importance to women and present papers on women's condition. It was designed to provide information and science to women.

104. Higginson claimed that Julia was the spirit behind the Town and Country Club, a literary and philosophical gathering of intellectuals who presented papers and critiqued each other's work. TWH, Houghton (1148), TWH letter to Fields, July 25, 1877; TWH letter to Anna, Aug. 15, 1875.

105. BFP, Peabody, Box 13, folder 3, Alice Stone Blackwell letter to WIB, Oct. 6, 1893.

Chapter 7. Bringing Together the Professional and the Political

Epigraphs: HIB, Harvard University, MJ, July 30, 1880, Henry Ingersoll Bowditch's reference to Samuel Sewall. New England Hospital for Women and Children, *Marie Elizabeth Zakrzewska: A Memoir* (Boston: the Hospital, 1903).

1. Sophia Smith Collection, Smith College, Box ME2, folder 30.

2. New England Hospital, *Marie Elizabeth Zakrzewska*, 14.

3. HIB, MHS, Scrapbook; *Annual Report*, 1892. Marie found in Boston "a group of noble men and women zealous in all attempts toward elevating and broadening women's life." New England Hospital, *Marie Elizabeth Zakrzewska*, 14.

4. When she first arrived in Boston Zakrzewska stayed with the Garrisons. GFP, Box 84, folder 2301 WLG, II, letter to Wendell Phillips Garrison, March 9, 1857. See also the letter read at her funeral, May 1902.

5. Marie Elizabeth Zakrzewska, *A Woman's Quest: The Life of Marie E. Zakrzewska, M.D.* , ed. Agnes C. Vietor (New York: D. Appleton, 1924), 238. She was also identified with the woman's suffrage movement, a member and active supporter of the AWSA and a close friend of Lucy Stone and Julia Ward Howe. Sophia Smith Collection, Smith College, Box 84, folder 2301, *Boston Herald*, May 16, 1902.

6. Zakrzewska, *A Woman's Quest*, 293–95.

7. Sophia Smith Collection, Smith College, Box ME 2, folder 30, Emma Call letter, 1928.

8. Also a supporter of the hospital was Walter Channing, Higginson's father-in law and dean of Harvard Medical School. HIB, MHS, *Annual Report*, 1892. Bowditch and Cabot's reputations were such that "their names were sufficient guarantee to the public for the honor and usefulness of our institution" (8). Sophia Smith Collection, Smith College, Box 21, File 54, Mrs. E. D. Cheney letter to HIB 1885.

9. HIB, MHS, *Annual Report*, Sept. 1892.

10. HIB, MHS, The others who came forward were Bowditch's friend Dr. Jarvis and James Freeman Clarke. Despite the presence of male doctors as consulting physicians, the New England Hospital was definitely a female institution. The overwhelming majority of its board of directors were female, as were all the officers of the organization. The membership was a veritable who's who of female abolitionists or younger children of abolitionist families. Mrs. J. F. Clarke, Abby May, and Sarah Russell were all abolitionists. The first president, Lucy Goddard, was the child of an abolitionist family whose aunt was Mary May. Henry Ingersoll Bowditch's daughter Olivia became a member of the board and her younger brother Vincent joined as a consulting physician as his father had been. *Annual Report*, Sept. 1892, 391.

11. Bowditch, *Life*, 212.

12. HIB, MHS, Box 3.

13. Bowditch, *Life*, 182. Bowditch joined the women's issue section of the National Association for the Promotion of Social Science.

14. HIB, Harvard, bMs c75.2, "Report of the Committee on Admission of Women to the Massachusetts Medical Society," MS.Ds Oct. 1, 1875.

15. HIB, Harvard, bMs c75.2, W.W. Wellington and Samuel Fisk, Minority Report of MMS, Oct. 6, 1875.

16. Ibid. Fisk went on to note that since women were "led by their fancies," it would be impossible "to keep them within the rules of the society and the gallantry of many and the fear of the outcry upon them would prevent any exercise of discipline upon them. . . . Once we let a violation of its ethics go un-rebuked . . . then farewell to the . . . MMS. Ibid. Fisk then noted he hoped "no one will charge me with wishing to deprive women of education" since he was a supporter of Smith College.

17. Ibid.

18. Fisk claimed that the MSS mission was to suppress "quackery," and that admitting women would disrupt the harmony of the organization and prevent it from doing its job. Besides, he argued, no "respectable women [would want] to unite with any society" where they were not welcomed by a sizable minority. HIB, Harvard, Samuel Fisk letter to HIB, Sept. 22, 1878.

19. Sophia Smith Collection, Smith College, Box ME2, folder 22.

20. Bowditch, *Life*, 2: 212.

21. TWH, Houghton (1095), TWH letter to his sister, March 8, 1873.

22. TWH, Houghton, James Freeman Clarke letter to TWH, Nov. 18, 1873.

23. HIB, Harvard, bMs, misc., HIB letter to Edith Varney, Sept. 24, 1890.

24. HIB, Harvard, MJ, Clipping, *Boston Advertiser*, April 3, 1889.

25. HIB, Harvard University, bMs, misc., HIB letter to Edith Varney, Sept. 24, 1890. Varney eventually gave her money to Boston University's Homeopathic Medical School.

26. Sophia Smith Collection, Smith College, Box ME2 folder 30.

27. BFP, MHS, Scrapbook.

28. See Harry Moore, *Public Health in the United States* (New York: Harper Brothers, 1923); C. E. A. Winslow, *The Evolution and Significance of the Modern Public Health Campaign* (New Haven, Conn.: Yale University Press, 1923); George Rosen, *History of Public Health* (New York, MD Publications, 1958); John Duffy, *A History of Public Health in New York City, 1866–1966* (New York, Sage, 1974); Duffy, *The Sanitarians: A History of American Public Health* (Urbana: University of Illinois Press, 1992); James H. Cassedy, *Charles V. Chapin and the Public Health Movement* (Cambridge, Mass.: Harvard University Press, 1962); Barbara Gutmann Rosenkrantz, *Public Health and the State: Changing Views in Massachusetts, 1842–1936* (Cambridge, Mass.: Harvard University Press, 1972); Paul Starr, *The Social Transformation of American Medicine* (New York: Basic Books, 1984).

29. Shattuck's study was based on the radical English reformer William Farr's work on contagious diseases in England. Shattuck was in communication with Farr and Farr had encouraged Shattuck to develop a standard for disease identification and registration. See Rosenkrantz, *Public Health and the State*, 24. Curtis became secretary of the Boston Association for the Promotion of Sanitary Science and pushed for a state board. In a letter to Jarvis in 1861 he urged Jarvis to get doctors around the state to petition the legislature for this. Edward Jarvis Papers, Countway Library, Harvard University, Josiah Curtis letter to Edward Jarvis, Feb., March 8, 21, 1861.

30. Jarvis also helped Shattuck put together his report on the conditions of the poor in Boston. Rosenkrantz covers this history in great detail, so I only sketch it here.

31. Chadwick Papers, University of London, School of Public Hygiene and Tropical Medicine, Letter10, Chadwick letter to J. Hill Burton n,d, probably 1840s; Letter 33, Chadwick to J. Hill Burton, Dec. 7, 1843.

32. Chadwick Papers, University College London, Special Collections, Copy Book II, 38, Chadwick letter to Frederick Hill, 1844. See also William Farr letter to Chadwick, Feb. 13, 1837; Chadwick Papers, University of London, School of Public Hygiene and Tropical Medicine, Letter 7, Chadwick letter to J. Hill Burton, n.d, probably 1840s; Letter 38, Chadwick to J. Hill Burton, July 31, 1844. Chadwick championed reforming the poor laws to make them less repressive to the poor. Chadwick Papers, University College London, Special Collections, Harriet Martineau letter to Chadwick, n.d.

33. Chadwick Papers, University College London, Special Collections, Edward Jarvis letter to Chadwick, June 9, 1853. Chadwick regularly sent Jarvis reports on Sanitary Reform and data gathered in Great Britain. Jarvis also asked Chadwick's advice on the issue of Irish immigrants. In one letter to Chadwick, Jarvis comments "we are indebted to you and your nation for all the first steps

in the sanitary movement, for your reports, your arguments, for the undertakings, for the amelioration of the conditions of the poor."

34. Rosenkrantz notes that Shattuck's focus was pietistic, and he was mostly concerned about personal morality and behavior. She argues that the politics of Massachusetts in the 1850s was no longer about personal reform and morality but about power, hence Shattuck, despite his involvement in electoral politics (being an elected Whig) was less able to command an effective hearing at the state political level. Rosenkrantz, *Public Health and the State*, 34.

35. Henry Ingersoll Bowditch, "The Massachusetts Board of Health, Its Origins, Its Reputation at Home and Abroad, Its Grotesque Metamorphosis and Death Under Political Fear and Chicanery, Its Reconstruction With Vastly Increased Powers," undated manuscript, Monograph, Vol. VIII, Harvard University, Boston, 3. Here after cited as "Origins." Bowditch was already inclined to a broad epidemiological view toward medicine. His early commitment to Louis's numeric system fitted nicely with the new public health focus.

36. George Hoyt Bigelow, "Henry P. Walcott," *New England Journal of Medicine* 207, 23 (Dec.1932): 1002; "Origins," 3. The State Board of Health was one of a series of state boards created in the 1860s. The state created the State Board of Charities (1864), the Rail Road Commission (1869), and a State Commission of Inland Fisheries (1866). See Rosenkrantz, *Public Health and the State*, 52.

37. Governor Andrew, the old abolitionist, had supported the Board since the beginning of his administration, when Curtis, Jarvis, and Bowditch first tried to get the legislature to create a state board. The legislation failed until Plunkett's wife got Plunkett to back the bill.

38. Davis had also been involved in sanitary improvements for the soldiers during the war. Edward Jarvis Papers, Countway Library, Harvard University, Josiah Curtis letter to Edward Jarvis, Sept. 12, 1862.

39. Sanborn wrote for that board that "3/4 of what is technically called crime among us is the direct result of poverty," and that to successfully deal with crime the legislature must work to alleviate poverty and that means addressing the "question of labor and its compensations." Massachusetts Public Documents, Annual Reports of the State Board of Charities, Massachusetts, 1865 (Boston, 1865) (hereafter SBC, Annual Reports)

40. "Notes to the Class of 1828, Henry Ingersoll Bowditch," Harvard University.

41. Derby's interest in sanitary issues led him to be appointed as health inspector of slum buildings in Boston. He resigned in protest because he believed the laws were not being adequately enforced. Rosenkrantz, *Public Health and the State*, 67.

42. Josiah Curtis, a Republican Party supporter, joined the Union army with Lincoln's call to arms. While working on sanitary conditions in the field, he wrote home to organize activity on the home front in support of sanitary reform. Edward Jarvis Papers, Countway Library, Harvard University, Josiah Curtis letters to Edward Jarvis, Sept. 17, Nov. 15, Dec. 19, 1861, Jan. 22, 30, 1863.

43. Bowditch called his campaign to get a national government run ambulance service for soldiers his "contest for the rights of the soldier." Bowditch, *Life*, 1: 30.

44. "Origins," 2–5.

45. Ibid., 25, 26.

46. Ibid., 8–9, 15.

47. HIB, Harvard, Seq., Bowditch journal entry on funeral of Dr. and Mrs. Jarvis.

48. "Origins," 8–9.

49. HIB, Harvard, Vol. 8, Address to the Board, 9.

50. HIB, Harvard, Edward Jarvis letter to HIB, Dec. 17, 1869.

51. HIB, Harvard, Harvard Medical School, Bowditch letter to Jarvis.

52. Bowditch, *Life*, 2: 228.

53. HIB, Harvard, Archives A9.20 Vol. 7, 1878 AMA Conference.

54. "Preventative Medicine and the Physician of the Future," SBC, Fifth Annual Report, 1874.

55. Bowditch Papers, Countway, Vol. IV, No. 31. Bowditch listed his reasons for leaving the Board, among them that the Board was not forcibly going after the practice of dumping effluent into millstreams "by the mills owned by evil capitalists."

56. Bowditch felt that Derby's caution was unnecessary yet came from a genuine commitment to the larger vision of the board. See Bowditch's statement on the 1874 death of George Derby, Harvard University Archive, Pusey Library, "He [Derby] did not feel as I have ever felt that certainly, in the present condition of the world, if our board should be for any reason abolished by any legislature, its immediate successor would be compelled by public opinion, to call another board of similar character into existence. State or preventative medicine, has taken so deep a root into the conscience of the English speaking race, that hereafter boards of health or in other words for the prevention of disease, must forever exist, and they will have more and more weight upon the policy of states and of nations.".

57. "Origins," 26.

58. See Rosenkrantz, *Public Health and the State*, 66.

59. HIB, Harvard, MJ, May 26, 30, 31, 1870. Going to Europe, especially England, to investigate actions taken there was a well established pattern in the nineteenth century. When Samuel Gridley Howe took over as director of the Massachusetts Institute for the Blind his first act was to tour Europe to investigate institutions. In 1873 the Massachusetts State Board of Charities sent its secretary to visit England, France, Belgium, and Germany to study penal and charitable institutions and approaches. Like Bowditch he visited the Barnetts and Octavia Hill.

60. HIB, Harvard, MJ, May 26, 30, 31.

61. HIB, Harvard, MJ, Bowditch's Journal, 154. In a letter to his wife, Bowditch comments that he went to a meeting of the National Association for the Promotion of Social Science in Newcastle and attended the health section that debated the issue of sewage. See Sanborn's SBC, First Annual Report, 1865.

62. OH, LPE, letter to Yetta, Nov. 12, 1876.

63. Bowditch, *Life*, 2: 230.

64. HIB, Harvard, Seq., Nov. 9, 1884. Bowditch argued that the role of the state was to control not the "poor sot" who drank, but those who made money off exploiting the poor and the "drunkard-maker." Bowditch, *Life*, 1: 114. Like Bowditch, Julia Ward Howe believed that although drinking was a problem, the prohibitionists' "method always appeared to me questionable," because it "involved one person trampling on another's rights." JWH, Houghton (320), Box 13. Bowditch's nonpaternalistic view was also reflected in his attitude toward abortion. When H. R. Storer attempted to get the Massachusetts Medical Society to endorse legislation against abortion, Bowditch argued against the action, noting that there were reasons for abortions, and that unlike most laws like theft, where there was an injured party, in the case of abortion both the woman

and the doctor voluntarily initiated the act. HIB, Harvard, HIB letter to H. R. Storer, April 20, 1857.

65. HIB, Harvard, MJ, Bowditch's Journal, 154. Bowditch's abolitionists friends Howe and Sanborn were making the same points in their State Board of Charities Reports. See SBC, Annual Reports, 1865, 1866, 1874.

66. Rosenkrantz, *Public Health and the State*, 62, 63. Bowditch continued long after the Civil War to rank people in terms of where they stood on slavery during the hard years of the abolitionist struggle. He never forgave Emerson for being late to the abolitionist cause and had no time for those who defended Emerson by claiming he was a poet and intellectual who needed to focus on writing and thinking rather than action. "Notes to the Class of 1828, Henry Ingersoll Bowditch," Harvard University.

67. That was the lesson of slavery for Bowditch and explained his intense hostility to New England's religious leaders who had not aggressively attacked slavery. His condemnation of institutional religion grew out of his belief that in failing to come out stronger against slavery, religious leaders helped sustain it.

68. See George M. Fredrickson, *The Inner Civil War: Northern Intellectuals and the Crisis of the Union* (New York: Harper and Row, 1965) for the appreciation of the power of the state to accomplish social ends.

69. Franklin Sanborn, Samuel Gridley Howe, and the State Board of Charities called for state laws limiting hours of labor, restricting overly exhausting labor, and providing fair livable wages for employees. See SBC, Annual Reports, 1865, 1886, 1874, 1875. For Bowditch's support of recreation for children and adults see HIB, Harvard, "Address to the Graduating Class of Harvard Medical School, 'An Apology; or the Medical Profession as a Means of Developing the Whole Nature of Man,'" Boston, 1863.

70. Quoted in Rosenkrantz, *Public Health and the State*, 67.

71. Bowditch, *Life*, 1: 189–90, Oct. 31, 1846.

72. Katherine Day Putman Papers, 1862–1876, MHS, bound papers, 1871, HIB letter to Katherine Day Putman, 1871.

73. "Preventative Medicine and the Physician of the Future," SBC, Fifth Annual Report, 1874.

74. See Rosenkrantz, *Public Health and the State*, 67. Tenement house reform occupied Bowditch's attention even before his involvement with the board. In 1848 he noted that he "was determined that something ought to be done about improving the tenements of the poor." Bowditch, *Life*, 1: 189–90. He continued to work for tenement house reform. In 1871 he was involved in the founding of the Boston Cooperative Building Company, along with fellow abolitionist James Freeman Clarke, to try to build model tenements. "Notes to the Class of 1828, Henry Ingersoll Bowditch," Harvard University. Tenement house reform was also a major concern of other Boston reformers. Bowditch's old friend and anti-slavery comrade Samuel Gridley Howe, as the first chair of the State Board of Charities, tried to focus attention of the Board on housing and clothing for the poor.

75. Massachusetts State Board of Health, Fourth Annual Report, 1872, 81.

76. *Edward Haskill v. City of New Bedford* (Oct. 1871), MA Reports, Brown, Vol. 12, 208.

77. Massachusetts State Board of Health, Ninth Annual Report, 1878, 59; Lyman Family Papers, MHS, Vol. 22, Theodore Lyman Papers, Diaries, July 10, 1865.

78. In Howe's State Board of Charities Report, he also argues that happiness was a right denied to those in poverty.

79. Bowditch argued that human nature had certain desires, including "enjoyment of the outward world experience, friendship and love." Since doctors and society had a responsibility to help" in people's love and emotional state," they needed to expand the authority of "state medicine," to protect peoples ability to experience the happiness of friendship love and the enjoyment of the outward world experience. HIB, Harvard, "Address to the Graduating Class." Since individuals could not enjoy their right of pursuit of happiness if they were forced to live in indecent conditions, the state would protect them by providing a decent environment. "Preventative Medicine and the Physician of the Future," Massachusetts State Board of Health, Fifth Annual Report. Other boards, particularly in New England, picked up on the Massachusetts position that a clean environment was a natural right. In its first report the New Hampshire Board stated, "we believe that every person has a legitimate right to nature's gifts, pure water, air and soil- a right belonging to every individual and every community upon which no one should be allowed to trespass." New Hampshire Board of Health, First Annual Report (Concord, 1882), 133.

80. See John T. Cumbler, *Reasonable Use: the People, the Environment, and the State* (Oxford: Oxford University Press, 2001) 144–160 for court support of corporations' argument that pollution was in the greater good. See also Theodore Steinberg, *Nature Incorporated: Industrialization and the Waters of New England* (Cambridge: Cambridge University Press, 1991); Morton J. Horwitz, *The Transformation of American Law, 1780–1860* (Cambridge, Mass.: Harvard University Press, 1977).

81. Connecticut State Board of Health, Second Annual Report (Hartford, 1880) 25.

82. Quoted in Rosenkrantz, *Public Health and the State*, 83.

83. BFP, MHS, Box 3, WIB letter to Vincent Bowditch, Jan. 8, 1903. See John T. Cumbler, *Reasonable Use* for the history of this conflict.

84. See Cumbler, *Reasonable Use*, for corporate resistance to the anti-pollution campaign; see also Rosenkrantz, *Public Health and the State*. See Sanborn and Howe, SBC Annual Reports for continued references to greedy capitalists, monopolists, and landlords as being responsible for poverty and crime as much as moral failure.

85. HIB, Harvard Medical School, Bowditch Monographs, Vol. VIII, no. 31, 245.

86. Ibid., 48. Donnelly assumed the chair of the merged board and immediately ran into conflict with Bowditch, eventually leading to Bowditch's resignation. Unlike his resignation from Massachusetts General Hospital, this time it did not produce reform results. Donnelly continued on the board until a conflict with Butler, who saw Donnelly as a conservative Cleveland Democrat opposed to Butler's attempts to dominate the state Democratic Party, led to Donnelly's removal from the board. But this action did not bring Bowditch's visions back. The state industrialists still opposed an activist board and worked to have even moderate public health reformer Henry Walcott removed after Republican George Robinson was elected governor and Donnelly was reappointed.

87. See Cumbler, *Reasonable Use*. Walcott, removed from the merged board under Donnelly, was put on the new board as chair. It also added Hiram Mills, an engineer from the Lowell textile industry, who was concerned about water quality.

88. See Nancy Tomes, *The Gospel of Germs: Men, Women, and the Microbe in American Life* (Cambridge, Mass.: Harvard University Press, 1998).

89. In a letter to Fredrick Shattuck in 1911, Sir William Osler wrote from Oxford that Bowditch created a community among people not just in one country but across borders. HIB, Harvard Medical School, Sir William Bart Osler letter to Fredrick Shattuck, April 5, 1911.

Chapter 8. "Public Society Owes Perfect Protection": The State and the People's Rights

Epigraphs: Julia Ward Howe's last statement before the Massachusetts State House on the cause of pure milk, spring 1910, Laura Richards and Maud Howe Elliot, *Julia Ward Howe, 1819–1910* (Boston: Houghton Mifflin, 1925), 434–35; James Brewer Stewart, *Wendell Phillips: Liberty's Hero* (Baton Rouge: Louisiana State University Press, 1986), 323.

1. *Commemoration of the Fiftieth Anniversary of the Organization of the American Anti-Slavery Society in Philadelphia* (Philadelphia: T.S. Dando, 1884), 15.

2. Ibid., 51.

3. Franklin Sanborn, *Dr. S. G. Howe, the Philanthropist* (New York: Funk and Wagnalls, 1891), 345.

4. Samuel Gridley Howe, who later came to champion aggressive state action to alleviate poverty, argued against the ten-hour day bill in the 1850s on the grounds that it would limit the independence of workers, and that a ten-hour day bill would legitimate a ten-hour day when in fact workers should not work more than six to eight hours. See Harold Schwartz, *Samuel Gridley Howe: Social Reformer, 1801–1876* (Cambridge, Mass.: Harvard University Press, 1956) 269.

5. Massachusetts Public Documents, Annual Reports, *First Annual Report of the Board of State Charities* (Boston: Wright and Potter, 1865), hereafter RBSC, 409.

6. Ibid., 410.

7. Ibid. See Nathan Irvin Huggins, *Protestants Against Poverty: Boston's Charities, 1870–1900* (Westport, Conn.: Greenwood Press, 1971), for a different view of New England charity reformers.

8. Quoted in Schwartz, *Samuel Gridley Howe*, 269. Howe went on to argue that the rich should take note, "for our people will ask questions about the rights of property, which will be hard to be answered and they will not be bamboozled by any superstitions, religious or social."

9. Ibid. Howe wrote to Sumner that his reform ideas might lead people to call him "red, very red perhaps they think me green."

10. Second Annual RBSC, 1866, xiv–xxii.

11. Ibid., xxx.

12. Ibid., xxxiv.

13. Ibid., xliv.

14. Fifth Annual RBSC, xxiv. The board also continued to fight for the passage of child labor laws (18).

15. Ibid., lix. Howe believed that if the state performed its duties of protecting the basic natural rights including the right to pursue happiness, which Howe believed was predicated on fair wages and decent living conditions, there would not be class conflict in society. He rejected socialism because it was based on the "false theory" that antagonisms in society are "inherent and essential"; he argued they were phenomenal and a product of societal failure. Ibid., xxxviii.

16. Ibid., xxiv.

17. Ibid., xxix, 18.

18. Barbara Rosenkrantz, *Public Health and the State: Changing Views in Massachusetts* (Cambridge, Mass.: Harvard University Press, 1972), 67. English work on model tenements as well as campaigns for washing and bathing establishments went back to the first half of the nineteenth century. HIB, Harvard, Josiah Curtis letter to Edward Shattuck, March 8, 1855.

19. Tenth Annual RSBC, 1874, 127–28.

20. OH, LSE, OH letters to Yetta (Mrs. Barnett), March 9, 1875; Nov. 12, 1876; March 3, 1877; March 22, 1884.

21. OH, LSE, letter to Yetta , Nov. 12, 1876.

22. OH, LSE, letter to St. Mary's Church, Nov. 1, 1874. In a letter to Barnett, Hill reminds him that charity work is "for Christ's sake," and that this must be made clear to the poor. Indeed she chides Barnett for letting the central point of their work "to bring the poor to God . . . slip just a little out of [his sight]." OH, LSE, letter to Barnett, Aug. 1, 1880.

23. Barnett Papers, London Metropolitan Archives F/Barr/548.

24. OH, LSE, letter to Yetta, Nov. 12, 1876. Barnett opposed any act of the state that would provide direct aid to the poor to overcome poverty (Barnett Papers, London Metropolitan Archives F/Barr/548). Hill and Barnett were at odds with Ruskin over this. Ruskin's views on poverty and the need for workers' housing were closer to those of the 1870s New England reformers. This brought him into conflict with Hill and Barnett. OH, LSE, letter to Yetta, Feb. 1878. Bowditch used the British example of housing reform to encourage public action in Massachusetts. He purposely closed his eyes to the differences in approaches between his advocacy of state action to protect a basic right and Hill's and Barnett's of action to control the poor and bring them closer to God. See Bowditch's reports to the Massachusetts State Board of Health, 1871. MSBH, Annual Reports.

25. Barnett Papers, London Metropolitan Archives, F/Bar/04, William Barnett letter to Frank, March 1884.

26. Bowditch, *Life*, 2: 154. Bowditch noted that in the "casual wards," the shelters for the homeless, those who came in were provided with a hot bath, bread and a cot. "Is not this casual ward business a step in a worthy direction? The authorities here undertake to provide shelter." He goes on to suggest following the logic of the casual wards "the public authorities eventually [should] build houses to be let at moderate prices and to be kept forcibly if necessary clean?"(2: 171).

27. Ivid., 2: 171. Hill was also involved in charity relief work. She was one of the major forces behind the Charity Organization Society where upper-class visitors would visit the homes of the poor and decide if they were worthy of relief. In addition to opposing public relief, she opposed the idea that visitors should be paid by the government. She wanted wealthy volunteers who would mingle with the poor and provide the proper uplift. OH, LSE, 2, OH letter to Yetta, Feb. 5, 1878. For Hill's vision of housing see OH letter to Yetta, Feb. 16, 1873.

Bowditch was not the only ex-abolitionist-housing reformer to visit Hill. When James Freeman Clarke went to England in 1882, he and his wife had tea with Octavia and her mother. James Freeman Clarke Papers, Houghton Library, Harvard University, bMs Am 1569.7 (311), OH letter to JFC, May 1882.

28. HIB, MHS, Box 3, *Medical and Surgical Journal of Boston*, Jan. 1903. Also in-

volved in the Cooperative Building Company was Abby May, also an old aboli-tionist. May Goddard Collection, Schlesinger Library, Harvard University, Box 2, letter 33, Phillips Brooks to Abby May, Jan. 18, 1871.

29. Katharine Day Putman Papers, 1862–1876, MHS, Bound Papers, 1871, HIB letter to KDP, 1871.

30. HIB, MHS, Scrapbook.

31. BFP, MHS, Box 3, William Bowditch letter to Vincent Bowditch, Jan. 8, 1903.

32. BPL, Samuel May letter to Mary Carpenter, Bristol, Dec. 29, 1843.

33. Laura E. Richards and Maud Howe Elliott, *Julia Ward Howe, 1819–1910* (Boston: Houghton Mifflin, 1916), 299.

34. Henry Ingersoll Bowditch, Harvard College, class notes of class of 1828. In a series of letters between Chadwick and Bostonian D. F. Lincoln, Lincoln noted that "the American system of public schools based on the Massachusetts method, is free to all and satisfied the demands of most." Any system that was seen as not in "the spirit of equality," would be opposed as stigmaticizing the poor. Chadwick Papers, University College London, Special Collections, D. F. Lincoln letter to Chadwick, Oct. 6, 1877.

35. For Howe's support of the eight-hour-day movement and also public own-ership of utilities see Richards and Elliott, *Julia Ward Howe*, 302.

36. See James Brewer Stewart, *Wendell Phillips: Liberty's Hero* (Baton Rouge: Louisiana State University Press, 1986), 261.

37. Quoted in Stacey M. Robertson, *Parker Pillsbury: Radical Abolitionist, Male Feminist* (Ithaca, N.Y.: Cornell University Press, 2000), 179.

38. BPL, Theodore Parker Sermons, Sermon 14, "Dangers Which Threaten the Rights of Man in America," July 2, 1854, 13, 14.

39. Ibid., 56.

40. May Goddard Collection, Schlesinger Library, Harvard University, Box 2, #35, Henry George to Abby May, Feb. 4, 1886. See also Robertson, *Parker Pills-bury*, 179.

41. TWH, Houghton, 784, Edward Bellamy letter to TWH, Dec. 21, 1890.

42. JWH, Houghton (322) manuscript, n.d. probably 1860s.

43. Julia Ward Howe noted in her travel book on Cuba that "the negro of the North is an ideal negro: it is the negro refined by white culture, elevated by white blood, instructed even by white iniquity," while the blacks of Cuba were "coarse, grinning, flat-footed, thick-skulled . . . chiefly ambitious to be of no use to any in the world." She argued that a slave needed to be sent "to school to the white race and his discipline must be long and laborious." Quoted in Deborah Pickman Clifford, *Mine Eyes Have Seen the Glory: A Biography of Julia Ward Howe* (Boston: Little, Brown, 1979), 136.

44. JWH, Houghton (320), manuscript "Aliens in America." Howe's vision of seeing all as neighbors seeking justice not as aliens applied to other persons as well. She became close friends with Oscar Wilde when he visited America, and they corresponded regularly. When Wilde was attacked for his homosexuality, Julia stood by him despite the fact he had become "an outcast from human sym-pathy" (322), Notebook 23.

45. HIB, Harvard, Seq., July 28, 1885.

46. BPL, Samuel May letter to Mary Carpenter, Bristol, Dec. 29, 1843. James Buffum noted that when he was in England working on anti-slavery he had to speak out against the "starving in Ireland because of the failed potato crop." *Commemoration of the Fiftieth Anniversary*, 45.

47. May Goddard Collection, Schlesinger Library, Harvard University, Box 2, folder 25, Samuel Gridley Howe letter to HIB, Jan. 30, 1867. Howe had asked Bowditch for support and Bowditch had sent $220. Sanborn, *Dr. S. G. Howe*, 309. Howe raised close to forty thousand dollars for Cretan relief, most from abolitionist friends, 312.

48. JWH, Houghton (320), speeches.

49. Julia Ward Howe, *Reminiscences, 1819–1899* (Boston: Houghton Mifflin, 1899), 320.

50. Richards and Elliott, *Julia Ward Howe*, 313. Two years later Julia organized the Boston Armenian Relief Committee and again looked to her old abolitionist friends, but fewer and fewer were alive or physically able to lend support.

51. Ibid., 302.

52. JWH, Houghton (322), notebook 7.

53. Howe, *Reminiscences*, 328.

54. Ibid., 329.

55. JWH, Houghton (320), Box 10, manuscript.

56. Howe, *Reminiscences*, 330–33. At the public debate on schools for women at Albert Hall, the bishop of Manchester attacked the idea as ludicrous because it would let upper-class children to sit next to children of shopkeepers. Howe responded that just such a situation existed in America and because of it, it was impossible to tell the difference between children of different classes (334).

57. JWH, Houghton (320), Box 10, manuscript.

58. Quoted in Richards and Elliott, *Julia Ward Howe*, 187. These Mother's Day Festivals for Peace were organized by women each year throughout the nineteenth century. The last was held in 1912 in Riverton, New Jersey, by the Pennsylvania Peace Society and the Universal Peace Union.

59. TWH, Houghton (1124), TWH letter to his sister May 31, 1875.

60. JWH, Houghton (322), Notebook 6.

61. Howe, *Reminiscences*, 84, 85. Howe also said that he "explored the most crying evils of society seeking to discover, even in their sources, the secret of their prevention and cure." She proudly noted his work with Dorothea Dix "to improve the condition of the insane," and Horace Mann to "uplift the public schools" (88).

62. Quoted in Richards and Elliot, *Julia Ward Howe*, 421.

63. Marie Elizabeth Zakrzewska, *A Woman's Quest: The Life of Marie E. Zakrzewska, M.D.*, ed. Agnes C. Vietor (New York: D. Appleton, 1924), 391.

64. New England Hospital for Woman and Children, *Marie Elizabeth Zakrzewska: A Memoir* (Boston: the Hospital, 1903), 29–30.

65. Ibid., 27.

66. New England Hospital, *Marie Elizabeth Zakrzewska*, 18.

67. Fifth Annual RSBC, 1869, xxxiii.

68. Ibid., xxxvi-xxxvii.

69. Sanborn, *Dr. S. G. Howe*, 336.

70. Tenth RSBC, 1874, 126–27.

71. See OH, LPE, London, Collection 512, Octavia Hill letters to Samuel Barnett and his wife Yetta.

72. *Tenth RSBC*, 1874, 127.

73. Katherine E. Conway and Mabel Ward Cameron, *Charles Francis Donnelly: A Memoir with an Account of the Hearings on the Bill for the Inspection of Private Schools in Massachusetts, 1888–1889* (New York: privately printed, 1909).

Chapter 9. "A Relative Right"

1. Julia Ward Howe, *Reminiscences, 1819–1899* (Boston: Houghton Mifflin, 1899), 258–59.

2. Quoted in James McPherson, *The Abolitionist Legacy: From Reconstruction to the NAACP* (Princeton, N.J.: Princeton University Press, 1975), 49.

3. In 1861 he and Samuel Gridley Howe planned to organize a company of men under John Brown, Jr., to move into northern Virginia, but the plan never materialized.

4. Higginson was not the only abolitionist to fight the war with black troops. Two of William Bowditch's sons fought with the Fifth Massachusetts Cavalry, a black regiment.

5. TWH, Houghton, THW letter to his sister, Sept. 3, 1870.

6. James Freeman Clarke and his family, as well as the Motts, up from Philadelphia, Whipple, the Chaces, and others, came to Newport for visiting and social events. TWH, Houghton (1074), THW letter to Anne, July 23, 1871. That same year Melville and his family stayed with the Higginsons. (1076), TWH letter to Anna, ? 20, 1871. See Howe, *Reminiscences*, 401–3.

7. Howe, *Reminiscences*, 402.

8. TWH, Houghton (1189), Nov. 1888.

9. James Tuttleton, *The Life of Thomas Wentworth Higginson* (Boston: Twayne, 1978), 46.

10. Quoted in ibid., 45. See also TWH Houghton Box 6 (1079), TWH letter to his sister, Jan. 15, 1872.

11. GFP, Anne Weston letter to Samuel May, Dec. 31, 1885. Higginson's review in the *Atlantic Monthly* was critical of Garrison but not as vicious as Weston implied. It was more a review of a person wanting to disassociate himself from the radical abolitionists rather than a rejection of abolitionism itself. *Atlantic Monthly* 57 (Jan. 1886): 123–28.

12. See James McPherson, *The Abolitionist Legacy: From Reconstruction to the NAACP* (Princeton, N.J.: Princeton University Press, 1973), 131.

13. Quoted in Tuttleton, *Life*, 46.

14. The restoration of Democratic rule in the South meant among other things a radical reduction of spending on schooling. The amount spent per pupil in nine southern states in 1880 was only 60 percent of that in 1875 under Reconstruction. Only two-fifths of black students were enrolled in school at all and most for only three months. Under these conditions it was hard to see how the southern black community could achieve the progress it was argued they needed before suffrage.

15. Quoted in Tuttleton, *Life*, 47.

16. Ibid., 48; see also McPherson, *The Abolitionist Legacy*, 379–86.

17. Thomas Wentworth Higginson, *A Part of a Man's Life* (Boston: Houghton Mifflin, 1905), 120, 136.

18. Chadwick Papers, University College London, Manuscript Collection, Charles Folsom letter to Chadwick, Dec. 6, 1878.

19. See Louis Menand, *The Metaphysical Club* (New York: Farrar, Straus, Giroux, 2001).

20. See McPherson, *The Abolitionist Legacy*, for the abolitionists' continued struggle to realize racial equality.

21. See David W. Blight, *Race and Reunion: The Civil War in American Memory* (Cambridge, Mass.: Harvard University Press, 2001) for the nation's attempt to

refocus its memory of the war around the valor of both northern and southern troops. See also George Fredrickson, *The Inner Civil War: Northern Intellectuals and the Crisis of the Union* (New York: Harper and Row, 1965) for how many conservative northern intellectuals saw the war as proof of the need for an elite role in society.

22. BFP, Peabody, Box 13, folder 4, Amos Lawrence letter to WIB, Oct. 1874.

23. See Richard Hofstadter, *Social Darwinism in American Thought* (Boston: Beacon Press, 1955) for a discussion of conservative use of natural rights.

24. Amy Dru Stanley argues that northern reformers grasped a contract ideal of free labor that saw equality and rights centered around a male head of household freely entering into a contract for labor. Amy Dru Stanley, *From Bondage to Contract: Wage Labor, Marriage, and the Market in the Age of Slave Emancipation* (Cambridge: Cambridge University Press, 1998).

25. See Hofstadter, *Social Darwinism*, for the conservative embrace of Spencer and Social Darwinism.

26. By the late 1870s the work of Herbert Spencer was increasingly popularized on this side of the Atlantic. Spencer claimed that Darwin's theories of evolution applied to humans and society. Those who succeeded in the struggle for survival were those most fit to survive, and a society that allowed those most fit to rise to dominance and did not through charity or other social intervention allow the weak to persevere would itself be strong and thrive, while a society that held the fittest back and burdened them with maintenance of the weak would itself decline.

27. Spencer's most influential work, *Social Statistics*, was first published in this country in 1864. Herbert Spencer, *Social Statistics* (New York: Appleton, 1864). Spencer was soon more popular on the western side of the Atlantic than in his home country. Part of the reason may have been that with some significant exceptions the dominant reform voices in England in the second half of the nineteenth century had not based their agenda on the radical idea of natural rights and full equality as the New England reformers had. The paternalism of the English reformers never threatened the basic social hierarchy, while in America reformers made fundamental radical claims on the state for action. Faced with this challenge, American conservatives found great comfort in Spencer's new natural science.

28. See William Graham Sumner, *What Social Classes Owe to Each Other* (New York: Harper and Row, 1883).

29. Quoted in Hofstadter, *Social Darwinism*, 51.

30. In an 1883 lecture before the Liberal Union Club Henry Ingersoll Bowditch denounced Social Darwinism as against nature. He claimed that cooperation not competition was the natural condition of man and that society should work toward furthering cooperation. HIP, MHS, Miscellaneous Volumes, Box 2, Journal compiled by Vincent Yardley Bowditch, "Biographical Contribution to the Class of 1828, Harvard College."

31. Sumner's attack on an activist state helping the poor was more in response to calls such as Sanborn's and Howe's than to what the state was actually doing in the 1870s.

32. JWH, Houghton (320), manuscript "Aliens in America."

33. See Sumner, *What the Social Classes Owe Each Other*.

34. See Henry Adams's *Democracy: An American Novel* (New York: Holt, 1880) for a vision of American politics as corrupt and a cynical view toward any claims of politics as a reforming venture.

35. HIB, Harvard, Seq., Nov. 9, 1884. Cleveland's affair did not bother Bowditch because Cleveland claimed paternity for the two children and provided for their education.

36. See John T. Cumbler, *Reasonable Use: The People, the Environment and the State, New England, 1790–1930* (Oxford: Oxford University Press, 2001) for Theodore Lyman. Lyman's family owned thousands of dollars worth of stock in textiles, textile machinery, and railroads as well as significant real estate in the Boston area.

37. Although the public notices of the deaths of these old activists did not stress their continued struggle for social justice, they did note it among themselves. In a letter to William Bowditch in 1895 Mary Grew noted that there were not many "of the old guard" left from "those grand times," but "doubtless our comrades who have preceded us to the other side are doing noble work there. . . . What glorious days of struggle, labor and conflict we few survivors can look back upon. What a blessing it is to us that we have been permitted to know them by experience." WBP, Peabody, Vol. 5, Mary Grew letter to W. B., Dec. 19, 1895.

38. GFP, Harriet Winslow Sewall letter to Francis J. Garrison, March 2, 1889.

39. Richard Hofstadter, *The Age of Reform: From Bryan to F.D.R.* (New York: Knopf, 1955).

Index

Acknowledgments

Most academic works, especially mine, accumulate scholarly debts along the way to publication. This one is certainly no exception. There have been so many people who have helped me along the way I fear many may be missed in this note of appreciation. Sam Bass Warner, as always, has been a tremendous help in this project. He encouraged me and then read through and provided editorial help for the entire manuscript. The title is also his contribution. Chad Montrie and Tracy K'Meyer also read through the entire manuscript and provided important help. Chad was also helpful early on in pointing to important themes that needed emphasis. Lewis Erenberg, as he has for many of my manuscripts, encouraged me, pointed me in new directions and has been one of those friends one can never fully thank. Mary Elizabeth Hawkesworth emphasized the importance of natural rights and social justice, pointed me to relevant literature in women's studies and along with Avery Koler helped me think through my understanding of Locke. My colleague Ann Allen's expertise in women's history was an important help. Mary Blewitt pushed me to think internationally and Kathryn Kish Sklar, Judi Jennings and Walter Licht supported me in seeing my activists as perceiving themselves as social justice agents. My students, particularly Gene Sublett, my fellow activist Bani Hines-Hudson and my long time friends Sally Benbasset and Steve Miller pushed me to do this work not for myself but for those involved in the struggle for social justice. My son and daughter-in-law read early versions of the opening chapters and my daughter and John Low provided listening boards, opened up their apartment and shared many a meal with me while I was doing research in Boston. Julia and Ed Berman provided me with a place to stay in western Massachusetts while I used the archives at Smith College whose librarians were the friendliest and most helpful I have ever encountered in 35 years of research. The librarians at the Massachusetts Historical Society, the Countway Library of the Harvard

Medical School, the Schlesinger Library, and the Houghton Library not only put up with my every demand but helped make a hard task pleasant. The Boston Public Library provided an incredible place to do research. My wife Judith Cumbler not only supported me through the many years of research and writing of this work, but she also tolerated me falling in love with Julia Ward Howe. Robert Lockwood is an ideal editor. He not only moved the manuscript through the various hurdles, but he understood exactly what I wanted to accomplish with this manuscript and worked with me to improve the manuscript so that it would achieve this end. Jim O'Brien, as always, proved a superb indexer. Without the help of these people and many others, including the hardworking production staff and copy editors at UPenn Press, this manuscript would be significantly weaker. Much of its strengths are the products of the collective efforts of these and many other friends and colleagues. The book also is an outgrowth of my years in the movement and is dedicated to all those who struggle "to break every yoke."